BESTSELLING
BOOK SERIES

GoldMine® 8 For Dummies

D0472826

Navigating the GoldMine Main Menu

If you're an experienced GoldMine user, you will notice that some functions have been moved. The following table provides a handy guide to finding your favorite functions under the various menus.

The GoldMine Menu Commands

File	Edit	GoTo	Tools	Actions
New	Cut	Activities	Synchronize	Send E-mail Message
Import and Export	Copy	Calendar	Automated Processes	Send Outlook Message
Print a Report	Paste	Mail	Services	Send Pager Message
Switch User	Copy Contact Details	Contacts	Process Monitor	Write Letter to Contact
Log Away	Undo Change to Contact	My Contacts	Databases	Write Memo to Contact
Exit	Delete Contact	Opportunities	Data Management	Write Fax to Contact
	Record Properties	Sales Scripts	Filters and Groups	
		Projects	User Groups	
		Campaigns	Users' Settings	Write Fax to Contact
		Lead Management	Configure	Begin Mail Merge
		Literature Fulfillment	QuickStart Wizard	Begin E-mail Merge
		Document Templates	Options	Call Contact
		Service Center	Logs	Take a Phone Message
		Knowledge Base		Timer
		Analysis		
		Reports		

Schedule	Complete	Web	Window	Help
Call	Scheduled Call	GM+Browser	New Contact Window	GoldMine Help
Next Action	Unscheduled Call	My GoldMine	Tile Horizontal	GoldMine Online
Appointment	Message	Launch Current Contact's Primary Web Site	Tile Vertical	FrontRange Forums
Literature Request	Next Action	Search Online	Cascade	Update GoldMine
Forecasted Sale	Appointment	Publish Calendar	Close All	About GoldMine
Other Action	Sales	Setup Web Import	Arrange By	Release Notes
Event	Other Action	Setup GM+View	(A dynamic list of open tabs)	
To-do	Event			
GoldMine E-mail	To-do			
	Correspondence			
	Pending Activities			

For Dummies: Bestselling

GoldMine® 8 For Dummies®

Decoding Your License Serial Number

You need your HDA (a.k.a. Account Number) whenever you call FrontRange for support, and you need your license type, number of users, and version whenever you upgrade or undock licenses for remote users.

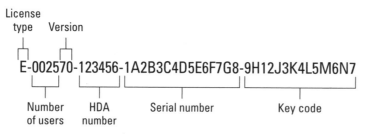

License type | Version

E-002570-123456-1A2B3C4D5E6F7G8-9H12J3K4L5M6N7

Number of users | HDA number | Serial number | Key code

- ✔ **License type:** Alpha-prefix denotes the type of Master license.

- ✔ **Number of users:** First four numbers indicate the license count or seats available in the license. The license count determines the number of users who can log on to GoldMine at one time but does not limit the total number of named users.

- ✔ **Version:** A two-digit version number.

- ✔ **HDA number:** Your six-digit HDA number. This is also your customer number that FrontRange uses.

- ✔ **Serial number:** Fifteen-character (alphanumeric) serial number uniquely identifying the license for an organization. It is used for registration and support and identifies all sublicenses as part of the same organization. Collected in three groups of five characters during licensing.

- ✔ **Key code:** Fourteen-character (alphanumeric) key code is a computer-generated check used by GoldMine to verify the license's validity. Collected in three groups of five characters during licensing.

Note: The key code is required during installation. Keep the license number and key code in a safe place in case you have to reinstall the software.

For Dummies: Bestselling Book Series for Beginners

GoldMine® 8

FOR

DUMMIES®

GoldMine® 8
FOR
DUMMIES®

by Joel Scott

Wiley Publishing, Inc.

GoldMine® 8 For Dummies®

Published by
Wiley Publishing, Inc.
111 River Street
Hoboken, NJ 07030-5774

www.wiley.com

WILEY

About the Author

Joel Scott is the president of the Computer Control Corporation, a technology consulting company founded in 1985. Mr. Scott began selling GoldMine software in 1991. The company has been awarded FrontRange's "GoldMine Top-10 Dealer" award eight times since then and has received numerous other awards for GoldMine training and best practices.

In 2007, Computer Control Corporation joined with Core Solutions, Inc., headquartered in Newton, Massachusetts. The newly combined company continues to sell and support GoldMine as well as several other well-known CRM products, such as Microsoft CRM and SalesLogix.

This is Mr. Scott's fourth *GoldMine For Dummies* book, and these sit on his bookshelf right next to the two Microsoft *CRM For Dummies* books that he has co-authored.

Always happy to hear from readers, Mr. Scott can be reached at dummy@ccc24k.com. To assure a response, please include all your contact information.

Author's Acknowledgments

This is my sixth *For Dummies* book. Wiley, the publisher, may contend it's the fifth. Opinions vary on this issue. In any event, it's been great fun, a great challenge, and a great learning experience. Each time it's been different because the editors change, the rules change, and the software changes.

I had two editors this time, and, to be honest, they were two of the best. Gary Klingler was, without a doubt, the best technical editor I have ever worked with. It makes a big difference working with someone who not only knows the product but also can make congenial and constructive suggestions rather than just saying "that's stupid!"

Susan Christophersen had the unenviable task of turning my English into *For Dummies* English. Those are apparently two separate dialects of the English language. I have to thank her for her patience and grace under pressure. But I still think "select" and "choose" are pretty much the same thing.

I also want to be sure I acknowledge the one and only FrontRange employee who understood that having another *GoldMine For Dummies* book could only be a good thing for everyone. The only person who made sure I had early copies of the software so that I could start writing. Politics at FrontRange being what it is these days, I think I will have to keep that name a secret so that I don't get anyone in trouble. But, I do thank you.

In Memoriam:

GoldMine Standard has met its demise — a victim of negligent homicide. It didn't need to be discontinued and surely not the way it was.

So many of my good friends from the glory days of GoldMine have moved on. It was so much fun. Now it's time for me to do something else, too.

Publisher's Acknowledgments

We're proud of this book; please send us your comments through our online registration form located at www.dummies.com/register/.

Some of the people who helped bring this book to market include the following:

Acquisitions, Editorial, and Media Development

Project and Copy Editor:
Susan Christophersen

(Previous Edition: Christine Berman and Jean Rogers)

Acquisitions Editor: Bob Woerner

Technical Editor: Gary Klingler

Editorial Manager: Jodi Jensen

Editorial Assistant: Amanda Foxworth

Sr. Editorial Assistant: Cherie Case

Cartoons: Rich Tennant
(www.the5thwave.com)

Composition Services

Project Coordinator: Patrick Redmond

Layout and Graphics: Melanee Prendergast, Alicia B. South, Christine Williams, Erin Zeltner

Proofreaders: Susan Moritz, Sossity R. Smith

Indexer: Valerie Haynes Perry

Anniversary Logo Design: Richard Pacifico

Publishing and Editorial for Technology Dummies

Richard Swadley, Vice President and Executive Group Publisher

Andy Cummings, Vice President and Publisher

Mary Bednarek, Executive Acquisitions Director

Mary C. Corder, Editorial Director

Publishing for Consumer Dummies

Diane Graves Steele, Vice President and Publisher

Joyce Pepple, Acquisitions Director

Composition Services

Gerry Fahey, Vice President of Production Services

Debbie Stailey, Director of Composition Services

Contents at a Glance

Table of Contents

Introduction

*Y*ou finally decided to get your professional life organized! Great. You bought and installed a copy of GoldMine 8 (also known as GoldMine Premium), or your boss decided to buy it, had it installed on your computer, and then told you to figure out how to use it. If either of these situations applies, then *GoldMine 8 For Dummies* is for you.

GoldMine 8 is part of a larger family of GoldMine products. And GoldMine itself belongs to a larger family of CRM software. Most people believe that "CRM" stands for "Customer Relationship Management." A better way to think of CRM is as "Client Relationship Management." Clients are customers about whom you actually know something, and GoldMine will definitely help you keep track of what your clients are all about.

Reading this book and, more important, using this software will dramatically improve your life. You will soon be taller and thinner. Smarter and faster. Rich and famous (or richer and more famous), too. Anyway, it has worked for me.

The Various Flavors of GoldMine

Back in the day, that is, back in the late 1980s when GoldMine first appeared, it had just one flavor. It was based on an old, venerable file structure called "dBase." Then, GoldMine was just called "GoldMine." There was no need for any further distinctions.

As we speak (it's the summer of 2007 as I finish this), GoldMine comes in several varieties. It depends on how you count. FrontRange, the manufacturer, calls them "editions." Before you get any further into this book, it's important to understand just a little of the history as well as the differences between the several editions.

GoldMine Standard

GoldMine Standard (a.k.a. "GoldMine," "GoldMine BCM," or "GoldMine dBase") was where it all started. The latest version within this edition is 6.7. FrontRange has announced that it has "sunsetted" this edition. Sunsetting means that no further development will occur. Support from FrontRange will be discontinued, and eventually you will not even be able to purchase this edition. The same scenario applies to GoldSync.

As Microsoft continues to develop new operating systems and as you inevitably convert your computers to these operating systems (for example, Vista), eventually your GoldMine Standard Edition may no longer even work.

Perhaps a groundswell of public opinion could convince management at FrontRange to rethink its position.

GoldMine Corporate

GoldMine Standard's big brother is the Corporate Edition, which is powered by Microsoft SQL. It made its first fledgling appearance back in the days of GoldMine 4 when it was originally called "Front Office" or "Service and Support."

The SQL engine makes the Corporate Edition of GoldMine capable of handling more users and more records, and it has much more capacity for integrating with other applications.

On the surface, GoldMine Corporate and GoldMine Standard look and function in very much the same way.

GoldMine Corporate has *not* been scheduled for sunsetting. In fact, there is a continuing development and support plan at least through 2009. The current version of GoldMine Corporate is 7.0.

GoldMine Premium

GoldMine Premium, also known as GoldMine 8, is the topic of this book. From this point on, I refer to GoldMine 8 simply as "GoldMine."

If you are running any edition prior to GoldMine 8 or GoldMine Enterprise, you are about to begin reading the wrong book. GoldMine 8's user interface is so dramatically different from its predecessors' interface that you will find this book to be nearly useless as a navigational aid for any prior edition. Of course, if your intent is to learn the new features in case you might want to upgrade, just keep reading.

FrontRange has almost completely overhauled the user interface, bringing it into the twenty-first century. Also, FrontRange has added a customer-support module. This is the area in which to track and manage customer or product issues and is the long-awaited answer to the many competitive systems out there with such capabilities.

GoldMine Enterprise

GoldMine Enterprise is definitely not your mother's GoldMine. In fact, it has very little to do with any other edition of GoldMine. It is a much higher powered, more expensive, .NET product with more capability than any other edition of GoldMine. Its table structure, its screens, its potential for customization, and its price tag far exceed those of all its relatives.

How to Use This Book

GoldMine 8 For Dummies is divided into eight parts. You should be able to comfortably read the book from start to finish, if you want, with one or two breaks. Well, maybe a few more than that. On the other hand, this book is designed as a reference book, with each chapter standing on its own.

You'll get the most benefit from this book by sitting in front of your computer with GoldMine on the screen. It's easy to convince yourself that you've _got it_ by just reading, but you'll find no substitute for trying the steps yourself. Experimenting with sample data is sometimes just the ticket to an epiphany.

I try to provide the easiest method to accomplish any particular task. If you find another way, by all means use it.

Foolish Assumptions

I assume that you have some basic computer and Windows skills and that you've used some sort of e-mail before. Regarding CRM, however, I assume that you've just returned from a long mission to Mars and need to start using CRM by tomorrow.

I also assume that you have a basic understanding of database concepts. If you're comfortable with fields, records, files, folders, and how they relate to each other, you'll be fine. If this is already sounding bad, you can seek help at most community colleges or local computer-training facilities. Or just ask any 12-year-old.

If you intend to be your own CRM administrator (backing up files and assigning user names, passwords, and access rights), you need to understand records, files, folders, and networks. If you just want to be a good day-to-day user of CRM, make sure that you understand what a file is and how to locate one using Windows Explorer.

How This Book Is Organized

This book has too many parts. Each part stands on its own, but you're best off if you at least skim through the basics before diving into the more complex material.

Part 1: GoldMine Premium Basics

This part gives you an overview of what GoldMine is all about and provides a tour of the main GoldMine screen. I discuss navigating within the new user interface in detail. I explain how to set up all your custom preferences and your options for accessing your GoldMine data remotely.

Part 11: Managing Contacts

This part shows you how to enter new records and find the ones that are already in the system. Additional contacts, a concept unique to GoldMine, is the next topic. You learn how to make use of the one-to-many Details and Referrals. And, to gather together similar kinds of records, I review filters, groups, and SQL Queries.

Part 111: Managing Activities

In this part, you learn how to schedule activities for yourself and others and how to make sure that nothing ever falls through the cracks. All scheduled activities need to eventually be completed in some fashion, and I show you how to do this — five different ways. If you're in sales, you will also want to visit the chapter on sales forecasting. If you're in support, you'll benefit from the special activities called "cases" that I discuss in Part IV.

Part 1V: Marketing and Support

In this part, I discuss how to manage all your leads and how to monitor the marketing you do through GoldMine. The new Customer Support section is discussed in detail because it is one of the most important new features in GoldMine 8.

Part V: Managing Documents

GoldMine has long had its own e-mail client; it can also integrate with Outlook. I discuss the pros and cons of each and show you how to use both. Linking to Microsoft Word and using template documents is a very powerful feature of GoldMine; I discuss that here in Part V. Last, I show you how to handle documents that need to be linked to individual records in GoldMine.

Part VI: Organizing and Distributing Information

The InfoCenter is a poor man's intranet, and Part VI starts with this topic. The Opportunity Manager is essentially Sales Forecasting's bigger brother, and that is the next topic along with the Project Manager. The Organizational Chart allows you to relate separate records to each other and is yet another organizational tool for you. Everyone likes graphics. Some people even like statistics. GoldMine has both, and I discuss them next. Everyone needs reports, and I discuss the many options you have to run and even develop reports.

Part VII: Customizing GoldMine

If you're a bit of a do-it-yourselfer, you can use this part to get started on modifying GoldMine to precisely fit your organization. You learn how to create new fields and field labels and how to manage lookup lists. These are the most basic and common of customizations. Automated processes are my favorite part of GoldMine; these give GoldMine the power to do all the mundane tasks that we are supposed to do but rarely get around to. GM+Browser is a great place to attach a GoldMine record to the Internet or to some outside data files. If you'd like to automate some of your lead collection by integrating GoldMine with your organization's Web site, the last chapter in this part is for you.

Part VIII: The Part of Tens

Many programs work with GoldMine; some are from FrontRange and others from dealers or development shops. Chapter 30 discusses the top ten add-on products. Chapter 31 summarizes the most important changes in GoldMine since the last *GoldMine For Dummies* book, which covers version 6.0.

Conventions Used in This Book

We use some conventions throughout this book that merit a little explanation. When you see a phrase such as "choose File➪Edit My Profile," it means to click through a given sequence of menu commands. In this example, those commands are File followed by Edit My Profile.

Whenever I tell you to click something (most likely it's a button or an icon), you use the left mouse button and click just once. On those rare occasions when clicking twice is required to get the job done, I tell you to double-click.

To *select* an item, you either highlight it or click in a check box or radio button, depending on the item. Text that I tell you to enter (that is, type) into the program, such as in a text box, appears in **boldface** type. Web site addresses and on-screen messages show up in `monofont` type. To signify hyperlinks, otherwise known as just plain links, I underline the text of the link. On your computer, clicking such links transports you to another location altogether, such as a Web page.

Finally, to avoid confusion (and to follow *For Dummies* rules), I use title-style capitalization for option names and links, even when the program doesn't.

Icons Used in This Book

You don't want to skip the helpful reminders noted by this icon.

This icon lets you know that some particularly geeky, technical information is coming up. You can look past this if you want.

This icon points you to a trick that will save you time and effort.

Look to this icon to find out what to avoid if you don't want your database to blow up or cause you other types of anguish.

Where to Go from Here

If you're new to GoldMine and to CRM, in general, reading and planning will work a lot better right now than will just jumping in and implementing in haste.

Those who fail to plan, plan to fail.

Any but the most trivial of implementations deserves some level of needs analysis. You can approach this by downloading a planning guide from one of several Web sites.

As your implementation grows beyond the "seat of the pants" level, paying a professional to do a formal needs analysis is usually worthwhile. I know one whom I respect, but most of the more experienced GoldMine dealers can help with this as well.

But if it's reading this book that's really on your mind right now, and you're somewhat new to GoldMine 8, I recommend that you pay particular attention to Chapters 1–5 before jumping into the software. After you properly digest that material, you can pick and choose your chapters at will. They each stand on their own and are waiting for you.

Part I

GoldMine Premium Basics

The 5th Wave   By Rich Tennant

"Well, she's fast on the keyboard and knows how to load the printer, but she just sort of 'plays' with the mouse."

In this part . . .

A little planning goes a long way toward the success of any project. This part provides you with some of the basic building blocks needed to set yourself up for a successful implementation. In addition to a general overview of what GoldMine can do for you and how to navigate the main screen, this part also contains a discussion of user preferences.

You can probably ignore the user preferences if you just want to play a little at the beginning. But, if you're really serious about getting the most out of your investment, put some time into Chapter 3 and use the Preference settings to fine-tune GoldMine to your own best advantage.

Whether you intend to work from home, while on the road, or at the beach, Chapter 4 provides a great overview of the best choices for remotely accessing GoldMine.

Chapter 1

GoldMine: An Overview

In This Chapter

▶ Understanding what GoldMine can do

▶ Examining some things that GoldMine isn't designed to do

▶ Preparing for a successful project

▶ Providing training

*G*oldMine 8 (also called GoldMine Premium) is a tool for sales, marketing, and customer support and is one of many CRM (Customer Relationship Management) systems available today. GoldMine is for you if you ever have contact with customers or with business prospects. Right out of the box, GoldMine lets you track all the basic information to manage your client relationships. And with a little effort or money, you can customize it to your specific needs.

In the late 1980s, my company was growing a bit too fast and was getting a little out of control. I began searching for some kind of tool that could help us sustain our growth without causing additional pain. I chose GoldMine because it

✔ Won't let us forget to return a phone call

✔ Ensures that we remember all our appointments and we never double- or triple-book ourselves

✔ Provides a central place to store all client information

✔ Links all our documents to clients' records so that we can't lose proposals

✔ Makes sure that we all get home for dinner on time every night

The developers at FrontRange Solutions, Inc (formerly GoldMine Software Corporation) don't really know the special needs of your organization; your work may require some fields or functions that just don't come in the box with GoldMine. For example, you may want to track each client's anniversary so that GoldMine can automatically send flowers to your client's wife. The bad news is that GoldMine doesn't come out of the box knowing how to do this. The goods news is that you can easily add an anniversary field and a process to completely automate this activity.

One of the advantages of joining the GoldMine community is the widespread level of expertise available to you from experienced GoldMine dealers all over the world. These dealers are trained professionals who have focused on CRM and GoldMine in particular. Admittedly, FrontRange has thinned the ranks of dealers and consultants today, but if you are looking for good and experienced dealers, they can still be found. Feel free to contact me for a local referral.

Discovering Everything that GoldMine Can Do

GoldMine tracks all the names, addresses, phone numbers, and basic contact information you will ever need. If you never use GoldMine as anything more than an electronic Rolodex, you will have gotten your money's worth. But if you use GoldMine in such a limited way, you will be missing out on most of the power for which your company paid good money.

Consolidating all your prospect and customer information

You will reap tremendous benefits from consistently entering every lead and every account into GoldMine. And if you can convince everyone in your organization to do the same, you have not only one organized location for all your data but also the following advantages:

- Everyone with authorization in your organization can share data and schedules.

- You can link e-mail and other documents to appropriate records, enabling you to maintain a complete audit trail.

- When a salesperson leaves your company, you can easily transfer her accounts to her replacement without missing a beat.

- You can set up all sorts of imaginative Automated Processes to help you with sales, marketing, and support.

Keeping track of your life

You can use GoldMine to track your business schedule and, in fact, your entire life. Just as important, GoldMine can keep schedules for all users and can help you coordinate your activities with theirs. This capability is one of the compelling reasons to use a CRM system such as GoldMine.

GoldMine lets you see what everyone else on your team is doing (although it also offers many provisions for privacy); at the same time, it lets everyone else track what you are doing. Or, at least what you claim you're doing. GoldMine can even coordinate the data for remote salespeople who rarely venture into the office.

If your entire team uses GoldMine consistently to schedule both professional time and personal appointments, here are some results you may see:

✔ You can eliminate most instances of overbooked or double-booked staff.

✔ You can feel reasonably safe in scheduling appointments for others in your organization.

✔ You can let GoldMine automatically find a time when everyone on your team is available to meet.

✔ You have a complete audit trail of team members' activities.

Communicating with your team and the world

You can use GoldMine to send a single letter to a customer or to send batches of letters or e-mail messages. Twenty years ago, sending notices to your thousand best customers telling them about tomorrow's price increase would have been an almost impossible task. Now you can name that tune in three notes.

To do all this, you can use GoldMine's built-in e-mail client or you can use Outlook, which can be tightly integrated with GoldMine. I am stubbornly sticking with GoldMine's e-mail client because I see no advantage to complicating my life with Outlook.

Keeping tabs on opportunities and projects

GoldMine has a simple sales forecasting system built-in, but that may not be enough to track your more complex sales. To meet that need, GoldMine has a much more sophisticated Opportunity Manager, designed to manage deals that may take months or even years to close and to involve multiple people in your organization — and possibly multiple people at your prospect's organization. The Opportunity Manager is also ideal when you want to link activities and documents to one of these larger pending deals.

When you succeed at landing that behemoth deal, GoldMine can turn your opportunity into a project so that you can just as easily keep track of all the work that is being done. I like to refer to this as Microsoft Project "light."

Setting up Automated Processes

My favorite feature of GoldMine is its Automated Processes, with which you can automate almost any business process you can design. With Automated Processes, you can have GoldMine send out follow-ups to sales calls or remind you to call a client or escalate an issue to your boss when you ignore GoldMine's first or second notices.

There is a great example of a series of Automated Processes within the AdvisorsGold add-on for the financial services industry. You can read more on that in Chapter 30.

Doing some great marketing

GoldMine can gather leads from your Web site (see Chapter 29) and automatically turn them into records in your database. Then, with a little planning, you can set up marketing campaigns to clients and to prospects directly from your GoldMine database. GoldMine is just great at scheduling calls and sending batches of e-mails, faxes, and snail-mail letters. The best campaigns use combinations of several strategies. E-mails and faxes will both benefit from some add-on products discussed in Chapter 30.

Organizing your customer support

Along with a completely reworked user interface, GoldMine Premium now boasts a customer service module that allows GoldMine to manage service issues by associating each issue with an account. It also assigns issues to a queue until someone deals with it and maintains a library of service-related documents.

Investigating a Few of the Things GoldMine Isn't Designed to Do

There's no point in reinventing the wheel and, for the most part, GoldMine hasn't. Rather than build a word processor, a quotation system, or an expense reporting system, FrontRange has relied on other developers to build great products. Many of these products are now tightly integrated with GoldMine.

Integrating word processing and spreadsheets

GoldMine has no built-in word processor, so you can't really use GoldMine to write a letter. The designers long ago decided not to reinvent this wheel and have long relied on what has become the de facto word processor — Microsoft Word. Just as GoldMine tightly integrates with Word, so it also integrates with Excel, just in case you need to output some data in that direction. Chapter 16 provides details on connecting GoldMine and Word.

Faxing

Faxing comes and goes. It was the hot technology before e-mail became so prevalent. Now that marketers are having more and more trouble penetrating everyone's spam filters, faxing is hot again. GoldMine, however, relies on one or two well-established faxing programs to carry the load here. Chapter 30 discusses these.

Quoting and accounting

Don't rely on GoldMine alone for help with accounting or with quotations. You can, and should, buy separate programs for these tasks. And again, you can refer to Chapter 30 for details about each of my favorites in these categories.

Planning a Successful Project

If you have five people in your office using GoldMine and your goal is to just consolidate your data and use GoldMine as an expensive Rolodex, you might be able to get away without too much planning. Plenty of people use this approach. Of course, that may be part of the reason that so many studies have cited CRM's rather shocking failure rate.

Any but the simplest of systems must have a real, professional planning phase. My own rule is that any CRM implementation that might involve ten or more days of work should have a formal Needs Analysis done first. A good Needs Analysis is done by an experienced dealer and is almost always a billable event. But it's money well spent to document goals, develop specifications, and assign tasks and timetables.

Perhaps you don't want to spend the money. Maybe you're a Type A and just want to get on with it. Resist the urge. Invest 10 percent of the total project budget in the analysis phase, even if you do the analysis yourself.

Planning and analysis is one thing. Installation is another. Back in the day of GoldMine Standard Edition, it was relatively easy to install GoldMine. Now that GoldMine Premium runs on MS-SQL, installation is a lot more involved. Definitely not something you want to do by yourself at home. Call an experienced professional if the thought of doing it yourself makes you at all queasy.

Providing Training: The Key to Success

Don't shortchange yourself or your company when it comes to training. At least 80 percent of my clients use less than 10 percent of GoldMine's power. That's usually because they just never made the effort to find out what else GoldMine could do after they solved their initial crisis.

You can get GoldMine training in several ways, and any one of them is certainly better than expecting someone to just figure it out. The following list shows some effective training methods, starting with the most effective and ending with the least effective.

 ✔ Send every user to an authorized GoldMine Dealer for training.

   In the old days, the manufacturer used to certify select dealers as Authorized Training Centers or Authorized Trainers. I am one. They don't do this any more, so any dealers with that designation is telling you that they have been around a long time and may or may not be up-to-date. You will need to do your own investigation to find a good trainer, or, again, contact me for a referral.

 ✔ Bring an experienced trainer to one of your regular company meetings and allocate a half day or a full day to GoldMine training.

 ✔ Bring an experienced trainer to your facility for training (make sure to temporarily confiscate all cell phones and pagers).

 ✔ Sign up for some Web-based training that several dealers offer. Some dealers actually specialize in Web-based training, and this is especially cost-effective if you have users in many locations or you want to schedule the training in bite-sized chunks.

 ✔ Buy some computer-based training CD-ROMs and set aside time for each person to work through them. *Note:* It's difficult to ask a CD a question if you're confused about something.

✔ Buy each staff member a copy *of GoldMine 8 for Dummies*. Tell each person that she will get a one-week paid vacation upon finishing the book.

✔ Tell your staff to just figure it out. I've never seen this actually work very well, but it might for you.

GoldMine manuals are available electronically — either on the initial CD or as a download. Printing hundreds of pages may not be practical, but the option is there. One advantage is that you can print just the chapter related to the subject you are trying to master.

Chapter 2

Getting Around in GoldMine

*F*or almost fifteen years, even as features were added, the GoldMine screens always looked the same. No more. The most obvious enhancement in GoldMine 8 is the complete overhaul of the user interface.

If you are a GoldMine veteran upgrading to the latest version, you will immediately be trying to figure out how to do all the things you used to do. In case these new screens are already making you nervous, be assured that every function you are used to is still there. You may have to press a different button or maneuver to a different area of the screen, but all the good stuff is still there. It took me about 15 minutes to accommodate myself to all this new navigation. It probably won't take you any longer, except that you are required to read this chapter first.

In this chapter I discuss and you discover how to navigate the corridors of GoldMine in the most efficient ways possible.

Understanding the GoldMine Interface

If you are sitting in front of GoldMine for the first time, you will quickly become comfortable with the navigation because it's very much like many other twenty-first–century applications.

In addition to looking different, GoldMine now has some new terminology for you to get used to. GoldMine 8 has a Global Toolbar, a Navigation Pane, and a Taskbar. On top of that, some of the functions are in different places now. Figure 2-1 shows as many of GoldMine's work areas as possible, and I refer to this figure throughout this chapter.

Main menu

Global Toolbar   Standard Toolbar   Taskbar   Work area

Figure 2-1:
All the
important
new areas
of the
GoldMine
screen.

Navigation Pane   Status bar

The Main Menu

The Main menu bar appears at the top of the screen just below the title bar. It contains all the general categories of functions, each of which displays a pull-down menu when you click the mouse over it.

Those of you coming from an older version of GoldMine can have your "old timers" menu structure back by choosing Tools➪Options➪System and selecting the Use Classic GoldMine Menu option. Of course, doing so will delay your effort to get used to the new screens.

The following list describes all the options available to you from the Main menu.

- ✔ **File:** Create new contact records, print reports, Import/Export data, and log in options. You also exit GoldMine gracefully from here.

- ✔ **Edit:** Cut, copy and paste your data; edit various record properties; edit, delete, and undo changes to Contact records.

- ✔ **Go To:** Access all of Goldmine's modules, as well as Analysis and Reporting tools.

- ✔ **Tools:** Access tools and wizards for synchronization, configuring GoldMine, managing databases, creating and running Automated Processes, Server Agents, globally replacing data, Synchronization tools, territory realignment, and launching the Database Alias Manager and QuickStart Wizard.

- ✔ **Actions:** Access GoldMine communication tools and timer commands, and manage mail merge functions.

- ✔ **Schedule:** Access scheduling options for the contact record, including scheduling a call or an appointment, scheduling literature to be sent out, scheduling forecasted sales, follow-up actions, and GoldMine e-mails.

- ✔ **Complete:** Access completed action options for scheduled and unscheduled calls, appointments, sales, other actions, correspondence, and other pending activities.

- ✔ **Web:** Access GM+Browser, Web publishing, and other online options.

- ✔ **Window:** Window display and status bar display options. Also open new Contact Record windows.

- ✔ **Help:** Online Help, the GoldMine Web site, NetUpdate, and important system information in About GoldMine.

The Global Toolbar

The Global Toolbar, shown in Figure 2-2, is located directly beneath the Main menu. It is completely customizable. It has two sections — the Standard Toolbar and the Taskbar. The buttons displayed throughout the Global Toolbar provide shortcuts to specific functions that you regularly perform.

Figure 2-2:
The default
Global
Toolbar.

The Standard Toolbar

The Standard Toolbar contains a customizable selection of functions, some or many of which you probably want to use regularly. You can customize the Standard Toolbar by clicking the drop-down button at the far right of the toolbar. Select Add or Remove Buttons⇨Standard. The Standard Toolbar list appears, as you can see in Figure 2-3. Using the checkboxes, select or deselect the elements you want to use.

The Taskbar

The Taskbar is comprised of the Getting Started and Customize tabs on the Global Toolbar. You control what options appear, the same way you customize the Standard Toolbar.

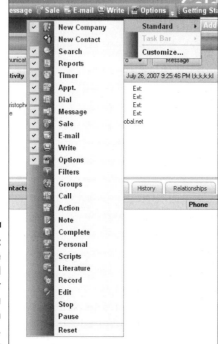

Figure 2-3:
All the
Standard
Toolbar
options you
can
customize.

The Navigation Pane

The Navigation Pane, shown in Figure 2-4, is a new feature in GoldMine Premium Edition. It essentially mirrors the Go To option from the Main menu.

Figure 2-4: A typical Navigation Pane with all four sections displayed.

The Navigation Pane also offers additional viewing and navigation options, depending on the module selected. The Navigation Pane contains the following four sections:

✓ **Search field:** The Search field enables you to search for one or more records in your database. Enter a contact name and click the Go button or just click the Go button. The Contact Search Center appears in the work area with the search criteria you just entered already filled in. Clicking the Go button here, or the Search button in the Standard Toolbar, you get to the same place: the Search Center. From here, you can do simple or complex searches for individual records or for sets of records that match your criteria.

✔ **Title bar:** The Title bar displays the title for the currently selected module. Click the Title Bar or the double arrows to the right to minimize or maximize the Navigation Pane.

✔ **View window:** The View window displays the most recent records you've accessed. The records you see here are context sensitive, changing as you change categories from the section just below it. Selecting a record from this list is usually the most efficient way to return to a record you have recently been working with.

✔ **Module menu:** If you reduce the size of the Navigation Pane by dragging down the dotted line that appears just above the Contacts list, the system replaces the menu options from the Navigation Pane with icons in the Module menu. If you are comfortable with using these icons, you can increase the real estate available in the View window.

The Work Area

The screen's center is the official Work Area. The GoldMine Work Area displays active windows, including the open contact records, Calendar, Activity List, and Contact Search Center. The Work Area also displays the scheduling dialog boxes, tools, and wizards. In short, this is where you do all your work.

Each time you select a contact record or an activity, or have the Work Area display anything, GoldMine builds a screen for display in the Work Area. That is, if you elect the tabbing option by maximizing your Work Area. GoldMine tiles these screens, in effect putting the most current screen on top of all the previous screens and displaying a series of tabs, with each tab linking to a recent screen you've been to.

Over the course of a day, you could build up a very large number of screens on top of each other, taking up a lot of memory space and potentially causing yourself to get pretty navigationally confused. That's why, when I finish with a screen in the Work Area, I usually close that screen. Just below the Global Toolbar, GoldMine displays the most recently accessed records or activities. You can close any of these screens by clicking the X on the right side of the tab. You can see these tabs in Figure 2-5.

Figure 2-5:
Closing an
opportunity
record in
the Work
area. You
can see the
"X" on the
right side
of the
Opportunity
tab is
highlighted.
Clicking this
closes the
Opportunity
record.

The status bar

The bottom line of the window is called the status bar and contains the following information:

- ✔ The name of the open Contact Set on the left side.
- ✔ Whether the Caps Lock and Num Lock keys are activated.
- ✔ When active, the timer, showing hours, minutes, and seconds.
- ✔ The username for the logged-in user.
- ✔ The date and time on the local computer.

Getting Help

GoldMine 8 includes a searchable Help Center. You can enter a keyword or a phrase and GoldMine displays all the relevant (and sometimes irrelevant) topics. For many topics, you get to see step-by-steps instructions, tips, and other miscellaneous reference materials. GoldMine's Help Center should be the first place to go when you're confused, frustrated, or just feel like reading.

One way to navigate to the Help Center is to click Help⇨GoldMine Help from the Main menu. However, the Help Center is designed to be context sensitive, meaning that you simply click F1 from whatever window or dialog box you're in to go directly to the Help Center. GoldMine then highlights the topic most likely to help you.

Figure 2-6 shows the Help screen you encounter if you click F1 while trying to schedule an appointment.

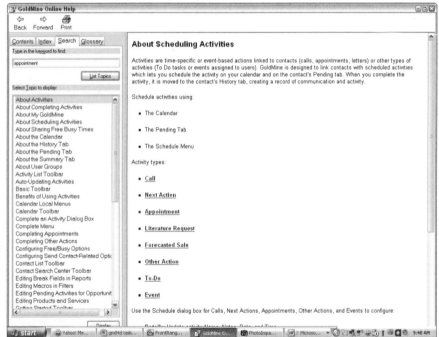

Figure 2-6:
A little help scheduling appointments.

In the Navigation Pane of the Help screen you encounter the following tabs (as you can see in Figure 2-6):

- ✓ **Contents Tab:** Displays a table of contents for Help. Topics are organized in "books." Expand books to display topics. To view a topic, highlight it and see it displayed in the right pane of the HTML Help viewer.

- ✓ **Index Tab:** Displays an index of Help topics. To locate a topic, scroll through the list or type a keyword or phrase for which to search. To view a topic, double-click the topic or highlight it and select Display. The topic displays in the right pane of the HTML Help viewer.

✔ **Search Tab:** Search for words in topics. Once the word is located, the topics containing that word display in a list. To view a topic, select it and click Display. The topic displays in the right pane of the HTML Help viewer.

✔ **Glossary Tab:** Displays a glossary of GoldMine terms. To display a definition, select a term from the list; its definition displays in the lower pane.

Getting help online

The second choice you encounter when you select Help from GoldMine's Main menu is GoldMine Online. Choosing this option takes you to the support center at www.goldmine.com. From this area of the FrontRange Web site, you can select several options for getting additional help. Most of the choices here require you to have your credit card handy if you don't have a current Maintenance and Support Plan in place.

Although you can eventually get to the GoldMine Support Center with a lot of clicking on the GoldMine Web site, a more efficient way is to go directly to www.goldmine.com/micro.aspx?id=4403 or call FrontRange at 800-755-2100. My clients report an average of about a 20-minute wait on hold when calling.

The GoldMine forum

The third choice on the GoldMine Help menu is the GoldMine forum, which you can also access at www.goldmine.com.. In this forum, dealers, consultants and other users share their insights, assistance, and complaints for free. Some of the advice here is quite good and usually very technical. Steel yourself for insults, however. Some of the more technical consultants have difficulty with social graces.

Chapter 3

Setting Up Your Preferences

. . . .

In This Chapter

▶ Customizing your Tabs

▶ Exploring the various preferences tabs

. . . .

*T*he preference settings in GoldMine enable you to put your own stamp on your copy of the software. If you're one of those eager beavers who just has to get right at it, you can probably skip this chapter. Read it later, or maybe never. Most of GoldMine works fine without your ever touching the settings. If you intend to use GoldMine's e-mail, you definitely need to establish your Preference settings.

On the other hand, if you're serious about making GoldMine work for you rather than the other way around, this is the chapter for you. In this chapter, you discover many interesting and powerful parameters you can set, and you don't need any programming knowledge to do so.

You can control hundreds of settings and options in GoldMine. Many of them deal with pretty technical stuff, however, so I skip over some of those in favor of the most commonly used and important settings.

You can access all user preferences through the Toolbar by choosing Tools⇨ Options, which gives you access to 12 separate areas. You can also get to your Option dialog box via Getting Started on the Taskbar. Behind each door of the Options settings are some of the secret tricks that GoldMine dealers use to set things up.

One of the most often requested changes is to the order of those tabs two-thirds of the way down the main GoldMine screen. In this chapter I also show you how to get the less valuable ones out of your way and promote the important ones to the front.

Customizing Your Tabs

Out of the box, GoldMine comes with 18 defined tabs, such as Fields, GM+View, Notes, and others. You can't see all of them simultaneously unless you click the down arrow to the left of the tabs being displayed. You then see a drop-down list of all available tabs, and you can even navigate to each of these areas by clicking any item in the drop-down list.

Early versions of GoldMine had just one row of nine tabs. Over the years, as the number of features expanded, so did the number of tabs. Now there are just too many to see all at one time in a horizontal display.

The Links tab helps you keep track of all the documents and files associated with each record. I discuss the Links tab in detail in Chapter 19, but it is far too important to live in relative obscurity. In fact, the Links tab is generally more important and more often used than several of the original tabs that are displayed by default.

There are several candidates for demotion from the first tier to the second. My recommendation is to demote the Summary tab to the second tier and replace it with the Links tab. I've used GoldMine since the early 1990s and have never once felt a need for the Summary tab. My second choice for demotion is the Referrals tab. Although I do use the Referrals tab, I don't use it all that often, and most of our clients don't use it at all. The Notes tab is another candidate for demotion. You probably shouldn't be using it, but as with most GoldMine users, you probably do.

Follow these steps to demote a tab and promote another tab at the same time.

1. **Click the down arrow to the left of the tabs.**

   A drop-down list appears.

2. **Click Customize at the bottom of the list.**

   The Display Tabs screen appears, as shown in Figure 3-1.

3. **Highlight the tab you want to promote or demote.**

   You do not need to touch the checkbox to the left of the tab description. Just highlight the name of the tab and then click the Move Up or the Move Down button as many times as you want. You can see the selected tab moving up or down as you click.

4. **When you're done rearranging all your tabs, click OK.**

   GoldMine returns you to the main work area. Your changes have taken effect.

Figure 3-1:
Use the
Display Tabs
dialog box
to rearrange
your tabs.

These changes apply only to the current logged-in user and do not affect anyone else. There is no global or company-wide setting for this.

If any of the tabs annoy you so much that you just want to eliminate them, you can do so from your Options screen by deselecting the box next to whatever tab you want to remove. Click the Reset button to restore all the original, default settings in case you change your mind. You could use this feature to eliminate certain tabs from the reach of certain users. For example, you could remove the History tab from the office snoop's system so that she can't see any e-mails.

Customizing All Your Preferences

You can do a lot of customizing of GoldMine without knowing how to program at all. In addition to adding custom fields, reports, and automated processes, you can tell GoldMine exactly how you expect to work and make sure that GoldMine conforms to that. In the following sections, I discuss the 12 tabs for setting preferences.

Personal Preferences

From the Preferences dialog box, click the Personal tab to see a dialog box like the one shown in Figure 3-2. The Personal tab is one of the simplest of the Preferences tabs and enables you to see your user name and full name, and to change your title, department, phone number, and fax number. In addition, by clicking the Change Password button, you can create a new password for yourself, thus preventing the resident office snoop from checking out too much of your stuff.

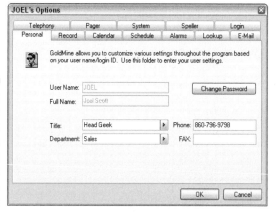

Figure 3-2:
Enter your
personal
information
on the
Personal
tab.

Be sure to use upper- and lowercase letters when entering your title and
department, because you may want to use these later as part of your e-mail
signature file.

You can move to another level of personal preferences and change your password by clicking the Change Password button from the Personal Preferences
dialog box. In the dialog box that appears, type your current password in the
Current Password text box. (Presumably, you know this password or you
wouldn't have been able to log on to GoldMine in the first place.) Then press
the Tab key and type a new password in the New Password text box.
GoldMine asks you to confirm your new password by retyping it in the New
Password Again text box.

Keep your GoldMine password cryptic and short, or you may become
annoyed if you have to enter something long and complicated every time you
start GoldMine.

The whole point to password protecting GoldMine is that your data is safe
because the password is secret, which means that no one else can access
your data. The downside to passwords is that if you forget yours, you're
going to be doing some reinstalling to get back to your data. You may want to
write down your password and keep it in a safe place, such as in a locked
cabinet in your office, or, like most people, on a sticky note stuck to your
monitor.

Record preferences

You can click the Record tab to customize the appearance of the main screen
(see Figure 3-3). Two radio buttons enable you to set the shading of the
screen background. You have two choices, either dark or bright background,
and the one you choose is purely a matter of taste. Give each a try.

Figure 3-3:
Change the main screen's appearance on the Record tab.

GoldMine also gives you a choice on the font size. Selecting the Use Large Font check box makes the characters larger on-screen. If your eyesight isn't quite what it used to be, using large fonts may be the best choice for you. You do pay a small price for this choice, however, because you can't see quite as many lines in your browse windows as you can see with small fonts.

You can also change the colors that labels and data appear in by clicking the Label Colors or Data Colors buttons on the Record preferences dialog box. Be sure to use contrasting colors to distinguish the labels and data from the background. You can have some real fun by setting the labels and data to the exact same color as the background. (Please don't actually do this, because it renders everything invisible!)

Following the Label Colors and Data Colors buttons, you see five check boxes that you can check to specify how data is entered or displayed:

- ✔ **Select Contents of Fields:** If this box is checked when you enter a data field, the existing data is highlighted, and whatever you type immediately overwrites the existing data. If this box is not checked, your new data is appended automatically to the existing data. Generally, you should leave this box checked.

- ✔ **Use a Word Format for User-Defined Dates:** This option applies only to user-defined fields, not to standard date fields such as those that appear on your Pending or History tabs. If you select this box, a typical date appears as Apr 1, 03. If this box is not selected, the same date appears as 4/1/03. Take your pick.

- ✔ **Show Numerics Aligned to the Right:** If you have a bunch of fields with numeric entries, sometimes the numbers are easier to read right-justified. Checking this box does just that for you.

✔ **Show Sort-by Field on Status Bar:** If you check this box, the currently active index appears on the status bar.

✔ **Show Contact Name on Activity Tabs:** Don't select this option unless you plan to make major and frequent use of the Relationships feature. Relationships connect or relate separate records in GoldMine to one another. For example, if you have separate records for each location of Burger King, you might use the Relationships feature to show how they are each related. See Chapter 24 for more about relationships.

The next section of the Record preferences dialog box enables you to determine how the system deals with entering ZIP codes. If you select the No Validation radio button, you then have to type the city, state, and ZIP code. Don't do this.

Behind the scenes, GoldMine builds a ZIP code database for you as you enter records. GoldMine builds on its ZIP code file and continues figuring out what city goes with what ZIP code. This is a great feature: The second time you enter a record from the same ZIP code, GoldMine automatically fills in the city and state for you.

You can buy several ready-made ZIP code files that will save you considerable effort. Check the Web site at www.ccc24k.com for a utility called ZipCodes+ And, a word of caution: In the mid-90s, the then-GoldMine Software Corporation pulled a ZIP code utility off the market. The company had been selling it for less than $20, but it had become so obsolete at that point that it was no longer of much value. There is now a dealer selling this same database or giving it away and claiming that it's worth $120. Let the buyer beware!

Make sure you select the Show Window of Cities radio button. With this option selected, you can

✔ **Enter the ZIP code and then enter the city and state.** GoldMine automatically fills in the city and state if the city and state are unique.

✔ **Select the correct city and state.** If multiple choices are possible, GoldMine displays a browse window that enables you to do this.

Calendar preferences

When you click the Calendar tab to display the Calendar preferences dialog box, most of the choices are pretty self-explanatory. You can set up GoldMine to reflect your normal working hours and the days of the week you usually work. These choices affect how your calendar is displayed, as shown in Figure 3-4.

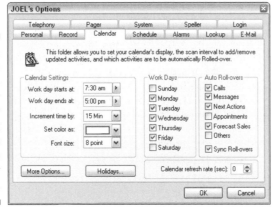

Figure 3-4:
Tell
GoldMine
what your
regular
work
schedule is
on the
Calendar
tab.

Click the Holidays button, and on the dialog box that appears, enter company holidays so that GoldMine won't schedule activities on those days. If you don't have Master access rights, ask your system administrator to take care of this task. The holidays are entered only once and are then in place in the schedule for everyone in the company.

You can actually schedule holidays based on the country in which you operate, as well as schedule personal holidays, such as your birthday or anniversary.

If you're like me, you may find that the Auto Roll-Over options are some of the most significant ones available in the Calendar preferences dialog box. Many are the days when I come into the office and have an overwhelming number of phone calls scheduled for me. Try as I might, I never seem to be able to make them all. If I do manage to make most of them, I want the remaining ones to be on my schedule for the next day. That's exactly what Auto Roll-Over does. It takes activities that you have not completed by the end of a particular day and moves them to the next day's schedule. It works very well. Maybe *too* well — at this writing, I now have 1,712 items on my activity list for tomorrow. I will be more diligent tomorrow, and I'm sure I'll get them finished.

You should select all the Auto Roll-Over options except auto-forwarding of appointments. Just because you didn't make it to that appointment with the IRS yesterday at 2:00 p.m. doesn't mean that you should show up there today at 2:00 p.m. (Well, maybe you should, but then again, I'm not a qualified tax adviser.)

If you are part of a corporate GoldMine installation and you use GoldSync, then the Sync Rollover option needs to be checked. It never hurts to check it, anyway.

Schedule preferences

When you click the Schedule tab, the Schedule preferences dialog box appears, as shown in Figure 3-5. This dialog box is fairly simple and offers you the following eight check boxes:

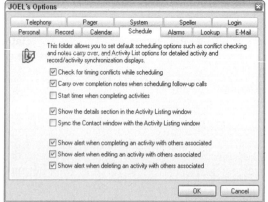

Figure 3-5: Set up your preferences for scheduling activities on the Schedule tab.

✔ **Check for Timing Conflicts While Scheduling:** As long as you have this check box selected, GoldMine warns you if you schedule yourself for two activities at the same time. Scheduling conflicts usually aren't an issue if you regularly schedule directly from the Calendar as I recommend, but selecting this option can't hurt.

✔ **Carry-Over Completion Notes When Scheduling Follow-Up Calls:** When you complete an activity and schedule a follow-up activity from the completion window, your notes are carried over to the follow-up activity if you have this option selected. I recommend that you select this one.

✔ **Start Timer When Completing Activities:** This option may be useful if you're tracking a telemarketing effort. In most cases, however, you don't need to select it.

✔ **Show the Details Section in the Activity Listing Window:** If you select this option, additional data fields appear at the bottom of the Activity Listing window. I recommend that you select this option.

✔ **Sync the Contact Window with the Activity Listing Window:** If you select this option and your monitor has an adequate resolution (greater than 640 x 480), you can see the related contact record when you highlight an item from the Activity List. I use this option also.

✔ **Show Alert when Completing an Activity with Others Associated:** If the activity you are completing has other users also assigned to it, GoldMine will alert you to this and allows you to complete the activity for everyone. For example, if you are all on a scheduled conference call, you may just want to complete the call for everyone.

✔ **Show Alert when Editing an Activity with Others Associated:** Same concept as the previous option, except this refers to editing. An example might be if you are rescheduling a conference call that has multiple users assigned to it.

✔ **Show Alert when Deleting an Activity with Others Associated:** Similar to the previous two options, you can delete that conference call for everyone.

Alarms preferences

When you click the Alarms tab, you see the Alarms preferences dialog box, as shown in Figure 3-6. This dialog box contains the following options (as well as a few more esoteric ones that I intentionally leave out):

✔ **Disable Alarms:** Selecting this option turns off your alarms so that GoldMine doesn't remind you to keep your dentist appointment. Assuming that you use GoldMine to help keep you organized, selecting this option is counterproductive. My advice: Do not disable your alarms.

✔ **Pop-Up Alarms:** By default, GoldMine displays alarms in a pop-up window on the right side of the screen. You can't miss one when it's triggered, and sometimes it becomes annoying when you get a barrage of alarms. You may want to consider a compromise solution, which is to have the alarm appear in the Taskbar.

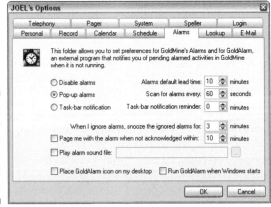

Figure 3-6:
Set up how GoldMine alerts you on the Alarms tab.

✔ **Alarms Default Lead Time:** The amount of time (in minutes) before a scheduled activity that the alarm window appears on-screen. To set the alarm to appear 15 minutes before each activity, type **15** in this field. Of course, 15 minutes is not always appropriate, so you can adjust this setting manually for every activity. Mine is set to 10 minutes, which usually works for me.

GoldMine includes the GoldAlarm program to remind you of scheduled activities even if GoldMine is not running. GoldAlarm is a separate program that runs alarms for you when you select the Run GoldAlarm When Windows Starts option.

✔ **When I Ignore Alarms, Snooze the Ignored Alarms for X Minutes:** This option works like the Snooze button on an alarm clock. If you ignore the alarms, they stop for a little while and then alert you again in a designated amount of time. The default snooze value is three minutes, but you can set it for whatever amount seems right to you.

✔ **Page Me with the Alarm When Not Acknowledged within X Minutes:** This option sets GoldMine to call your pager if you do not respond to an alarm within the specified number of minutes. Obviously, this option is valuable only if you have an alphanumeric pager set to work with GoldMine. The default waiting time is 10 minutes. To disable this option, just leave the check box blank. By default, it's blank anyway.

✔ **Play Alarm Sound File:** This option sets GoldMine to play the WAV sound file entered in the field to the right of the option. Windows comes with a number of WAV files that you can use if you want your alarm to play something other than the standard alarm sound.

Lookup preferences

If you click the Lookup tab, the Lookup preferences dialog box appears, as shown in Figure 3-7. This dialog box deals with some of the parameters involved in helping you locate a particular record in GoldMine. Figure 3-7 shows the selections I prefer.

E-mail preferences

GoldMine plays very nicely with the Internet. In fact, working with the Internet is one of the most important aspects of using GoldMine.

If you click the E-Mail tab, you can access all your options for setting up your e-mail.

Before you can use GoldMine with the Internet, you must sign up with an Internet service provider (ISP); you can choose a regional, national, or international provider. One important consideration when deciding on an ISP is how much, and where, you travel. If you want to avoid long-distance charges when you travel, hook up with a provider that has local coverage in the places you travel to most often.

Your ISP can provide you with most of the information you need to fill out your Internet preferences. Figure 3-8 shows some sample entries for these fields.

Note that GoldMine's e-mail client requires POP3 and SMTP for its e-mail client. For instance, if your company uses Microsoft Exchange and does not have POP and SMTP enabled, you will not be able to use GoldMine's e-mail client.

Figure 3-7: Set up your display options when querying the database on the Lookup tab.

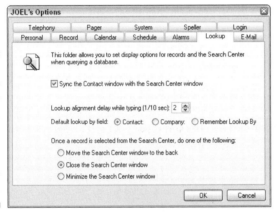

Figure 3-8: Tell GoldMine where to find your e-mail servers on the E-Mail tab.

The Network Connection section determines how GoldMine connects to the Internet. If you use another program, such as Internet Explorer or Netscape Navigator for your Internet connection, you don't have to select the Use Dial-up Networking option; if you want GoldMine to dial in and make the connection, however, select this option.

Login preferences

If you click the Login tab, the Login preferences dialog box appears (see Figure 3-9).

The settings on the Login preferences dialog box apply to everyone on your network, and your GoldMine administrator should establish the login settings. You probably shouldn't change any of the other Login preferences options. The other parameters are meant to be used in a network environment and are set by the GoldMine administrator. (But if you're working alone with a single user license, *you* are the GoldMine administrator!)

You can elect to bypass the login banner only if you're not using a password. I always recommend using a password, even if you're a single user sitting at home. If you do select this option, GoldMine doesn't pause at the initial logon dialog box but goes directly to the main data screen. This is a small time-saver if you're not worried about security issues.

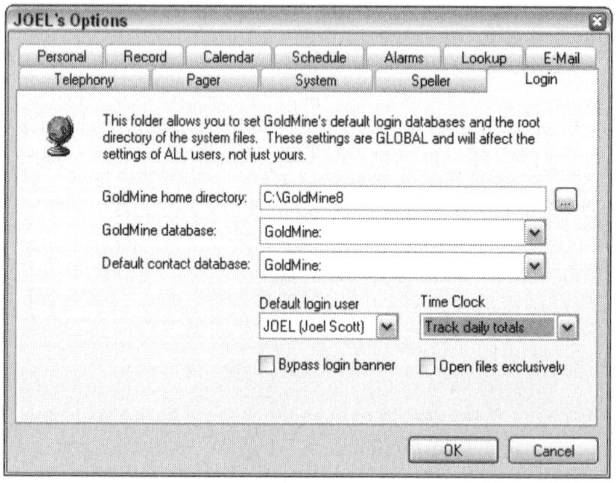

Figure 3-9:
Setting up
your Login
information.

Speller preferences

Finally, back in version 6.0, GoldMine gave in to all those users who just can't spell or aren't the greatest typists. (Sorry, but GoldMine can't help you yet if you're grammatically challenged.) Preference settings now include a series of settings for controlling how you want GoldMine to spell check your various notepads and e-mails. Specifically, GoldMine now enables you to check the spelling in all the activity-related notepads.

Figure 3-10 illustrates the settings that I use and that I recommend for most users. The following list describes what the options do when the spell check runs:

- ✔ **Ignore Capitalized Words:** Skips any words that begin with a capital letter. Use this option if your text typically contains many proper names.

- ✔ **Ignore All-Caps Words:** Ignores words containing all capital letters. Particularly in the high-tech and medical fields, it might be worthwhile to ignore things such as HTML and EKG because roughly half the words people in these fields use are acronyms.

- ✔ **Ignore Words with Numbers:** Skips over words containing embedded numbers, such as Win98. Mixing numbers in with words is also a popular specialty of the high-tech industry.

- ✔ **Ignore Words with Mixed Case:** Skips any words containing an unusual mixture of upper- and lowercase letters, such as GoldMine.

- ✔ **Ignore Domain Names:** Ignores any words that appear to be Internet domain names (such as `www.ccc24k.com`).

Generally, I have the spell checker ignore all kinds of words that have unusual capitalization or punctuation. There are just too many different kinds of words like this, particularly for those of us in the high-tech field. Simple capitalized words aren't so strange, so I allow the spell checker to do its thing on those words.

You can build your own dictionary of strange words you commonly use. If you do this religiously, it might then make sense to deselect some of the ignoring options.

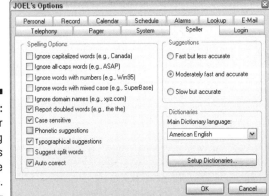

Figure 3-10:
Setting your spelling parameters on the Speller tab.

- **Report Doubled Words:** Reports any word appearing twice in a row. I have a habit of typing "the the" often, so I select this option.

- **Case Sensitive:** Makes a distinction between capitalized and noncapitalized words. For example, "france" is considered different from "France," so "france" would be reported as a misspelling. When the option is disabled, "france" and "France" are considered identical. Selecting this option noticeably slows the spell checker.

- **Phonetic Suggestions:** Suggests alternative spellings based on phonetic (sounds-like) similarity to the misspelled word. This option tends to improve suggestions for badly misspelled words. Enabling this option increases the time required to locate suggestions.

  Note that either Phonetic Suggestions or the Typographical Suggestions option must be selected or GoldMine offers no spelling suggestions.

- **Typographical Suggestions:** Makes suggestions based on typographical (looks-like) similarity to the misspelled word. This option is appropriate for people who are generally good spellers — like me, of coarse.

- **Suggest Split Words:** Suggests two separate words as replacements for a misspelling containing two joined words. For example, the spell checker suggests "are you" to replace "areyou."

- **Auto Correct:** Changes words marked with "Auto Change" actions automatically are changed to their specified replacements. When this option is deselected, GoldMine prompts you before it changes the words.

- **Main Dictionary Language:** Allows you to set the language of the main dictionary used to check spelling. The list shows only languages for dictionaries installed on your system. To check spelling in a language other than English, select the language from the list.

- **Suggestions:** Determines the speed and accuracy of the initial search for suggested replacements for misspelled words. When a misspelled word is found, a search is automatically made for suggestions. Clicking the Suggest button in the Check Spelling dialog box causes an increasingly more accurate (but slower) search for suggestions. My preference is faster *and* more accurate, but that one isn't offered yet.

System preferences

In the System tab you deal with a few menu and date settings. You can cling to the old-timers' GoldMine menu system, and you can specify how you want dates displayed.

The Epoch setting refers to how you want GoldMine to handle dates from other centuries. This was actually important back in 1999 when users were possibly scheduling activities for 2000 and GoldMine was sometimes confused. The Epoch setting isn't really critical now unless you are scheduling into the twenty-second century.

You can see the recommended settings in Figure 3-11.

Pager preferences

You can have GoldMine automatically track you down via Pager. The Pager feature is useful and is connected to alarms in GoldMine. When an alarm is triggered, it can automatically send a message to a pager if the Pager preferences are filled out. I don't have too many clients who use this feature (none?), but I am displaying the screen in Figure 3-12 for the sake of completeness.

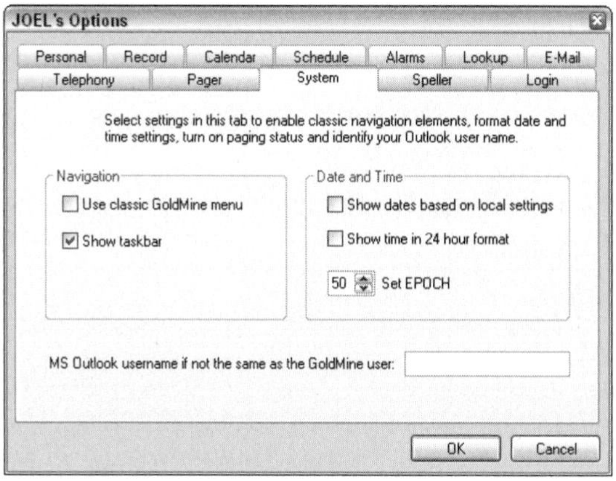

Figure 3-11:
System
settings.

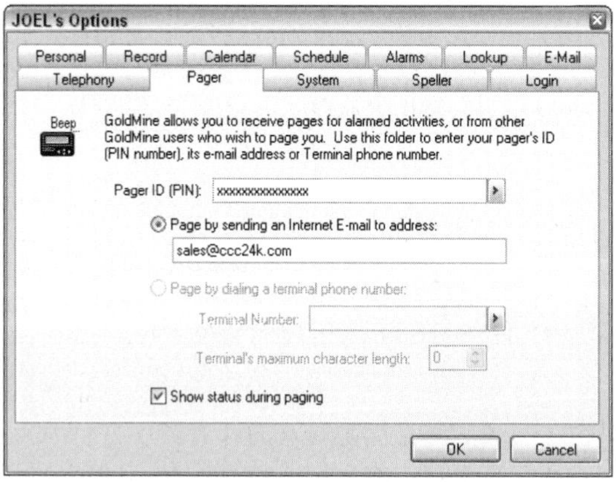

Figure 3-12:
Pager
settings.

Telephony preferences

The Telephony tab combines the old Modem preferences with the newer SoftPhone options. The Telephony tab is shown in Figure 3-13.

The options for the Modem preferences are most significant for those users who want GoldMine to actually dial the telephone based on a phone number in a contact record. If you're sitting at home with a simple telephone and telephone line, or if you're in an office in which you have your own line, this feature is simple and useful.

Figure 3-13:
Set up your
dialing
preferences
on the
Telephony
tab.

If your office has a central telephone system with multiple lines, however, you may need some technical help, along with additional hardware and software, to make GoldMine handle the dialing for you. That's what the SoftPhone options are about.

Unless you have some in-house telephony expertise, I do not recommend going down the SoftPhone route without a GoldMine consultant. And even then, you may want to investigate very thoroughly.

Chapter 4

Accessing GoldMine Remotely

. . . .

. . . .

*O*ne of the great strengths of GoldMine is its ability to provide you with important client data, whether you are sitting in the main office or you're in a submarine under the Arctic icepack. This strength is also a potential liability because the more available you make GoldMine to your staff, the more available you may inadvertently make the same critical data to people who shouldn't see it at all.

I find it amazing how many of my clients insist that they must have all their GoldMine data available while they are on airplanes. It's more realistic to think about bringing one or two documents associated with client accounts, but really, who actually works for hours on an airplane reviewing calendars and forecasts? As I write this, several U.S.-based airlines just announced plans to provide wireless Internet service to passengers in their main cabins. I'm sure there will be a fee for this, but it should minimize the requirement for having GoldMine data always loaded on everyone's laptop.

In this chapter I discuss most of the common ways you can work with your GoldMine system when you're at home, at a client-site, at a hotel, in an airplane, or at the beach. I've never actually used GoldMine while at the beach, but I have sent e-mails and even written a chapter or two while sitting outside at the pool. And you thought this writing stuff was hard.

GoldSync and CompanionLink are the two utilities most often used by people who can never be without their data. With each of these utilities, the data is loaded (synchronized) into your laptop or your handheld device respectively.

For those who are content to use GoldMine and its data while connected to the Internet, iGoldMinePlus and Remote Desktop are good solutions for laptop users. wMobile is a similar solution for handheld devices like BlackBerries and Treos.

Securing Your Data

For most of my clients, GoldMine contains their organization's most critical information the entire list of prospects and clients. Of course, any salesperson would feel crippled if he didn't have access to a phone number for a client who was about to place an order or who was on the verge of cancelling one.

The very requirement that you always have your data with you leads directly to a serious security issue. When your laptop is lost or stolen, some unknown person, and very possibly a bad one, may have your data. Wouldn't it be nice if that person worked for your fiercest competitor? Or, just as bad, what if the thief were clever enough to figure out who that competitor is and then realized that the data he now has might be worth something?

That probably won't happen, right? In the past few years at my company, we have had two cars broken into and laptops stolen. We had an employee leave a laptop at a girlfriend's house (in another state). And, one of us, in a rush to get on a plane, left a laptop in the trunk of a rental car. That last one was me.

None of those incidents ever made headlines. But all too often, we have seen headlines made by organizations (particularly in health care, financial services, and government) that have allowed employees to run around with sensitive data that should never have gotten out of the office. Social Security numbers and financial and medical information all demand that you take great care. People lose jobs and occasionally go to jail when they let data leak out.

So, here are my rules for remotely accessing data:

✔ If you don't need it, don't take it. You're not going to call any clients while you're flying to Paris. At most, you're probably going to edit a document or two. Just bring the documents.

✔ If you do need GoldMine data with you, take only the records you really need.

✔ The more people there are from your organization running around with the database, the greater the likelihood that a breach of security will occur.

Syncing Up with GoldSync

If you need to run GoldMine even when disconnected from the Internet, your only choice is to use the GoldSync utility that comes with GoldMine 8. GoldSync has been available for many years, first appearing in the mid-1990s as an add-on to GoldMine Standard Edition. Now GoldSync is actually included with every license of GoldMine Corporate and GoldMine Premium (a.k.a. GoldMine 8).

The basic principles behind GoldSync are as follows:

✔ **It requires licenses.** Each user who needs to run GoldMine remotely has to have a license broken off from the main group of GoldMine licenses and installed on a laptop. These licenses are called "undocked licenses." If licenses are scarce, an undocked license can be put back into the main group when not needed by a remote user.

✔ **It updates field by field.** GoldSync keeps each remote user up-to-date by sending all the data that has been changed since the last time GoldSync was run. This updating is done on a field-by-field basis, not record by record. This means that if the phone number in a particular record is changed, only the new phone number is actually sent back and forth. By crunching the data and sending only what has changed (not the entire record), GoldSync is very quick and efficient.

✔ **The last user to change a field wins.** Every time you change any data in a field, GoldMine saves a record of that change in its transaction log. If someone using GoldMine on the server changes a phone number and a remote user also changes that phone number, the transaction log makes sure that the most recent change is the one that sticks.

✔ **It runs automatically.** You can set GoldSync up to run automatically at regular intervals — typically once a day. You can initiate this process by either the remote laptop or by the GoldMine server, but the best approach is to have the remote user initiate each synchronization session. Otherwise, the server might be trying to communicate with a laptop that's stowed in the trunk of a rental car.

GoldSync has so many nooks, crannies, and gotchas that I have to recommend that you find an experienced GoldMine consultant if you insist on using it. Nevertheless, a wizard is embedded in GoldMine that you can use to set up GoldSync. You get to this wizard from the main menu by choosing Tools⇨ Synchronize⇨Synchronization Wizard.

Three main steps are involved in each synchronization session:

1. A transfer set is created based on changes to the data since the specified "cutoff" date.
2. The GoldMine data server and the remote computer connect via the Internet and exchange data.
3. The retrieving computer incorporates the updates into its database.

FrontRange has published three detailed documents that include information on GoldSync as well as on many other technical aspects of GoldMine. You can download each of these documents for free from `www.ccc24k.com`. The documents are as follows:

- ✔ GMPE 8 User Guide
- ✔ GMPE 8 Install Guide
- ✔ GMPE 8 Administrator Guide

Adding iGoldMine Plus

iGoldMinePlus is an add-on product that you can buy from your GoldMine dealer. With iGoldMinePlus, you can run the copy of GoldMine that is installed on your office server. In fact, you can run up to 35 different applications if you have an iGoldMinePlus license. These 35 applications can be almost anything (except HEAT). For example, your remote users might use iGoldMinePlus for access to accounting, inventory, or quotation systems. Each user may be restricted to just those applications that he is authorized to use.

You need to have one iGoldMinePlus license for each user — these licenses are "named," not concurrent. GoldMine licenses are concurrent, meaning that if you have a ten-user license for GoldMine, any ten people can use GoldMine simultaneously although you may have 20 or more total users. Named licenses require that anyone who might ever use the system has her own license. So if you have 20 total users, each of whom might at some point use iGoldMinePlus, you need to have 20 iGoldMinePlus licenses.

Due to some interesting and creative licensing from FrontRange, you can access GoldMine and up to 34 other applications with iGoldMinePlus, but if you want to access GoldMine and HEAT, you need two iGoldMinePlus licenses. HEAT, by the way, is a customer support system developed and supported by FrontRange. It integrates to a small degree with GoldMine.

FrontRange didn't actually develop iGoldMinePlus. It licensed a product called GoGlobal, which is available from a small group of GoldMine dealers. By purchasing GoGlobal instead of iGoldMinePlus, you might benefit from less restrictive licensing and, perhaps, more favorable pricing. Of course, you will then have to get your support for GoGlobal from your dealer.

Accessing GoldMine with Remote Desktop

Remote Desktop (formerly known as Terminal Services) is an alternative to both iGoldMinePlus and GoGlobal. It's an add-on to your Windows operating system and comes from Microsoft. Frankly, this is what I use when I need to get into GoldMine if I'm not in the office. Depending on what operating system you use, some number of Remote Desktop licenses may even be included.

Remote Desktop, which is included with Windows XP Professional, enables you to connect your computer via the Internet from almost any computer or Smartphone. After you are connected, Remote Desktop gives you mouse and keyboard control over the server to which you have just connected. In other words, you are dialing into your company's GoldMine server and using that computer as though you were sitting right in front of it. As long as you have a decent broadband connection, the speed is almost as good as it is when you are sitting in the office.

Using Handheld Devices

A handheld device, for this discussion, is any phone such as a BlackBerry or a Treo that can connect to the Internet and has a graphic display. These devices are inherently different from a laptop because they can't actually load and run GoldMine. Nor can they display GoldMine as you're used to seeing it. You just can't fit the entire GoldMine screen on a 2" by 2" display. And you can't expect to download your entire GoldMine database into one of these devices.

Depending upon how much memory is in your handheld and how many records are in your database, you can expect to keep your basic contact information (names, addresses, phone numbers, and so on) in your handheld. You can also expect to coordinate your GoldMine calendar with the calendar in your handheld. Many of my clients also send e-mails directly from their handhelds and then store those e-mails in their GoldMine database.

CompanionLink

CompanionLink has been around for a long time and is sold by most of the GoldMine dealers. You can check with your own dealer or log on to www.ccc24k.com for product details and to purchase CompanionLink. It allows you to plug your handheld into a cradle and download the static information (names, addresses, phone numbers, for example) for many, perhaps thousands, of records. Don't expect your BlackBerry to store all your history and linked documents, though. That's really asking too much.

You can edit the GoldMine data on your handheld and then sync it back into your main GoldMine database when you return to the office.

wMobile

wMobile is an add-on product produced by W-Systems and distributed by several of the more experienced GoldMine dealers. With wMobile, you can use almost any handheld device (for example, BlackBerry and Treo) that allows access to the Internet to actually run GoldMine. Well, not exactly GoldMine. As mentioned previously, the display on a handheld device is too small for the entire GoldMine screen. wMobile provides virtually all the essential GoldMine information in a condensed and simple format. You can customize the fields that you see, thereby turning your handheld into a very powerful remote access device. For example, if you have added some custom fields (perhaps a priority field or a credit limit field) to your GoldMine, wMobile comes with tools allowing you to add those same custom fields to the display you see on your handheld.

With wMobile, you don't store any of your GoldMine data in your handheld device. This is the main difference between CompanionLink and wMobile. You have access to your data only if you have an active Internet connection. You almost always have connectivity to the Internet with these devices, but you could be in trouble while on an airplane or if you're deep in a subway tunnel.

Additional information about each of these add-on products (and any good new ones that become available) is available at my company's Web site (www.ccc24k.com/add-ons.htm). Some of these products, at least at the time of this writing, offer free trials. Additional information about these products and possible trials is also available by writing to me at dummies@ccc24k.com.

Part II
Managing Contacts

The 5th Wave   By Rich Tennant

"Your database is beyond repair, but before I tell you our backup recommendation, let me ask you a question. How many index cards do you think will fit on the walls of your computer room?"

In this part . . .

The real point of GoldMine is the management of all your accounts. Assuming that you have customers, clients, or accounts, all of which are basically the same thing, this part of the book gives you a solid feel for entering and managing all the basic contact information in GoldMine.

How and when to enter free-form notes is an art form that may help keep you out of trouble later. Additional contacts that seem important enough to keep track of can be kept within the secondary contact system or managed within the newly enhanced Relationships tab. Random tidbits can be housed in the Details section. The Referral section allows you to relate one account to one or to many others.

Filters, Groups, SQL Queries, and the SQL Query Building Wizard are all tools you need to focus on specific types of accounts or activities. With these, you can tailor reports and marketing campaigns and truly automate your business.

Chapter 5

Creating and Viewing Client Records

*I*f you actively use GoldMine in your business, you probably need to create new records just about every day. And you may need to quickly locate existing records in the database many times each day. In this chapter, you find out how to do these tasks efficiently.

Out of the box, GoldMine is a terrific general contact-management system. But the developers don't know the details of your business, so they can't think of every field you may require. They're smart enough, however, to give you the ability to create these fields yourself. After you create fields, you can use your custom fields the same way you use all other fields. In this chapter, I show you how to enter a new record manually.

Creating New Records

A sure sign of a growing, healthy business is a steady increase in the number of records in its database. You can add new company records or new individual contact records that belong to company records.

Adding a new company

To add a new company, click the New Company button in the upper-left corner of the main work area. This brings you to a short drop-down list allowing you to decide to enter either a new company and primary contact or just a new secondary contact that relates to an existing company. Figure 5-1 shows the dialog box for entering a new company.

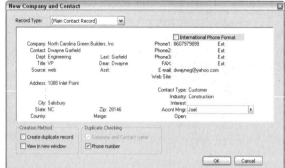

Figure 5-1:
Create a
record for a
new
company.

The first two fields that you see in Figure 5-1 are the Company name and main contact person's full name (Contact). When you enter information into these fields, type them in upper- and lowercase letters. You may eventually want to merge the data in these fields into a Word template. Then your word processor will display them exactly as you typed them into the database. I discuss this topic in Chapter 16. Most people use a combination of capital letters and lowercase letters for contact and address information in a letter, so type your field names in GoldMine that way.

If you forget to use standard, consistent capitalization when you enter data, don't panic. The software police will not come looking for you, and you won't suddenly be assaulted by horrendous error messages. However, your letter will surely look less personal. Your client may recognize that the letter was computer-generated and figure that no human being even touched it. So spend a little time properly capitalizing your entries, and you may benefit from some warm, fuzzy feelings from your clients.

Entering additional contacts

GoldMine 8 features a streamlined method for adding additional contact records for an existing company. *This does not create secondary contacts, but rather a completely separate record for the new contact — with a relationship automatically formed.* When you initially enter a new company, you also enter that company's primary contact person. Chances are, for many of your accounts, there are additional people also associated with the account. More details on handling additional contacts are in Chapter 6.

To add more contacts to GoldMine, follow these steps:

1. **Click the down arrow to the right of the New Company button to enter a New Contact.**

   The screen shown in Figure 5-2 appears. It's important that the primary contact's record is the active one as you are adding additional contacts to that same company.

2. **Select Auto-fill with Primary Address if the additional contact person is at the same physical address.**

   This grabs the address information from the primary record and copies it to the record you are creating. It does not copy phone information.

3. **Select the Create Duplicate Record option in the lower-left corner if you want to copy more than just the physical address.**

   This copies virtually all the fields from the upper portion of the screen and allows you to edit whatever you need to change in the newly created record.

Dealing with Jr., Sr., and III

GoldMine tries to determine automatically the last name of a contact by looking at the name you enter in the Contact field. It takes the last full word you type, assumes that this is the last name, and places it in the Last field on the main screen. This works fine if you type a simple name, such as *Jim Smith*. But if you type *Jim Smith, Jr.*, GoldMine mistakes *Jr.* for the last name and puts it in the Last field.

I often use the Last field to look up records in the database, and it's not helpful to have this field cluttered with hundreds of *Jr.*s rather than actual last names. The solution to this dilemma is to type the full name in the Contact field, including *Jr.* or *Sr.*; then, when you return to the main screen, manually correct the Last field by changing *Jr.* or *Sr.* to the actual last name of the contact.

Figure 5-2:
Adding
additional
contacts to
existing
companies.

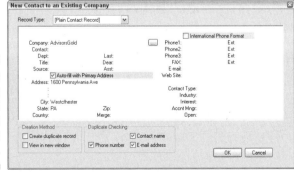

Entering U.S. telephone numbers

The Phone number field holds the primary telephone number for the client. Every telephone number can also include an associated extension of up to six characters. Six digits is the limit, even though it looks as though more space is available.

Type the 10 digits of the area code and telephone number without parentheses, dashes, or any other punctuation. GoldMine automatically applies the format (909)792-8636 to a U.S. telephone number.

You don't do any harm if you go ahead and type the punctuation; you're just working harder than you have to.

Entering telephone numbers for the rest of the world

Other countries use a variety of telephone number formats, so things get a little trickier when you're entering telephone numbers for clients outside the United States.

To enter a telephone number in a format other than the standard U.S. format, select the International Format check box on this dialog box. After selecting International Format, you can type the phone number any way you want, and GoldMine applies no additional formatting. The field can hold up to 20 characters, not including the extension field.

The extension field has one of those right-arrow buttons next to it, indicating that it has a lookup list. The list is taken from the Extension field associated with Phone1 on the main screen. If you modify that lookup list on the main screen, those changes also appear on the Add a New Record dialog box.

E-mail addresses — you've got to collect 'em

As with the fax machine, e-mail is here to stay. In fact, it's not hard to argue that, for many businesses, e-mail is rapidly overtaking the fax machine as the communication device of choice. Your clients likely have an e-mail address (or two or three). Making use of this technology is not just important, it's essential. Fortunately, GoldMine enables you to collect, store, and use e-mail addresses easily. E-mailing is discussed in Chapters 17 and 18.

If you religiously gather e-mail addresses for every new and existing account, you can send individual e-mails, broadcast e-mails, attached documents, photos, and almost anything else that is critical to business communication. But first you have to obtain the addresses and put them in the database.

The primary e-mail address is a piece of information you normally enter while you're creating a new record. There is no limit to the number of e-mail addresses a contact could have, so you can always go back to that contact's record and add more e-mail addresses. These are displayed in the Details tab, and you can get more information about this in Chapter 7.

Entering Web site addresses

You can also add a Web address for this new company. This address is clearly different from the client's e-mail address. The Web site defines the URL or address of the company's Web page.

If you enter the Web site address, GoldMine can easily direct you or any of your co-workers to this client's Web site. That is, you can pull up the client's Web page right from GoldMine.

You can enter only one Web site address on this dialog box. If a client has multiple Web sites, you can enter additional sites later within the Details tab of the main screen. See Chapter 7 for more information on using the Details tab.

Checking for duplicate records

As you enter new records into GoldMine, asking it to search for duplicate records is useful. GoldMine checks the following for you, based on up to three fields:

- ✔ Company and Contact name
- ✔ Phone number

I suggest that you select both the Phone number and the Company/Contact name. If you enter a phone number that exactly matches one already existing in your database, GoldMine notifies you before it adds your new record (but annoyingly, it does so only after you enter all the information into the Add a New Company and Contact dialog box), and then you have an opportunity to decide whether to proceed.

Contact name and Company name work a little differently. GoldMine checks to see whether what you just entered matches the beginning of any existing contact or company name. For example, if you enter **Computer**, the system warns you if it finds an existing record with Computer Control Corporation in the Company name field. This result may be desirable, or may not be. The Contact name field works the same way. Try it; you can always turn off this feature if it aggravates you when you're really doing what you intended to do in the first place.

If you do create some duplicate records, you can combine them by using the merge/purge utility. You can find that utility on the Tools main menu. Selecting Merge/Purge Records brings you to the wizard that walks you through the entire procedure. The merge/purge utility has the capacity to merge all your individual records into one record — probably not what you want! As always, make sure you have a recent backup before doing this or any procedure that affects multiple records. Just as "brush only the teeth you want to keep" makes sense, so does "back up all the data that matters to you." As soon as you click OK, you return to the GoldMine main screen. Your new record has now been created, and you can continue with all the additional fields on the main screen.

Finding a Record in Your Database

As you use GoldMine, the task you will probably find yourself doing most frequently is finding a record. Scheduling activities, writing notes, or checking a client's history requires you to look up the correct record. And every time the phone rings, you may want to quickly check the caller's record.

If you're like me, you get lots of calls every day. Some of these calls come from a person who clearly knows who I am, but for the life of me, I can't recall who he or she is. The last thing I want the mystery caller to know is that I don't remember him or her. So I sometimes need to quickly and quietly find a client's record while I'm saying hello and making small talk. With a little practice, you can find any record, no matter how many are in your database, in just a few seconds.

The semi-secret and fast way to find a record

Most of the fields on the main screen allow you to point your mouse at a *label* and double-click, which opens a browse window. For example, if you double-click the Last label, a browse window, like the one shown in Figure 5-3, appears. This browse window is actually called the Search Center, which was brand new in version 6.0. In Figure 5-3, I have already entered the letter "g" in the search field, so GoldMine is listing all my accounts that have a primary contact whose last name begins with that letter.

To make the browse window (Search Center) appear, be sure to double-click the field label — not the text box in which you enter data.

Figure 5-3:
Find records
quickly by
using the
Search
Center.

More sophisticated searches

The Search Center has gradually been getting more sophisticated and now allows you to do much more complex searches. In GoldMine 8, you can now search on multiple fields at the same time. For example, you could find all the accounts in California that have fax numbers. You expand your search from the simple kind of single field search described in the previous section to multiple fields by clicking the Search button in the upper-left corner of the GoldMine screen.

When the Search Center window appears, you can select which fields to display by clicking the Columns button in the upper-right corner of the Search Center. Doing so displays the screen shown in Figure 5-4.

You can add or delete fields (columns) from the Search Center display by highlighting the particular field and selecting the left or right arrows in the middle of the screen to add or delete the column.

If you click the small down arrow just below the Columns in the upper-right corner of the Search Center GoldMine immediately expands your search to multiple fields. This is a very powerful feature. You can see the example of California accounts that have fax numbers in Figure 5-5. You can use a series of AND or OR operators to separate each specification.

Figure 5-4:
Fine-tuning the fields you see in the Search Center.

Figure 5-5:
Using multiple fields to find records in the Search Center.

In Boolean logic, ANDs take priority over ORs. Also, you can't use parentheses to control the precedence as well as you can when building filters.

Using a Custom Field

Custom fields are fields that you, someone in your company, or your GoldMine dealer set up to meet your organization's specific needs. They don't come as part of the standard package; they are developed because you need to track some particular data.

If you have more than a few custom fields, you can group them into *custom field views*. Each view is set up with a separate file folder tab and may have its own access rights. Consequently, certain people or groups of people may not be able to see or edit the data in a particular field view.

Who needs custom fields, anyway?

Almost every business needs to track some unique information. GoldMine has all the common fields that almost every business needs to use. Your business is probably a little different from mine, so you may need some fields that I don't need.

Each department in your organization probably tracks different information. The following lists show some examples of information that particular departments may track.

- ✔ **Accounting department**
  - Credit limit
  - Credit terms
- ✔ **Marketing department**
  - Related interests
  - Will be a reference (Y/N)
  - Wants newsletter (Y/N)
- ✔ **Sales department**
  - Competition
  - Purchases YTD
  - Budget cycle

How custom fields get on-screen

Placing custom fields on-screen takes some design effort. Usually, an experienced GoldMine dealer handles this process, but nothing prevents you from doing it yourself.

Interview some people from the departments that use GoldMine to determine which custom fields you may need to add to your program. Review all the reports they currently use and any reports they plan to implement in the future. Reports always provide good clues as to what fields need to be available in the database. Ask as many questions as you can.

GoldMine provides three field types: numbers, text, and date. Yes, it would be nice if there were more field types and more formatting capability. When you create a custom field, you must define the field type, field length, F2 lookup list, and access rights for the field.

Accessing field views

GoldMine is capable of holding hundreds of custom fields. More than ten or so, however, becomes unmanageable if they aren't segregated into logical groups. These groups are called *views,* and each view is associated with its own tab.

Particular access rights are often assigned to an entire view. For example, the Accounting view may have data that the marketing department doesn't need to see or change.

If your system has any custom field views, you access them by following these steps:

1. **Click the Fields tab.**

2. **Position the cursor anywhere in the area below the tab and right-click.**

   A selection window appears, listing all the additional field views.

3. **Select the appropriate field view from the first section of the selection window, as shown in Figure 5-6.**

Figure 5-6:
Getting to a
field view by
right-
clicking.

Adding the same field to two different views is just fine, but they are only one field in the database. The information entered in one view will show up in the other. Just because they are placed on two views doesn't make them two different fields. This is good for something such as an account number that needs to be in the Accounting view along with all the items you don't want salespeople to see, but it may also be in the Sales view so that salespeople can know the correct account number for taking orders.

Chapter 6

Handling Notes and Secondary Contacts

*Y*ou can use GoldMine to maintain a complete audit trail of everything that has ever happened with each of your accounts. You use various notepads to record your notes about each of your accounts. Sometimes, this audit trail can get you out of trouble. Better yet, if you use it consistently, it can keep you from getting into trouble in the first place. The stark reality, however, is that you have to make it a habit to type in notes if you are to reap the benefits. That means that you actually have to enter your notes every time you complete an activity. And remembering to enter your notes may be the hardest part.

In this chapter, you find a discussion of the main Notes and Contacts tabs. Every contact record in GoldMine contains a series of file folder tabs in the lower third of the work area. In "The Main Notepad" section of this chapter, you discover how to view existing notes, how to enter new notes, and, most important, what notes you should actually put there.

Additionally, you discover how to find additional people listed in the Contacts tab and how to enter new or edit existing information in this chapter. You also discover how to determine when to use the Contacts section and when to create a separate record.

The Main Notepad

One of the standard tabs on the main menu is labeled Notes. When you click this tab for the first time in a particular record, the main notepad appears and is completely blank except for the Add note button in the upper-left corner. The main notepad, shown in Figure 6-1, is sitting there waiting for you to start typing.

Figure 6-1:
The main
notepad
before
you've
entered
anything.

If you type lots of notes for a particular record, you won't be able to see them all on-screen at the same time. Use the scroll arrows on the right to scroll through the notepad.

What to put in the main notepad

So what notes go in the main notepad? GoldMine contains many different notepads. In fact, a similar notepad is associated with every activity that you schedule or complete. You should particularly understand the distinction between the main notepad and those in the scheduled and completed activities sections. See Chapters 9 through 11 for more details.

You should put general comments concerning the account into the main notepad. If you hear a rumor about a pending IPO, make a note of it here. Any concerns you might have about your client's credit rating should go in the main notepad as well. If you had a problem with someone at the client site, put it here rather than in the Completed Activities notepad.

TIP

Take notes — stay out of court

Several years ago, a local attorney called our office and asked us to send a computer technician to his office to repair a computer. The same request was made twice more in the following months. All three times, the technician was dispatched, the computer was repaired, and the attorney was billed. By this time, the attorney had run up bills totaling $830.

On December 31st, this client sat down to pay his bills, apparently for the whole year. We received a check from him for $380. You might think that he mistakenly transposed the digits. But in two places on the check he had written, "Paid in Full." I knew that meant that if I cashed the check, I was accepting it as payment in full, and I would have no legal recourse toward collecting the money he owed us.

I called this client and convinced him to come over to our office. He initially refused to rewrite the check. In fact, he then claimed that he didn't

owe us any money at all because I could not prove that any of our technicians had ever been to his office!

I showed him the GoldMine screens where we had three pages of date- and time-stamped notes detailing everything we had done in the past three months at his office. He asked if I could print it all out. I told him, "Yes, but only for the judge." He literally ran out to his car to get his checkbook, and he couldn't pay us fast enough.

I am certain that we never would have been paid had we not maintained the complete notes about all the work we had done for him.

The moral of the story is that you should write *everything* down. And be especially careful and thorough with your notes if your relationship with an account seems to be headed in an uncomfortable direction.

Starting a new note

Starting with version 6.0, GoldMine made starting a new note and date and time stamping the note completely idiot proof. To start a new note, simply follow these steps:

1. **Click the Notes tab and then the Add Note button in the upper-left corner.**

   A blank space appears and you can just start typing.

2. **To have GoldMine check your spelling when you're done typing (but before you save the note), right-click within the text area and, in the drop-down list that appears, select Spell Check.**

   GoldMine goes through your entire note, letting you and your third grade teacher know which words were misspelled and suggesting corrections.

3. **Select the yellow Save icon to save your note.**

   GoldMine automatically date and time stamps the note and records your username on the note (see Figure 6-2). If you forget to save your note, GoldMine does it for you anyway.

Figure 6-2:
A note with
a date and
time stamp.

The main notepad lets you type anything you want. But be careful: Everything you write can be read by everyone else on your team and possibly by others outside your team. Never type anything that you wouldn't put out for public view.

In previous versions of GoldMine, you could edit or even delete your old notes or someone else's notes. That didn't make for a very secure audit trail and actually made the legal value of these notes somewhat questionable. In GoldMine 8, you can no longer edit existing notes in the main notepad, although it's easy enough to just delete a note by right-clicking within the note and then selecting Delete Note. There is no warning to make sure you really mean it, though.

Designing a coherent report based on information in the main notepad is difficult. Finding key words or particular items that belong together can be hard, but you can do a text search for a key word or phrase. This search will go through all your active records to locate those accounts that have that word or phrase in the main notepad. I mention "active records" because if you activate a filter, only those records that belong with that filter are available for the search. More information is available about filters and groups and SQL queries in Chapter 8.

To do a text search within the main notepads of all your accounts:

1. **Select Search from the Toolbar.**

   The Search Center appears.

2. **Select the down arrow to the right of the Search By box.**

   A drop-down list appears, showing Notes as one of the choices within the alphabetical listing of fields.

3. **Select Notes and then select the appropriate operator from the next box, as shown in Figure 6-3.**

   When the Search By drop-down list is invoked, press the N key on the keyboard. The first word that starts with *N* appears. Continue pressing N until the word *Notes* appears. Then select it.

4. **Click the Search button.**

   GoldMine begins cruising through all your active records. There is a per-cent complete area that shows you GoldMine's progress as it goes through your records. If you have a large database, this could take a while.

Figure 6-3:
The Search Center searching the main notepads of all active records.

If meaningful reporting is your thing, you will find it easier to create a report based on a particular user, a range of dates, or some kind of Result Code if those notes are in Pending or History records rather than in the main notepad.

When you come back from an appointment or hang up the phone and want to detail what went on, write those notes in the Completed Activity notepad. See Chapter 11 for more information on that.

The Contacts Tab

In many, if not most, of your accounts, you deal with more than one person. When you need to keep track of more than one person for an account, you can add the information for each additional person you deal with by using the Contacts tab. GoldMine refers to these additional people as *secondary contacts* or *additional contacts*. Entering information for primary contacts is discussed in Chapter 5.

When I am dealing with a major account (one for which I have many important contacts), I usually enter each of these people as a separate record and relate them via the Relationships function that is explained in Chapter 24. When I need to keep track of someone with whom I don't expect to have much communication, I enter that person as a secondary contact. In my own case, for example, someone in accounting might be a secondary contact, and that information is useful to me when I have to call to find out where my check is. Because I don't market my services to people in accounting, I can get away with this. If I were consulting on accounting software, I would approach it differently.

The Organization Chart was significantly enhanced in recent versions, although in GoldMine 8 that has morphed into the Relationships tab. I now use the Contacts tab to house only those people I don't intend to directly correspond with. An example might be someone in the Accounts Payable department. I might need to call this person sometime, but I probably won't include him or her in my quarterly newsletter distribution list.

The Contacts section is the first section that is relational in nature. A *relational system* implies that you have a one-to-many situation. In this case, *relational* means there may be many secondary contacts for each account. In fact, you have an unlimited number of secondary contacts that you can attach to each account.

Entering a new secondary contact

To enter a new secondary contact, follow these steps:

1. **Click the Contacts tab.**

2. **Move the cursor anywhere in the area below the highlighted Contacts tab and right-click.**

   You see a drop-down menu (shown in Figure 6-4) that enables you to enter new contacts or edit existing contacts.

3. **Select New from the drop-down list.**

   GoldMine then displays a data entry window in which you can enter a considerable amount of information about a new contact, as shown in Figure 6-5. The window contains four sections of information, same as the window for entering the primary contact's information. Read on for more information about these four sections.

Figure 6-4:
The drop-down menu for adding secondary contacts.

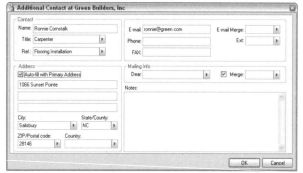

Figure 6-5:
Enter the
new
secondary
contact's
information
in the
Contact
dialog box.

In the first section, you see three fields:

- ✔ **Name:** Enter names just as you do on the main screen. Use upper- and lowercase letters, and enter the first name followed by the last name.

- ✔ **Title:** This field's purpose is obvious. You can make use of a lookup list with this field. The lookup list is the same as the Title lookup on the main screen.

- ✔ **Ref.:** The Reference field is really synonymous with the Department field on the main screen, and you should use it this way. See Chapter 5 for details on entering information on the main screen. The Reference field also has a lookup list.

The second section contains address information corresponding to the information in the address area of the main screen. If this secondary person's address is the same as the address for the main record, you can just select the Auto-Fill option. Auto-Fill automatically copies the address information from the primary contact's record to the secondary contact's record. It's a time-saving feature and is great if you are entering a lot of people all at the same address. Putting anything in the address fields, such as a room number or P.O. Box, turns off the Auto-Fill feature from the primary record.

If you intend to use secondary contacts for mailing, be certain that either NO fields or ALL fields of the secondary address are filled out.

The third section contains fields for an e-mail address, a phone number, and a fax number. Each of these fields is specific to the secondary person you're entering. Again, you can leave out the phone numbers if they are the same as the primary contact's phone numbers, but remember to collect as many e-mail addresses as you can.

This third section also has an E-mail Merge code field. You can regulate what e-mail correspondence goes to your secondary contacts. Also, this Merge code field is what allows you to specify this. For example, by entering "XMAS" as a code in just select secondary contact records, you can regulate who gets an electronic Christmas card. You can find a little more on this topic in Chapters 13 and 14.

The fourth section contains the Dear field, mail merge codes, and another one of the ubiquitous notepads.

The Dear field, or Salutation field, is the same as the Dear field on the main GoldMine screen. Enter into this field the greeting you want to use when you write a letter to this person.

The mail merge codes enable you to regulate what printed correspondence this person receives. The mail merge field has a lookup list, and you can have multiple entries from the lookup list, of course. These mail merge codes work together with filters and groups that you can build. Working with filters and groups is detailed in Chapter 8.

If you need multiple entries for mail merge codes, such as "XMAS, BD, ANN, NYD," keep your abbreviations short. You are limited to a total of 19 characters, and the commas and spaces between entries count. The E-Mail Merge field discussed previously has only 15 characters. The shorter your abbreviations, the more choices you can fit into one field. See Chapter 26 for more about using lookup lists.

Editing an existing secondary contact

Sometimes you create a secondary contact but you don't have all the important information at hand. You may need to go back and enter the contact's address or e-mail address later. Or perhaps this person's phone number changed. You can add or edit information in a secondary contact's record by following these steps:

1. **Click the Contacts tab.**

2. **Right-click the contact name that you want to edit.**

   A drop-down list appears.

   Double-clicking the secondary contact you want to edit also enables you to edit a secondary contact's information.

3. **Select Edit from the drop-down list.**

   You return to the original secondary contact window.

4. **Enter new information or edit existing information and then click OK to save your changes when you're done.**

Swapping the secondary contact with the primary one

Occasionally, someone who was secondary becomes more important in the scheme of things, and you need to promote him or her to primary status. GoldMine enables you to do this easily, as follows:

1. **Click the Contacts tab.**

2. **Right-click the current secondary person you want to promote to primary status.**

3. **Click Options.**

4. **Click Swap with Primary and then confirm that you really do want to do this.**

After you confirm, the person who was the main contact is dropped into the Contacts tab to join the rest of the commoners down there. The person who had been in the secondary section is promoted to the top. This swap can be temporary because you can reverse it very easily.

Converting a secondary record to a stand-alone record

Sometimes one of your secondary records deserves to become a separate record, either by itself or still somehow related to a main record. For example, a major change in the organization of an account may warrant a change to a stand-alone record.

To create a separate stand-alone record, follow these steps:

1. **Click the Contacts tab.**

2. **Right-click the current secondary person you want to deal with.**

3. **Click Options.**

4. **Select Convert to Record from the menu and then confirm that you really do want to make the change.**

GoldMine removes the secondary contact from the initial record and creates a completely separate record for the contact. You can still maintain a relationship between the original secondary contact and the rest of the people at that account by using the Relationships tab, which I discuss in detail in Chapter 24.

Chapter 7

Details and Referrals

In This Chapter

▶ Taking care of the details

▶ Using the Referrals tab

*T*he Details tab allows you to save random tidbits of information that relate to individual records. You can search for them and report on them as well. The Referrals tab enables you to relate one account in your database to another.

The Details and the Referrals tabs are two of the least understood and least used of the basic sections of GoldMine. But the truth is that they aren't that hard to understand, and they can both be very useful. In this chapter, you find out how to use them, and you find some recommendations on clever ways to make the most of them.

Taking Care of the Details

I like to think of the Details tab as containing random, relational information. By *relational,* I mean that one account in your GoldMine database may contain an unlimited number of detail entries. Another way to say this is to call it a "one-to-many relationship." You can use the Details tab to store data that isn't necessarily needed for every record.

For example, suppose you want to keep track of a credit card number for each account. You could create a user-defined field for the credit card number. A *user-defined field* is a new field that you define and place into the GoldMine database. It would be fine to use one of these fields until the first time a client tells you he has *two* credit cards you need to keep on file. You paint yourself into a corner by using a user-defined field for credit cards or for any other kind of data that might require multiple entries.

The Details tab solves this problem by enabling you to set up many different details and use each only when you need it. And you can use the same detail (such as the second credit card number) as many times as you need to for each account.

The Details tab also solves a problem sometimes involving the Fields tab. If you have any user-defined, custom fields, they are displayed in the Fields tab. For every record, whether or not you fill in any data in each of these fields, space is taken on your hard drive. So, if you've developed 50 custom fields, but on average use only three of them, the other 47 take up space but don't really do anything for you.

When you enter your data into the Details tab, only then does GoldMine create the storage space it needs. If you don't have credit card information for an account, no space is taken up on your hard drive.

Using existing details

The Details tab includes 3 preset, separate details that you can use immediately, as shown in Figure 7-1.

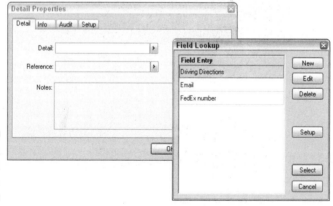

Figure 7-1:
The preset
details.

Without a doubt, the most important detail record is the e-mail address. When you create a new record for a contact (see Chapter 5 for information about entering new records), one of the entries you make is in the E-Mail Address field. When you enter an address in this field, GoldMine automatically puts this e-mail address directly into the Details tab for that record. The e-mail address is also displayed on the main GoldMine screen, along with the phone numbers. You don't need to do anything special to put the e-mail address in either place, or even to use it later.

You're not limited to just this one initial e-mail address. You can enter as many more addresses as needed, which is becoming increasingly common as more and more people acquire multiple e-mail addresses. GoldMine stores one e-mail address as the primary address and the rest as secondary addresses.

Aside from just storing data, the Details tab can also be actively used. For example, you can send an e-mail message to one of your accounts directly from its Details tab (assuming that you're using GoldMine's e-mail rather than Outlook) by following these steps:

1. **Click the Details tab.**

2. **Select the e-mail address you want to send the correspondence to.**

3. **Right-click and select Send E-mail from the shortcut menu.**

4. **Compose and send your e-mail message.**

Entering new details

If, for some reason, you didn't enter the e-mail address (or some other kind of detail) when the record was first created, it isn't too late. To enter an e-mail address after the record has been created:

1. **Click the Details tab.**

2. **Right-click in the area below the tab and choose New.**

   Immediately, the Detail Properties dialog box, shown in Figure 7-2, appears, enabling you to enter a new detail. This figure shows an example of driving directions.

The first field, Detail, stores the type of detail you're recording. This field wants to know, "What kind of information are you trying to set up here?"

Figure 7-2:
Enter new
information
in the Detail
Properties
dialog box.

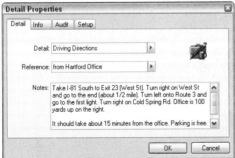

This Detail field has a lookup list that shows the preset details available to you. To access this list, click the arrow to the right of the Detail field. Select E-Mail Address and tab to the next field, labeled Reference. GoldMine stores the actual data for each detail in the Reference field. In this example, you enter the e-mail address into the Reference field.

Creating your own details

Creating your own, new detail isn't hard and you probably at least several kinds of Detail records that will be useful to your operation.

Remember, it's appropriate to use a Detail record for any field that won't be used for every single record or when multiple entries may exist (such as credit cards).

One of my favorite details to add to the system is one for driving directions to the client's location. To create this detail, follow these steps:

1. **From the main GoldMine screen, click the Details tab.**

2. **Right-click in the area below the tab and choose New from the shortcut menu.**

3. **Select the arrow to the right of the Detail field to see the Detail lookup list.**

4. **In the lookup list, click the New button.**

5. **Type** Directions **and click OK.**

The list of details now includes an entry for directions, and you can use it any time. You may not need the Reference field, but you can use the Notes field to write down the specific driving directions to get to this client.

Another common use of custom details is to track individual components of a piece of hardware. Check out Figure 7-3 to see a typical detail record tracking the parts of a computer.

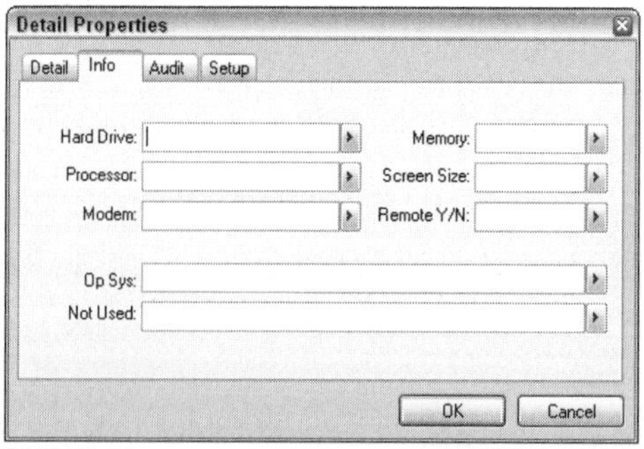

Figure 7-3:
Use a
custom
detail for
tracking
hardware
components.

Detail Properties	☒

| Detail | Info | Audit | Setup |

Hard Drive:		▶	Memory:		▶
Processor:		▶	Screen Size:		▶
Modem:		▶	Remote Y/N:		▶

| Op Sys: | | ▶ |
| Not Used: | | ▶ |

OK   Cancel

More fields you can use with details

Sometimes the Reference and Notes tabs together do not allow for enough information. Recent versions of GoldMine have provided eight more fields in the Info tab that goes along with each detail.

You can even eek out a few more fields within the Details tab by using an add-on product called Details Plus. I discuss add-on products in Chapter 30.

You may want to try using the Info tab to keep track of one or more shipping addresses for each account. Or if you sell computers, you may want to track the details of each computer — the processor speed, the hard drive size, modem speed, amount of memory, and so on, as shown in Figure 7-4. In this example, I have changed several field labels to reflect information appropriate for credit cards. Use the Setup tab to change field labels.

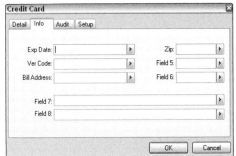

Figure 7-4:
The Info tab stores more details.

You may want to consult the GoldMine Reference Manual for further explanation of this advanced topic, or have an authorized GoldMine dealer actually set this up, and then you can access this data.

Finding specific detail records

GoldMine provides you with a way to easily look up particular records within the Details tab. For example, if an e-mail message comes to you with an address that you don't recognize, you can manually check your database to find out who the mystery sender might be by following these steps:

1. **From the main menu, choose Lookup⇨Detail Records.**

2. **Choose the appropriate Detail Record type from the lookup list.**

   For this example, choose E-Mail Address.

Getting directions online

Another technique for getting assistance with directions is to make use of the GoldMine Web interface. Directly and automatically from the client record, you can have GoldMine dial in to MapQuest on the Internet and provide you with a map and driving instructions. To do so, follow these steps:

1. From the main GoldMine menu, choose Lookup⇨Internet Search.

2. Select maps from MapQuest.

---

3. **Type the first couple of letters of the e-mail address you are trying to find.**

   GoldMine brings you to its main contact window, sorted by e-mail address and positioned at the first e-mail address, starting with the letters you just specified.

The Details Property Dialog Box, shown in Figure 7-2, has several tabs, one of which is the Audit Tab. GoldMine automatically tracks who initially created each detail record and who most recently modified it. With this information, one could create a report or a series of alerts each time a record is modified.

Making Use of Referrals

The Referrals tab on GoldMine's main screen enables you to link one record to another or, perhaps, one record to many other records. The Referrals tab is *relational,* meaning that one piece of data links to multiple pieces of other data. By linking one record to another, you can quickly see what the relationship between two or more records might be. Suppose for example, that your accountant referred 17 other clients to you. You thank her and record each of the referrals in your accountant's GoldMine record. Makes her look a lot more important, doesn't it?

An important note is that the Referrals tab is bi-directional, so after you link A to B, B is linked back to A. The relationship works like a toggle switch. By double-clicking a referral listing, the record that the referral is linked to appears. You can get right back to the original record by double-clicking the referral listing again. In Figure 7-5, you can see two records linked to each other in the Referrals tab.

Even if you don't have to track leads you have given out to dealers, you may want to use the Referrals tab for some kind of related activity. Working with an account that uses a consultant (or an accountant, or an attorney) presents an opportunity to employ the Referrals tab. A referral is especially useful if this same consultant pops up in other accounts of yours, and it's also relevant if you're part of a multi-level distribution system.

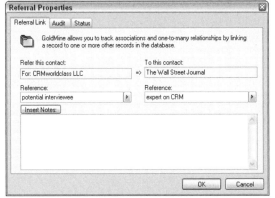

Figure 7-5:
Record leads from a client on the Referrals tab.

To create a referral link, follow these steps:

1. **From the main GoldMine screen, click the Referrals tab.**

2. **Right-click in the area below the tab and choose New from the shortcut menu.**

   A window displaying all the records in your database appears.

3. **Double-click the record you want to link to.**

   The Referral Properties dialog box appears, enabling you to enter the referral information. On the left side of the dialog box, you see the original record and an empty Reference field below it. On the right side of the dialog box is the listing for the record to which the referral is being placed. You use the two reference fields (one for each record) to indicate what the relationship is between the two records.

Each of these two Reference fields can have a lookup list. If you plan to make extensive use of referrals, you should set up these lookup lists to ensure some consistency in the relationships you use. Refer to Chapter 26 for more details on using lookup lists.

For example, if you were referring CRMworldclass to *The Wall Street Journal,* you might set up the referral as shown in Figure 7-6.

At my company, we prioritize our clients and prospects, usually based on projected or actual revenue. However, the Referrals tab can influence our priorities because an account that may never generate any revenue for us itself may refer so much business to us that we give it preferred status.

Starting in Version 6.5, GoldMine added another tab to the Referral Properties Dialog Box — the Status Tab. The Status Tab, shown in Figure 7-7, gives you a convenient place to track the progress of a deal that came to you via referral. It's all part of the Leads Distribution System that FrontRange has gradually been developing since the middle of version 6.

The Status fields are hard-coded but give you a 13 step plan for documenting this progress. Selecting a particular status does *not* remove the check marks anyone put in there previously.

If you've referred the lead to someone on your team who is also using GoldMine and either connecting directly to your database or synchronizing with it, you can both update these status fields. If you've sent the lead to some outside person who is not using GoldMine, you need to manually update the Referral Status fields.

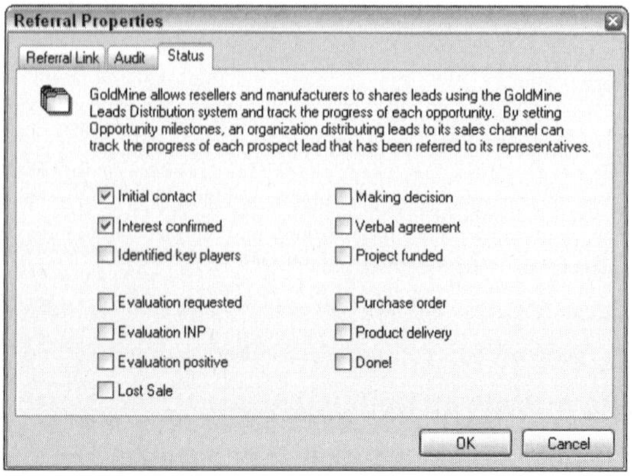

Figure 7-6:
A typical
referral.

Figure 7-7:
Tracking the
progress of
your
referrals.

Chapter 8

Using Filters, Groups, and SQL Queries

*A*s your contacts increase and your database grows, you'll quickly find a need to isolate certain kinds of records. For example, you may want to see all your accounts in Albany. Another time, perhaps just those accounts in Colorado. Yet another time, perhaps you want to see only Moe's accounts that have fax numbers. You can organize your records into subsets using filters and groups.

Filters are like spaghetti colanders. You can use a filter to drain away all the records you don't need, leaving just the ones you want — as long as you have some logical way to specify which records you want *and* as long as the fields that help you specify your criteria are the right kinds of fields.

Groups are like filters on steroids. Using groups allows for faster access to sets of records, and groups allow you to generate sets of records where no logical method exists to select them other than pointing at individual records. Selecting records by pointing at them is called *tagging*. See the "Building groups from manually tagged records" section for more information about tagging records.

Each time you activate a filter, GoldMine hunts for all the records that belong to that filter. If you've added a record since the last time you ran that filter, the filter will find it. That's why the term "dynamic" applies to filters. Groups, on the other hand, are "static." If you add a new record that belongs to a group, you need to manually add the record to that group or re-create the group based on the original parameters.

After you create either a filter or a group, you can use either tool to regulate exactly what data shows up on a report, or which accounts receive correspondence, or whom to schedule for a phone call via Automated Processes (see Chapter 27). These components of GoldMine are extremely powerful.

If the power of filters, groups, or both isn't enough, you can move right up to SQL queries. Such queries within GoldMine used to be the realm of the serious geek, but now GoldMine has a SQL building wizard that allows anyone to build sophisticated queries.

Building and Using Filters

Using GoldMine, you can build simple or sophisticated filters. A simple filter may depend upon just one field — for example, all the accounts in one city. A more sophisticated filter may be a function of several fields and requires some understanding of Boolean logic. (*Boolean logic* deals with the evaluation of mathematical expressions that contain one or more ANDs, ORs, NOTs, and parentheses.)

But don't worry. Even if Boolean logic isn't your cup of tea, the next few sections show you how to create almost any filter you'll ever need.

Accessing the filter system

To access the GoldMine filter system, choose Tools⇨Filters and Groups from the main menu or choose the Filters icon from the Toolbar. Either way, the Filters and Groups window appears, as shown in Figure 8-1.

The View Filters field displays either a specific user or Public. You can assign filters to particular users. In Figure 8-1, you can see the existing filters belonging to me (JOEL). You can assign more general filters as Public filters. This assignment process is really more a way of separating filters into manageable sections than anything else.

The window shown in Figure 8-1 displays all the existing filters that belong to me. To truly explore how to set up your filters, you need to create a new filter.

Creating and using a new filter

To create a filter, follow these steps:

1. **On the Filters and Groups window (refer to Figure 8-1), click the New button.**

   The New Filter dialog box appears, as shown in Figure 8-2.

2. **Enter a name for and assign an owner to your new filter.**

   GoldMine accepts almost anything as a filter name, but you should name your filters logically and specifically. When you come back in six months looking for some filter you're sure you've already created, you don't want to see a list of filters called Filter#1, Filter#2, and Filter#3. For example, if you want to create a filter to isolate accounts in Connecticut, name that filter something like "Accounts in Connecticut" or "Connecticut records."

   To assign an owner, either select yourself, Public, or another user who hasn't read this chapter and needs your help. Assigning an owner to a filter allows you to group your most commonly used filters together.

Also, when setting user preferences (see Chapter 3), you can prohibit a particular user from accessing someone else's filters. That way, GoldMine can somewhat regulate who sees whose accounts.

3. Click the Build tab to move on to the real action of building your filter.

The Build tab is shown in Figure 8-3. On this tab, you select the field or fields you want to base your new filter on, as well as operators and values.

A. Select the field you want to base your new filter on.

Click the down arrow to the right of the Field name (refer to Figure 8-3) to display all the available fields, and then select a field. If you want to isolate all your records for the state of Connecticut, you select the State field here and then go on to Operator and Value.

Figure 8-2:
Starting a new filter.

Figure 8-3:
Specifying a new filter's parameters.

TIP

Only GoldMine's standard fields and user-defined fields are available for use in Filters. You can access supplementary fields, such as e-mail address and those others in the Details tab, only by using Groups or SQL queries.

B. Select an operator from the lookup list.

For example, if you choose Equal to (the simplest of all the operators), you're asking GoldMine to locate all the records for which the field exactly matches the value you supply.

C. Enter a value in the Value field.

The value you enter must match entries in your records. For example, if you use State as your field name, your value must be the abbreviation of the particular state you chose. In other words, use "CT" as your value rather than "Connecticut" because the State field itself uses abbreviations rather than the full state name.

D. Click the Insert Condition button.

Your growing filter now displays in the rectangular area below the Field name box. Your filter is practically built, and your dialog box should look similar to Figure 8-4.

E. Click OK.

The dialog box that lists all available filters appears. You should see your filter listed alphabetically. Your new filter won't do anything yet because you haven't *activated* it. Activating a filter causes GoldMine to focus on just those records that meet the conditions of the filter.

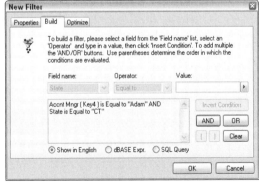

Figure 8-4:
A completed filter.

4. Activate your filter by clicking the Activate button.

The main GoldMine screen appears. In the title bar at the top, you see a statement that your filter is active, and the last record you were dealing with is on the screen. That old record may be in front of you even if it isn't part of your filter. This is curious but not harmful.

When your filter is active, as soon as you press Page Up or Page Down or scroll to another record, you begin seeing the effect of your filter. GoldMine ignores all the records in the database that don't match the filter, so you see only the records that match the criteria in your filter.

At this point, you can use your filter with

- **Any of the reports you want to run:** As long as your filter is active, any report you run will have only those records that the filter has found. See Chapter 22 for details on reports.
- **Mail, fax, and e-mail merges:** You can send correspondence to just a subset of your entire database by using a filter.
- **Automated Processes:** These processes are a great way to regulate your marketing efforts. Chapter 27 discusses the details of Automated Processes.

When you get the hang of filters, you'll discover that they're critical to your daily work and that they can help you with such things as

- Replacing fields globally
- Deleting unwanted records
- Merging/purging of records
- Creating transfer sets for synchronization
- Exporting
- Scheduling
- Running reports

Unlike Groups, when you use a filter it will find all the records that currently match the filter's criteria. This is called dynamic selection. With Groups, you see only those records that met the Group criteria at the time the Group was created unless you manually added records to the original Group.

Releasing a filter

As long as a filter is active, you won't be able to easily use records outside the scope of that filter. You can get your entire database back by releasing the active filter. You can release a filter by

> ✔ Clicking the Filters icon from the Toolbar
>
> ✔ Clicking the Release button on the Filters and Groups window

After you release your filter, the main screen returns, and the title bar shows nothing but the name of the current record.

Counting records in a filter

When you completely finish entering a filter, the Filters and Groups window appears. Every time you finish developing a filter, ask GoldMine for a count of the records that the filter finds. You can do so by highlighting the specific filter, right-clicking, and selecting Count from the menu that appears, as shown in Figure 8-5. Alternatively, you can use the Preview tab instead of Count. The Preview option shows you the specific records that are included in your filter.

GoldMine immediately begins counting how many records in the entire database fall within the scope of this filter. Many times when you develop a filter, you don't know ahead of time exactly how many records you will find. That's okay, but you may want to know approximately how many are within a filter.

Figure 8-5:
Counting records in a filter.

What you don't want is a filter that finds either no records at all or one that decides that every record in the database is part of the filter. In either of these cases, something is likely wrong with your filter expression. If you encounter this situation, go back and review your filter expression and adjust it with the assumption that the problem is the interface between your keyboard and your chair.

Generally, you get a record count somewhere between none and all records in the database and the percentage of the database included in the filter. You can use this number to help you manage the use of the filter. If your filter finds only three records, you may not consider that number to be enough people to invite to a seminar. If the filter finds thousands of records, you may consider that too many for the mailing you had in mind. Adjust the filter until it finds a number of accounts you're more comfortable with.

Reviewing Boolean logic

You may need to examine logical operators if you want to prepare for more sophisticated filters. If this section brings back bad memories of eighth-grade math class, I apologize in advance.

If two or more fields need to be involved in the development of a filter, they must be connected to one another with logical operators. The operators are

- ✔ ( )
- ✔ AND
- ✔ OR

The *order of precedence* specifies which of the preceding operators GoldMine evaluates first. Another way to look at it is, "Which of these is the most important?" It turns out that the order shown in the preceding list is the exact sequence that GoldMine uses to evaluate an expression.

This sequence corresponds with algebra. Everything within the parentheses is calculated first, and then the expressions separated by AND are evaluated, and the OR connections are done last. This order is critical to the proper development of sophisticated filters.

Looking at a more sophisticated filter

An instructive example of a sophisticated filter comes from real life at my company. We planned to host a User Group meeting and wanted to invite all our clients from Connecticut and Massachusetts. I decided to fax the invitations rather than mail them. I needed to develop a filter that isolated just the right accounts.

Sometimes patience is a virtue

One of the advantages of filters is that no matter when you want to use one, it finds all the records it's designed to find. Your filter can find records that didn't even exist when the filter was initially created. It does so by searching the entire database for records every time you activate the filter.

Sometimes, that strength also can be a weakness. If you have a large database (many thousands of records), finding those records may take a considerable time. A 10,000-record database may require several minutes for a filter to find all its records. You could view this as a good time to get a cup of coffee or to investigate the Optimize button on the Build Filter dialog box. Optimizing allows you to restrict the filter's search to speed things up a bit. Groups were developed, in part, to reduce your number of trips to the coffee machine and to speed things up a little.

Whenever you want to develop a filter that's even moderately complicated, write it out on paper first, and then copy it character by character into the GoldMine filter system. Editing a filter that isn't quite right is relatively difficult, so you may just as well plan a little up front to avoid frustration later.

In the User Group meeting example, three statements need to be coordinated:

- ✔ The State field contains CT.
- ✔ The State field contains MA.
- ✔ The Fax field contains a fax number.

The filtering system provides only the three previously mentioned operators — the parentheses, ANDs, and ORs. Each of the three statements needs to be connected with an AND or an OR. As I set up the filter, my first few attempts don't work correctly. To help you avoid making similar mistakes, I show you what's wrong and how to fix the mistakes.

Just take one piece of the projected filter and connect the first two expressions. I first try

```
State equals CT AND State equals MA
```

No matter what else follows in this filter expression, no records can be part of this filter. Using the AND conjunction effectively asks GoldMine to find accounts in both states. But no account can be in both states at the same time — only one State field exists per record, and you can enter only one state there. What I'm really looking for are any accounts either in CT *OR* in MA. Thus, the OR conjunction is the correct one here. So the correct expression for this part of the filter is

```
State equals CT OR State equals MA
```

Next, I need to make sure that each record the filter finds contains a fax number in the Fax field. I don't need to check for any specific value; I'm concerned only that something is actually in the field. I make the assumption that if anything at all is there, it's a valid fax number:

```
State equals CT OR State equals MA AND Fax Exists
```

Because the order of preference requires that expressions separated by AND be evaluated before expressions containing an OR, we still have a problem.

The computer first looks for accounts in MA that also have fax numbers. And that's fine. But next it looks for any accounts in CT regardless of the existence of any fax number. The way the preceding expression is configured, no connection exists between the fact that the account is in CT and also has a fax number. A set of parentheses fixes this problem:

```
(State equals CT OR State equals MA) AND Fax Exists
```

By enclosing the first two expressions within parentheses, you take advantage of the order of precedence again. First, the computer checks each account to determine whether it's in CT or MA. If it finds a record that complies, it then immediately checks whether it has a fax number. Any record that complies with all three expressions is counted as part of the filter. So the last expression is actually correct and produces the desired results. Yes!

Building and Using Groups

A *group* is a fixed set of records that meets a set of conditions you have defined. Using a group, you can isolate a subset of the data whenever you want. You can use groups with reports, mail-merge forms, and Automated Processes. Groups can be created based on scheduled and historical activities and on other supplemental fields, which filters can't handle. Groups can also be created based on an existing filter. Each GoldMine user can create an unlimited number of groups, and each group can have an unlimited number of records.

The number one advantage of groups is their speed. When you create a group, GoldMine automatically creates an index file that points to each record within the group. This index file allows you to access each record within the group almost instantaneously. In contrast to working with filters, you don't have to wait for records to be found when you activate a group.

The index file is created automatically only once — when the group is first created. As you add records to your database, those new records that belong within a group are *not* automatically put into the group. You must add them manually. That's the price you pay for the speed you get with groups.

GoldMine has a Group Building Wizard to assist in the creation of groups. A *wizard* is an intelligent system that walks you through a procedure, giving you your options and helping with questions. The Group Building Wizard allows you eight different bases for building a group:

✔ Filtered records

✔ Previewed records

✔ SQL queries

✔ Tagged records

✔ Search results

✔ Scheduled Calendar activities

✔ Completed History activities

✔ Supplemental contact data

Of these, filtered records and tagged records are the most commonly used bases. I explain how to create groups by basing them on a filter and by manually tagging individual records in the following sections. You may someday also want to create a group based on Calendar or History activities, or even on supplemental contact data.

Usually, the best candidates for groups are sets of records that don't change much over time. If a small percentage of your accounts are major accounts, according to whatever your definition of major is, these accounts constitute a good set of records to turn into a group.

Building groups from filtered records

If you already have a filter, its population is fairly stable, and you want to speed your access to those records, you can create a group from that filter. To create a group based on a filter or expression, go to the Filters and Groups window and follow these steps:

1. Select New from the Groups window.

A Group Profile window appears, requesting that you provide a name for your new group. After you've named your group, click OK. The Group Building Wizard begins.

2. **Select the Filtered records option.**

With this option, you can use any predefined filter to add records to a group. When a group is built based on a filter, all contact records that match the selected filter become permanent members of the group. The wizard also gives you the opportunity to create a brand new filter upon which your group will be built.

3. **Select a specific filter.**

The Build a Group Based on a Filter dialog box appears, containing the following options:

- **Build on a Filter:** Lists all the defined filters for the group's owner. Click the drop-down arrow and then select the desired filter.

- **Owner:** A GoldMine user who "owns" the filter. Selecting a different user from the drop-down list associated with this field changes the display of defined filters in the Build on a Filter field. To display a list of available user names, click the arrow to the right of the field. If you don't have access to other people's filters, don't get too involved with changing users here. Your access rights are determined in User Preferences, which I discuss in Chapter 3.

- **Build on an Expression:** Displays the expression corresponding to the filter displayed at the top of the list of predefined filters in the Build on a Filter option. To type a new filter expression, select the radio button corresponding to this option.

- **Build Filter:** Enables you to build a filter as opposed to picking one from the list of predefined filters.

You can also build a new Group based on a SQL Query that has already been defined. See the "Building and Using SQL Queries" section, later in this chapter.

Building groups from manually tagged records

Sometimes no logical way exists to select the records you want in a group. An example might be when you want to send a mailing to your ten best friends, but no field exists in GoldMine defining friends.

Instead of struggling with a filter to make your group, you can *tag,* or manually select, multiple contact records from the Contact Listing or the Activity list or the Search Center. As you select records, GoldMine indicates the total number of tagged records in the title bar.

To tag a record, you can do one of the following:

- ✔ Press and hold the Ctrl key and then click each record you want to include in the group
- ✔ Press and hold the Shift key and press the down-arrow or up-arrow key to move to the record that you want to select, and then press the spacebar

You can remove the tag from any record selected in the Contact Listing by repeating the same steps by which you tagged the record. This method works like a toggle switch.

Records remain tagged as long as you don't close the Contact Listing window. You can minimize the window, but if you actually close it, all tagged records lose their tags. To actually create the group, after records are individually tagged, use the Group Building Wizard to create the group.

After a group is created, you can perform any standard merge operation on those records, including printing, sending e-mail and fax messages, and scheduling. Groups, just like filters, need to be activated before you use them, and they need to be released when you're finished with them.

Building and Using SQL Queries

With SQL Queries you can go places that filters and groups just can't go. GoldMine now has a wizard that helps you build SQL Queries that allow the creation of "filters" that include data from pending and historical activities. Filters can't do that. You might, for example, want to create a SQL Query that shows all the calls that a certain salesperson was supposed to make last week, but didn't. You could then assign all those calls to someone else.

You can get to the SQL Query Wizard several ways, but the simplest way is as follows:

1. **Choose Tools from GoldMine's main menu.**

   A drop-down list appears that has an option for Filters and Groups. This brings you to the Filters and Group dialog box.

2. **Select he Filters and Group tab.**

   GoldMine displays the SQL Query builder, as shown in Figure 8-6.

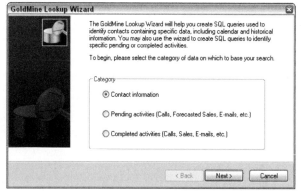

Figure 8-6:
Building a
SQL Query.

3. Click the Build option button shown in Figure 8-6.

This brings you to the GoldMine Lookup Wizard, through which you tell GoldMine whether your SQL Query will be based on standard contact information, custom fields, the details tab information, additional contacts, or pending or historical activities. This is way more than you can specify with filters.

The SQL Query Wizard leads you through the entire process of building or editing a SQL Query, right up to naming and saving it at the end.

Real SQL aficionados will realize that SQL Queries also allow you to modify data in SQL databases. GoldMine, however, has restricted this ability within the wizard to protect its data from you. If you're really confident of your SQL abilities and your knowledge of GoldMine's data structure, you can build your own SQL Queries and place them in the wizard for later use (at your own risk).

To find out more about SQL, check out *SQL For Dummies*, 6th Edition, by Allen G. Taylor (Wiley Publishing).

Part III
Managing Activities

The 5th Wave   By Rich Tennant

"WELL, SHOOT! THIS EGGPLANT CHART IS JUST AS CONFUSING AS THE BUTTERNUT SQUASH CHART AND THE GOURD CHART. CAN'T YOU JUST MAKE A PIE CHART LIKE EVERYONE ELSE?"

In this part . . .

*H*aving thousands of accounts is great, but you won't keep them for long if you never do anything with them. The real purpose of GoldMine is to enable you to schedule and track everything that's supposed to happen and everything that has already happened. This part of the book shows you how GoldMine can effectively nag everyone to make sure that nothing falls through the cracks and how all the history gets recorded for every account.

If you've ever tried to fool yourself or your manager with your sales forecast, you'll see how to accomplish that very same thing within the confines of GoldMine.

Chapter 9

Scheduling Activities

Keeping track of names, addresses, and phone numbers is the heart of GoldMine; recording pending activities in the Calendar is the soul. If you don't enter pending activities, you won't have a record of completed activities, and then you'll waste most of the power of GoldMine.

Plan on putting your entire life in the Calendar — whether you're using GoldMine's calendar or Outlook's. Sure, you're using GoldMine for all your business appointments, but you can put the Little League games and the dentist appointments in there, too. That way, GoldMine reminds you about all the things you don't want to forget (and nags you about the things you'd like to forget).

This chapter shows you how to harness the organizational power of GoldMine's Calendar to track the activities in your busy life. I also show you how to share your Calendar with other members of your team, a feature that my co-workers and I find really powerful and efficient. I also discuss how to share appointment information with people who don't yet use GoldMine. Don't worry — GoldMine has plenty of safeguards built in, and enough privacy so that no one will ever know about those weekly tee times or shopping trips. Trust me.

Defining Activities

GoldMine features nine types of activities, all accessible from the main menu by choosing Schedule (see Figure 9-1). You also can access all these activities from the Standard Toolbar (just below the main menu), although by default, only a few of them show up. You can add to this list by customizing the Toolbar (see Chapters 2 and 3 for customizing options). In the following list, I explain the different types of activities:

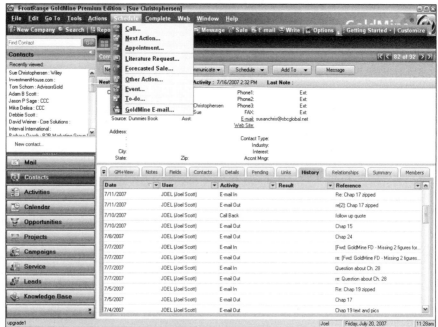

Figure 9-1:
Activities
within the
Schedule
menu.

✔ **Call:** Generally, outgoing phone calls are scheduled with this coding, although incoming conference calls may also come under this scheduling regime.

✔ **Next Action:** Often, when you complete an activity with a client, you need to schedule a follow-up. For example, after a fact-finding meeting, you might schedule a "Review of Proposal" meeting as your Next Action.

✔ **Appointment:** An appointment can be a meeting that is scheduled either inside your office or at some other location. Meetings are usually person-to-person affairs, but meetings may also occur through the Internet or via conference calls.

✔ **Literature Request:** This type of activity is used to schedule orders for your shipping or fulfillment department to send out. These could be marketing materials or actual products.

✔ **Forecasted Sale:** GoldMine has a simple sales forecasting system, and you actually schedule the closing of a sale in the same way you schedule anything else. I discuss sales forecasting in Chapter 12.

✔ **Other Action:** This is a catch-all category for activities that just don't fit nicely anywhere else. In my office, non-billable, R&D projects are scheduled as Other activities.

✔ **Event:** You use the event category to schedule daylong or multi-day activities. For example, a trade show that requires you to be out of the office for an entire day would be scheduled as an event. I don't like using Events too much, because they don't show up as obviously on your Calendar as other types of activities.

✔ **To-do:** To-dos don't have a time of day associated with them, so they never show up on the main Calendar. You see them listed below as special items just to the left of the Events. For example, a reminder to pick up milk and bread on the way home or to do some research at your competitor's store would fit in this category. You can see how To-do's and Events are displayed in Figure 9-2.

✔ **GoldMine E-mail:** From this selection you can create and/or schedule an outgoing e-mail to other users on your team.

Whatever type of activity you're scheduling, as soon as you click OK to actually schedule it, GoldMine automatically puts a record of the activity into the Pending tab of the appropriate record (unless it's a To-do, which is never linked to a record). You can always see it or edit the activity from the Pending tab. In addition, it shows up on your Activity List and on the Calendar itself.

Creating Activities

To schedule an activity, click the Activities button in the Navigation Pane. The Activities window appears, as shown in Figure 9-2.

Depending on your Preference settings, your calendar display may show less information than is displayed in Figure 9-2. I configured my Calendar display to show the maximum amount for purposes of this illustration.

Options include seeing a daily, weekly, monthly, or yearly view of the Calendar. I find the daily and weekly Calendar views to be the most useful. These views show enough detail for me to understand exactly what I have scheduled. As you progress to the monthly and yearly views, you see less and less detail about specific activities. You can select any of these views using the tabs on the Calendar View window.

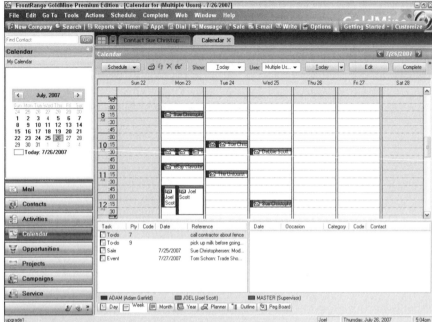

Figure 9-2:
The
Activities
window.

In addition to these presentations, you have a choice of several not commonly used views. These options are all additional tabs on the local scheduling window:

- ✔ **Planner:** Displays a Calendar for multiple GoldMine users. To display this Calendar, click the Planner tab.

- ✔ **Outline:** Displays a Calendar in an outline, or hierarchical, format. To display this Calendar, click the Outline tab.

- ✔ **Peg Board:** Displays a status chart of other GoldMine users. To access this display, click the Peg Board tab. This feature allows users to log in or log out and post a message regarding their whereabouts. It also checks for inactivity as measured by the existence or absence of keystrokes on the keyboard.

Entering Activities on the Calendar

You can schedule an activity either from the Calendar or by using the main GoldMine menu. Both of these methods land you at the same place — the Scheduling dialog box, shown in Figure 9-3. Scheduling from the Calendar, however, saves you the effort of manually entering the date, time, and duration of each activity; these items are automatically filled in. Doing it directly from the Calendar also allows you to easily check for scheduling conflicts before you create the activity rather than waiting for GoldMine to tell you there's a scheduling conflict. Using the main menu allows you to schedule activities that shouldn't really occupy a significant block of time, such as quick phone calls or short in-house meetings.

Make sure that the active record is the one you want to schedule an activity for. But if you need to schedule an activity for another record, you can temporarily switch records in the scheduling window by selecting the icon to the left of the contact person field. After you finish scheduling, GoldMine takes you back to your original record. This clever option is useful if you're in the midst of writing a summary of your recent meeting with Client A and suddenly remember that you need to schedule an appointment with Client B.

Scheduling activities directly from the Calendar is generally best for appointments or for any activity with a significant duration. Follow these steps:

1. **Open the Calendar by clicking the Calendar icon on the Toolbar or by clicking Calendar on the Navigation Pane.**

   The Calendar's main window appears.

2. **Select either the daily or weekly view by clicking the appropriate tab.**

3. **Click and drag the mouse over the desired time for your activity.**

   When you release the mouse, the main Schedule an Appointment dialog box appears, shown in Figure 9-3, where you fill in additional details. (See the next section for more information about the Scheduling dialog box.)

Figure 9-3:
Enter an appointment on your Calendar with the Scheduling dialog box.

To schedule an activity from the main menu without opening the Calendar, follow these steps:

1. **Choose Schedule from the main GoldMine menu.**

2. **Choose the appropriate type of activity from the Schedule menu.**

   See the "Defining Activities" section, earlier in this chapter, to find out about the different types of activities.

Creating a personal record for yourself is a good idea. When scheduling an activity for yourself, such as a dentist appointment, you can then attach that appointment to your own record in the database.

Always link pending and completed activities to an existing record in GoldMine. GoldMine, by default, links each activity you schedule with the record that's currently active. For personal appointments, you should have a record for yourself (complete with home address and phone numbers) and link your own personal appointments to that record.

Filling in the Scheduling Dialog Box

After you use one of the two methods for getting to the Scheduling dialog box, you see a series of fields you must fill out. I discuss each of these fields in the following sections.

The Contact field

The first field you see on the Scheduling dialog box (refer to Figure 9-3) is the Contact field. By default, this field contains the primary contact from the record you were just using. Click the icon to the left of the primary contact field to temporarily activate a different record in your database or to select a secondary contact person from this same record. You can also select multiple contacts or even multiple GoldMine users for the same appointment.

The Code field

The next field is labeled Code, which GoldMine uses to describe the nature of the appointment. Typical examples of activity codes are

- SLS — Sales
- ADM — Administrative work
- PER — Personal

You can see and use these choices by right-clicking in the field or by clicking the drop-down arrow to the right of the field. In the Code field, you should make up a short series of codes that cover pretty much every reason you may ever deal with an account. You can use these codes later to develop reports that select and sort based on your activity codes. See Chapter 26 for further information on adding codes to lookup lists.

The Activity Code and Result Code fields in "Schedule" and "Complete" only store three characters. I suggest they be all uppercase so they make sense when it comes to reporting (for example, LVM = Left Voicemail or NIN = Not Interested Now).

The Primary User field

The next field you see on the Scheduling dialog box is the Primary User field. GoldMine assumes that you're scheduling this appointment for yourself; therefore, you generally see your own user name showing up here. If you are indeed scheduling for yourself, you can just skip this field entirely.

If you double-click in the Primary User field or click the down arrow to the right of the Primary User field, the names of all the other users on your system appear. You can schedule for someone other than yourself by simply selecting his or her name. This feature is called *delegating* and is one of my favorite GoldMine tools. See the sidebar "The art of delegating," elsewhere in this chapter, for tips on using this handy feature.

Colors, colors, everywhere

Colors are a great way to specify types of activities. When you use different colors for different kinds of appointments, these colors show up very clearly on your Calendar. Then, whenever you look at your Calendar, you can very easily see what kind of day you're going to have.

My colleagues and I developed the following color-coding scheme at our company that works very well for us:

✔ **Red:** An appointment away from the office

✔ **Gray:** A tentative appointment that still needs to be confirmed

✔ **Yellow:** An assignment requiring us to be in the office, such as tech support

✔ **Blue:** An appointment in the office

✔ **Green:** Personal time

Feel free to develop your own scheme for your company. Any consistent color scheme that makes sense to everyone in your company is better than no color scheme at all. Although color scheme defaults can be set into your Preferences (actually, in your `lookup.ini` file), this is on a user-by-user basis and not for your entire organization. As a result, an organization-wide color coding scheme is a policy issue rather than a technical one.

The Reference field

Be sure to always use the Reference field to provide a short description of the activity. Sometimes you may schedule activities many months in advance. When an activity suddenly pops up on your activity list, the Reference field reminds you what the activity is all about. For example, you may use "Initial Sales Call," "Project Review Meeting," "Technical Support," or my personal favorite, "Close Deal." Make up your own list, and put it into the lookup list for this field. Again, you can refer to Chapter 26 for details on adding items to a lookup list.

The Notes field

You can use the Notes field as a reminder of specific information pertinent to this meeting, such as, "Remember to bring three copies of the proposal and a projector." Some people also use this field for directions to the account, but I prefer to put that information into the Detail section or have it mapped in GM+Views.

This Notes field does not require date or time stamping, so you need only click in the field and start typing.

The Date field

On the right side of the Scheduling dialog box is the Time section. Every appointment, of course, has a date and a time associated with it. If you don't enter a date and time, then the appointment won't show up properly on your Calendar, and you may not realize that you need to be doing something. If you began your scheduling directly from the Calendar, the Date and Time fields are already filled in for you.

The best way to change the date is to click on the right arrow adjacent to the date field. Voilà — a month's worth of the Calendar instantly appears, as shown in Figure 9-4. You can move ahead (or backwards) if necessary by clicking the Month or the Year scroll buttons. When you see the date you want, just double-click. GoldMine automatically fills in this date on the Scheduling dialog box.

Figure 9-4:
Select a
date for
your
appoint-
ment.

The Time field

The Time field works the same way as the Date field. Your preference setting for Calendar intervals (see Chapter 3 for setting this up) determine whether you can schedule activities every 5 minutes, 15 minutes, every hour, and so on. I have mine set to 15 minute intervals.

Every appointment has an expected duration. Make sure that you enter a duration either in minutes or in hours as seen in Figure 9-5. If you don't, you end up with conflicting appointments and a generally messed-up schedule.

Come up with a company-wide standard for dealing with travel time. Failing to account for travel time on your Calendar may result in someone's putting another appointment in your schedule right when you're driving back from the first appointment. Color codes work well for this kind of situation. (See the sidebar "Colors, colors, everywhere.")

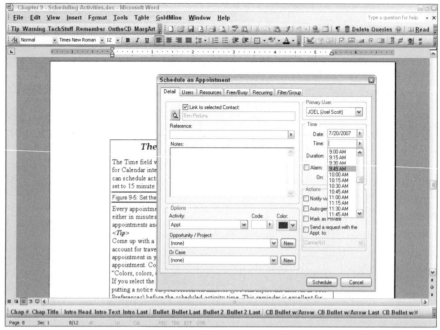

Figure 9-5:
Set the time
for your
appoint-
ment.

If you select the Alarm, GoldMine automatically reminds you of an activity by putting a notice on your screen ten minutes (you can adjust this interval in User Preferences) before the scheduled activity time. This reminder is excellent for out-of-the-office appointments, but if you overuse this function, you may find it a bit annoying. When I schedule an appointment for someone else in my office who tends to run late, I always make use of the Alarm feature.

Using the Options

You generally use most of the Options fields only if you're part of a team. I explain these Options and their purposes in the following list (refer to Figure 9-3 for the location of each of these options on the main Scheduling dialog box):

- ✔ **Link:** This button, which is on by default, links the activity to the account that's active. It's hard to imagine a reason to ever turn this off. Suggestion — just leave it alone.

- ✔ **Notify via E-Mail:** This button can be an extremely important tool to use whenever you schedule for someone else. If you click this button, GoldMine *immediately* notifies the person for whom you're scheduling the activity. This notification isn't the same thing as an alarm, which goes off shortly before the activity.

For example, if you schedule Harry to make a presentation to the Board of Directors next Thursday, you can be fairly sure that he would like to know about it more than ten minutes beforehand. Click the Notify via E-mail button, and GoldMine immediately sends Harry an e-mail message with the information about the activity you entered into his Calendar. Forget to use this button once or twice, and you're guaranteed to hear about it.

✔ **Auto-generate RSVP:** You can select the RSVP button when you schedule an activity for someone else. It allows you to keep track of when, and if, activities that you have scheduled for other users are completed. This field is particularly useful when activities are delegated to other network or remote users. GoldMine creates an RSVP message on your Calendar as soon as an activity you scheduled for another user is completed or deleted.

✔ **Mark as Private:** If you select Mark as Private, other GoldMine users can see that some amount of time is blocked out of your Calendar, but they won't be able to see exactly what you're doing or where you're going.

Use this option too much and your boss and co-workers are bound to be a little suspicious. And, because the boss or your GoldMine administrator probably has Master access rights, he or she can find a way to see what you're doing anyway.

You can assign an activity to an existing Opportunity, Project or Case. In the lower left corner of the scheduling dialog box (see Figure 9-3 again) you have the option to associate the current activity with either an Opportunity, a Project or a Case.

Rescheduling an Activity

In real life, most people usually look at a calendar before scheduling anything. GoldMine is no different. You can go directly to the Calendar by clicking the Calendar icon. Doing so immediately displays your Calendar so that you can see what is already scheduled. Most people think it is important to look before they leap.

The easiest way to reschedule an appointment is directly from the Calendar by using the drag-and-drop method (just like dragging cards when you're playing Solitaire). Click to select the appointment, hold down the left mouse button, and drag the appointment to the new date or time, and then release the mouse button. You can also make the appointment longer or shorter by dragging the top or bottom of the appointment to extend or reduce the time allotted to it.

Scheduling Activities for Other People

GoldMine enables you to schedule activities for other users by accessing their Calendars. This works very well in my office, and I highly recommend it. But you must consider several key elements when you schedule an activity for someone else:

- ✔ **Make sure that the other person is okay with this arrangement.** Also make sure up front that everyone on the team agrees to the efficiency of the idea.

- ✔ **Make sure to schedule directly from the other person's Calendar.** You do so by changing the User to the person for whom you're scheduling. When you change the User, you immediately see that other user's Calendar. (See the section, "The Primary User field," earlier in this chapter, for more information.) Because you're probably less familiar with someone else's Calendar than you are with your own, *check it first* to make sure you're not creating a conflict.

- ✔ **Make sure that you *always* use the Notify button.** Doing so is courteous and professional. Using a color-coding scheme, such as gray for an appointment that the user needs to confirm, is a good idea too.

Using the iCal Features

The iCal feature is a hottie, and it comes under the heading, "If you can't beat 'em, join 'em." You won't see *iCal* on the scheduling screen, but you access this feature by selecting Send a Request with the Appointment to on the scheduling screen. The developers at FrontRange realized that many people use tools other than GoldMine for their scheduling and their e-mail. The most common tool, of course, is Microsoft Outlook. The iCal feature allows you to use GoldMine to schedule meetings with anyone using a scheduling program that makes use of the iCal standards. You can translate that into Microsoft Outlook and Lotus Organizer. If you haven't convinced the Outlook stalwarts in your company to convert to GoldMine, you can use this feature to coordinate your schedule with theirs. If some of your clients or vendors use Outlook, you can use GoldMine to formally request a meeting with these people.

This feature works both ways. Anyone using Outlook can send a meeting request to you. You can accept, reject, or suggest an alternative. After you agree, that meeting appears in both the GoldMine Calendar and in the Outlook calendar.

The art of delegating

Delegating is an absolutely great way to avoid ever having to actually do any work yourself. On the other hand, a few rules of professional courtesy exist that you should probably be aware of before you start delegating activities:

✔ **Don't ever schedule anything for a co-worker without properly alerting him or her.** Properly alerting someone requires setting an alarm and clicking the Notify button. Although you may think that hollering across the hall is adequate, always cover yourself with an electronic notification.

✔ **Don't schedule appointments for people who will be upset that you're messing with their schedules.** You must understand and respect the pecking order in your organization.

✔ **Don't tell your client that the person you're scheduling for will absolutely be there.** Whenever you schedule for someone else, clarify to your client that you do so tentatively; the appointment still requires final approval by the user. Use the appropriate Calendar color (in the color scheme at my office, it's gray) for a tentative appointment.

✔ **Don't delegate all the nasty or boring stuff.** If people get the idea that you're doing that — well, remember that they can delegate things to you, too.

iCal standards still vary a bit from system to system, so not every function works properly with every iCal-based program. For example, recurring appointments in GoldMine may not translate perfectly to other programs. But for regular, simple stuff, iCal is great.

Scheduling a meeting with an Outlook user

The key to scheduling a meeting with someone using an iCal-based system is the little check box in the lower right side of the Scheduling dialog box. You can see this check box in Figure 9-3. Selecting this option sends an e-mail message to the recipient. The message is formatted in such a way that should the recipient accept your invitation, the meeting automatically posts itself in his or her Calendar.

The best way to test out all this iCal stuff is to schedule a meeting with yourself as the recipient. That way, you won't annoy all your friends as you experiment. When you're confident, you can try it with a real Outlook user.

Responding to a meeting request

You may receive a meeting request from an Outlook or Lotus Notes user. The fifth option on the window, shown in Figure 9-6, allows you to check your own calendar before deciding to accept, decline, or revise the meeting schedule.

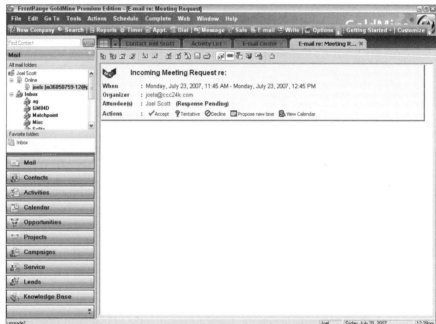

Figure 9-6:
An incoming meeting request.

Scheduling Recurring Activities

Many times, you have a regularly scheduled activity. For example, if you have a team meeting every Monday morning at 9:00 a.m., you don't have to painstakingly enter it on your Calendar for every week of the year. You can go into the Schedule an Appointment dialog box and click the Recurring tab, as shown in Figure 9-7. This tab enables you to automatically schedule a daily, weekly, or monthly activity from now until the cows come home.

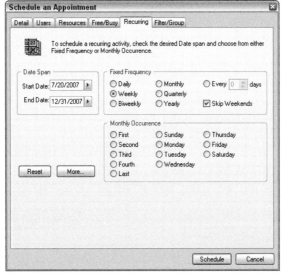

The recurring *appointment or activity* system is a great way to make sure you always remember to make the phone, rent, and tax payments on time. This applies to company and to personal activities. (Remember, the personal ones should be scheduled against your own personal record.) A color code for payments may also be helpful.

Chapter 10

Viewing Scheduled Activities

*W*hat good is scheduling activities unless you can easily view them? You can see scheduled activities in GoldMine by using either the Calendar or the Activity list. The Calendar displays the same basic information as the Activity list but in a graphical format. The Activity list displays all your open activities, or selected categories of open activities, in a list format for any user. (*Open activities* are any scheduled activities that have not yet been completed.)

If your GoldMine is integrated with Outlook, you can also view scheduled activities within Outlook. (See Chapter 18 for more about Outlook.)

In this chapter, you find out how to view your scheduled activities as well as those of your co-workers. You can look at completed activities as well as old, still pending activities that you wish you had completed. You also discover the different ways you can view activities. By viewing scheduled activities, you can determine what you and everyone else in your organization will be doing today, tomorrow, or any time in the future, and you can plan your time accordingly.

Viewing Activities Using the Calendar

Almost anything you can see from the Activity list you can also see from the Calendar view. The advantage of looking at the Calendar is that it provides a more graphical presentation, which, if you use color coding for your activities, can be a very clear way to look at your day's or week's action. (See Chapter 9 for more about color-coding your activities.)

You can get to the Calendar by clicking the Calendar button in the Navigation Pane.

Viewing open activities with the Calendar

The first thing I do when I arrive at work each morning is check my Calendar. I look at all my scheduled activities and then review the schedules for everyone else on my team. (See the "Viewing Groups of Users on the Calendar" section, later in this chapter.) That way, I immediately know who is on vacation, who is in the office, and who is scheduled to be out at some other location.

By consistently using the color-coding scheme, such as the one suggested in Chapter 9, your view of the Calendar gives you a quick and easy way to see what's going on for that day or week.

When you open the Calendar, the basic User's Calendar window appears, as shown in Figure 10-1. The default view is Day. You can change the view on the Calendar by clicking the following tabs:

✔ **Week:** You see seven days of activities, Sunday through Saturday, even if you don't work weekends. I select this Calendar view most often.

✔ **Month:** From this view, you can get an overall perspective of how busy a month you have, but few details are visible. You can see what each activity is by hovering the cursor over the activity and looking at the status bar. You see the contact's name and reference of the activity. This is true for the Year view, also.

Figure 10-1: You can see scheduled activities on the Calendar window.

✔ **Year:** As the highest level in the hierarchy, a year contains all activities grouped by months.

✔ **Planner:** You can check the schedule of one or more GoldMine users by clicking the Planner tab in the Calendar. Your settings in the Calendar tab of the Preferences window determine the period of days that the Planner tab displays. (See Chapter 3 to find out how to set preferences.) By default, the Planner shows 18 days of activities for the current user. Each activity is represented by a colored bar that shows the amount of time reserved for the activity, as shown in Figure 10-2.

✔ **Outline:** You can display your scheduled activities in a hierarchical structure by clicking the Outline tab. Each Calendar level is graphically represented by an icon. This view, shown in Figure 10-3, is a concession to those who are devoted to Day-Timers. The Outline view displays a tree with branches that correspond to the Year, Month, and Day tabs.

✔ **Date:** Each date lists all scheduled activities.

✔ **Peg Board:** In the Calendar, the Peg Board tab displays the login status and activity of individual users and system availability. For individual users, GoldMine tracks login/logout times, total logged time, and activity as determined by keystrokes and mouse use. When you need to leave your desk, you can log away, posting your location and expected time of return. See Figure 10-4.

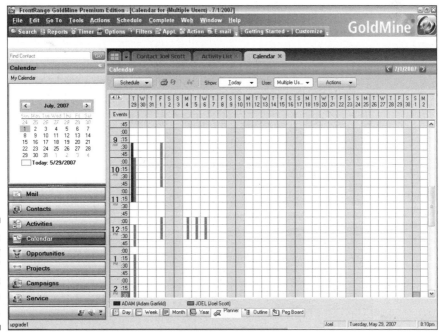

Figure 10-2: Check other users' schedules on the Planner tab.

Figure 10-3:
Display
activities in
a hierarchy
on the
Outline tab.

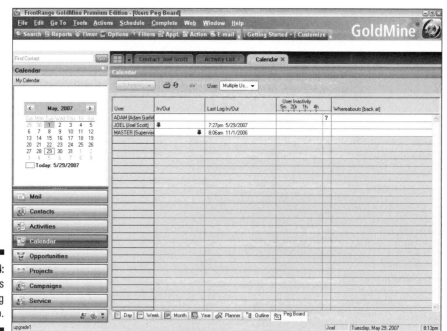

Figure 10-4:
Track users
on the Peg
Board tab.

Viewing completed activities from the Calendar

By default, when an activity is completed, it disappears from the Calendar. I discuss completing activities in Chapter 11. A setting also exists within the Calendar that allows even completed activities to remain on the daily or weekly view of the Calendar. I highly recommend using this setting. By using this preference setting, you can look at past days or weeks on your Calendar to see what you (or others) have done. This feature is often useful, for example, when compiling your long-overdue expense report. To retain completed activities on your Calendar, follow these steps:

1. **Display the weekly view of your Calendar.**

2. **Right-click anywhere within the Calendar and choose Activities from the shortcut menu.**

   The Select Activities to View dialog box appears, as shown in Figure 10-5.

3. **In the Completed Activities column, check all the activities you want to remain on your Calendar and then click OK.**

From this point on, your completed activities are displayed with a gray background and a horizontal line through the listing. That way, you can look at last week's Calendar to remind yourself what you actually did. Figure 10-6 shows an example.

Figure 10-5:
Selecting
past
activities to
keep on
your
Calendar.

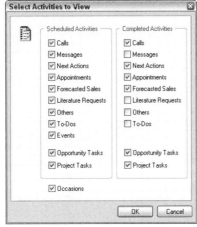

Figure 10-6:
Completed
activities
displayed on
the
Calendar.

Modifying the listing within each Calendar activity

You can use an option setting within the Calendar to determine exactly which fields display on the Calendar. Space is limited within each Calendar listing, so you don't want to view more than one or two fields at a time. The most important fields are probably the Contact Person and the Company fields, although you can elect to display any field or fields in the database. The following steps show you how to modify the display options on your Calendar:

1. **Display the weekly view of your Calendar.**

2. **Right-click anywhere within the Calendar and, from the shortcut menu, choose Options ➪Preferences➪More Options.**

   The Calendar Display Reference Properties dialog box appears, as shown in Figure 10-7.

3. **Select the fields you want to display and then click OK.**

Using the normally available selections, you can have the Calendar display either the company name or the contact name related to an activity. If you would like a little more information, you can arrange it by entering an expression in the dialog box, as shown in Figure 10-8. These expressions need to be written in dBASE, which is a little outside the scope of this book. But a good example can go a long way toward enabling you to create your own expressions in this case.

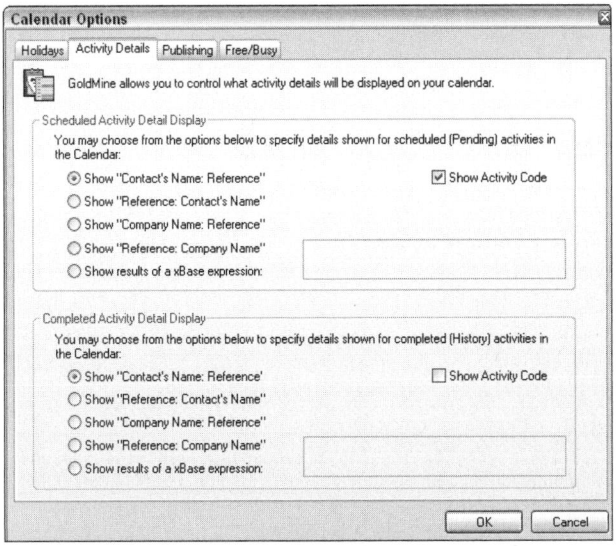

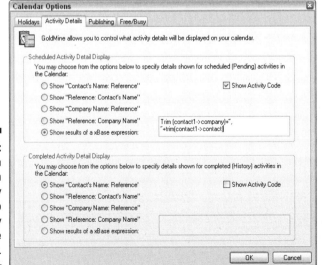

Figure 10-7: Calendar display options.

Figure 10-8: Using an expression to specify data to display on the Calendar.

If you want to see both the company name and the contact name on your Calendar, you can have GoldMine display exactly that by entering the following dBASE expression:

```
Trim(contact1->company)+", "+ trim(contact1->contact)
```

The `Trim` function removes all the unnecessary spaces surrounding the data. The expression within the parentheses specifies the name of the data file followed by the data field itself. The two fields are separated by a comma and a space.

Checking the Activity List

In addition to using the Calendar to view scheduled activities, another way to find out what your coming attractions are is to use the Activity list. By using the Activity list, you can see a little more information, such as the Reference field related to each activity. To access the Activity list, click the Activities button in the Navigation Pane. A window appears, just above the Navigation Pane, shown in Figure 10-9, allowing you to specify exactly what activities you want to see.

Figure 10-9:
View your activities as a list.

✔ **Open:** Displays all pending activities, regardless of category, for a particular user.

✔ **Actions:** Lists pending Next Actions.

✔ **Appts:** Lists pending appointments along with information about the date, time, duration, the primary contact, and reference.

✔ **Calls:** Lists pending phone calls. If you select auto-forwarding for calls (see Chapter 3), you may see pending phone calls that you were supposed to make but haven't gotten to yet.

✔ **Events:** Shows all scheduled events.

✔ **Forecasts:** Lists pending sales with data on projected close date, probability, amount of sale, product, and primary contact.

✔ **Others:** Lists pending Other Activities.

✔ **To-do:** Lists pending to-do activities.

✔ **Opp/Proj Tasks:** Shows scheduled tasks that are associated with either an Opportunity or an on-going project.

✔ **Alarmed:** Shows all pending activities with an alarm.

✔ **Completed Activities:** Lists all completed activities for a specified date range.

✔ **E-mail:** Lists pending GoldMine and pending Internet e-mail with information about the sender and the subject matter.

✔ **Inbox:** Lists Internet e-mail messages you have already brought into GoldMine.

✔ **Outbox:** Lists Internet e-mail messages that have been created but not yet sent. This situation arises if you choose to queue your outgoing e-mails rather than send them immediately. See Chapter 17 to find out how to send e-mail and use the Out-Box. When you're ready to actually send your outgoing e-mails, go to this tab, right-click, and choose Send to send all the previously queued messages.

✔ **Filed:** Lists all available information about GoldMine and Internet e-mails that have been received.

✔ **Occasions:** Shows personal holidays that you set up, such as birthdays and anniversaries.

✔ **Holidays:** Lists company holidays, such as New Year's Day and Christmas.

Getting back to the account

If you double-click any activity within the Activity list, GoldMine brings you directly to the proper account. From there, you can check either the Pending tab or the History tab. These tabs are often useful if you want to see more details, such as Notes, or if you want to make some modification to that activity.

Changing the focus of the Activity list

By default, the Activity list shows you the activities that are scheduled for the current date and the activities that are assigned to you (your user name). You can change either of these settings so that you can see activities assigned to others and activities scheduled for a future date.

By clicking in the Show field of the Activity list, you get a menu list of choices, as shown in Figure 10-10. From this list, you can choose a variety of time ranges.

Similarly, you can click in the User field and you get a drop-down list of all users. By selecting another user you immediately see that person's list of activities.

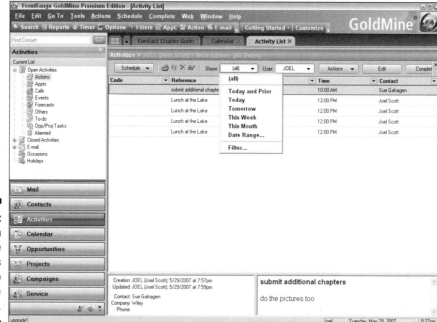

Figure 10-10: Homing in on just the activities you want to see in the Activity list.

More actions you can perform on activities

There are several other, more global actions you can perform. You access these actions by clicking the down arrow to the right of the Link button. The choices described in the following sections appear.

Link

The Link option allows you to re-assign an activity to the active contact record. You can do this only one activity at a time.

Roll-over

By selecting Roll-over, you can forward activities to yourself (presumably to complete at a later date) or to another user. This option is potentially danger-ous. More than one GoldMiner has come to grief using it. With one click of the mouse, you send all your scheduled activities to someone else, and no easy way exists for you to get them back, even if you really didn't mean to do it.

Leave Roll-over alone; it has bitten more than one user in the past. Instead, use Territory Realignment, which is a data management option under Tools in the main menu. The Territory Realignment Wizard walks you through the entire procedure.

Auto-Update

Auto-Update is a valuable feature that allows you to complete more than one activity at a time. One of the most useful times to employ this Auto-Update feature is when you've neglected to complete a bunch of pending activities. My office has people who always forget to do this, literally for months at a time. Rather than have hundreds of still-pending activities that someone claims to have actually done, we use Auto-Update occasionally to fix this.

Viewing Groups of Users on the Calendar

You can actually view up to 16 users' schedules simultaneously, which is useful if, for example, you want to see whether anyone from your Boston office is available to go to Halifax, Nova Scotia, next week. Viewing all these schedules is made particularly simple if all your Boston people are in a user group that you have already created. To see a list of all registered users, follow these steps:

1. **Click the drop-down arrow in the User field of the Calendar window.**

    A shortcut menu appears.

2. Select Multiple Users.

This choice leads you to a dialog box listing all the registered users, as shown in Figure 10-11.

3. Select as many users as you want, or a group, and then click OK.

You are limited to displaying a total of 16 separate users.

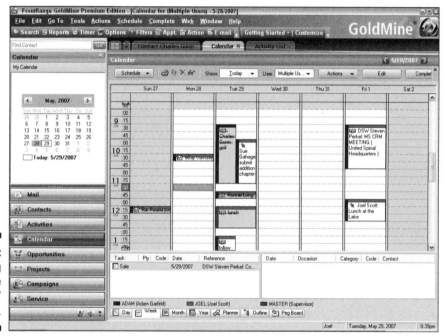

Figure 10-11: Displaying multiple users' Calendars.

Another approach to viewing multiple users is to select a group. A typical group may be the "Sales" group, or those people who work in one of your regional offices. Then, instead of selecting those individuals, you can select the group of which they are members.

Chapter 11

Dealing with and Completing Scheduled Activities

. . . .

In This Chapter

▶ Delegating activities to other people

▶ Rescheduling activities

▶ Deleting activities

▶ Ignoring activities

▶ Completing activities

. . . .

*T*he whole point of using GoldMine is for you to schedule all sorts of activities and then dispose of each of them in some logical fashion. In this chapter, you find out how to get all scheduled activities off your Calendar and get home for dinner on time. I promise.

You have three ways to view previously scheduled activities:

✔ **Directly from the Pending tab of an individual record.** Use this method when you want to focus on a particular account and have easy access to the Pending folder. See Chapters 9 and 10 for more details on how scheduled activities are related to records.

✔ **From the Activity list.** Use this method when you want to view all your different types of scheduled activities for some time period.

✔ **From the Calendar.** Using this method is often the best, particularly when you deal with activities that have a specific duration that you need to reschedule.

Regardless of the method you use to access your scheduled activities, you have five and only five things you can do with an activity: delegate, reschedule, delete, ignore, and complete. In this chapter, I explain these five actions and how to accomplish completing your activities by using these actions.

Four Ways to Complete Your Activities

In this section, I describe four of the five ways to complete an activity. Each of these methods is valid and gets the job done; however, these methods are temporary or weak solutions. To discover the fifth and best way to complete an activity, see the upcoming section, "The Best Way to Complete an Activity."

Delegating activities to other people

Remember, the fundamental design goal of GoldMine is to allow a team of people to coordinate themselves. In this fashion, one way to complete an activity is to delegate it to someone else, which is my personal favorite. To delegate an activity, follow these steps:

1. **In the Schedule an Appointment dialog box (see Figure 11-1), look for the Primary User field in the upper-right corner and click the down arrow next to the field.**

   A lookup list appears, and you immediately see all the registered Users on your team. If you don't see a list, then no other Users exist, and there just isn't anyone to delegate anything to. Too bad.

2. **From the list of registered users, select the person to whom you want to delegate the task.**

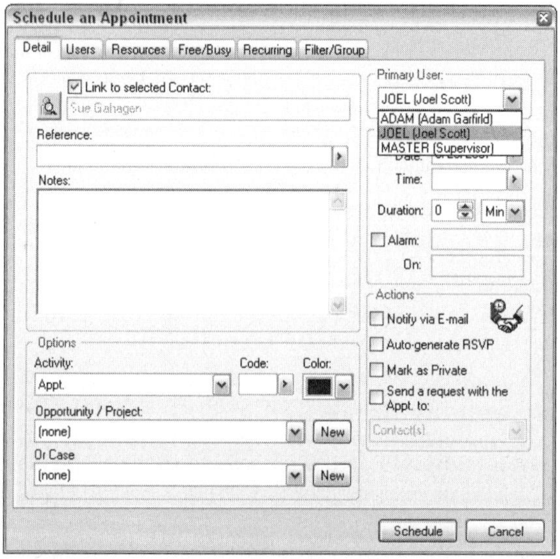

Figure 11-1:
Delegating an appointment.

3. **Click the OK button and GoldMine immediately places this task on your "delegee's" Calendar.**

You won't be very popular in the office, however, if you don't let people know you've just delegated some task. Even setting the Alarm to go off 20 minutes before the task is scheduled may not be enough time. No one wants just 20 minutes' notice before giving a presentation to the Board of Directors. Refer to Chapter 9 for delegating etiquette.

Always click the Notify button when delegating tasks to someone else. When you do so, GoldMine immediately sends an e-mail message to that person, letting her know that you have scheduled her for this activity.

Rescheduling activities

One of the most common actions you'll take with an appointment is to reschedule it. The easiest way to reschedule an appointment is to do it directly from the Calendar. Not only is the Calendar the best way to see what alternate times are available, but physically changing the time of the appointment from the Calendar is simple.

I like to use the drag-and-drop method for rescheduling. From either the daily or weekly Calendar view, simply highlight an existing activity and drag it to some other available time slot on either that day or another day. GoldMine automatically changes the time and date on the Pending tab and in the Activity list. If you need to make more than a minor adjustment to a scheduled activity, you can double-click the specific activity in the Pending tab. This brings you right back to the original Schedule dialog box, and you can defer the appointment for a year or more, or turn a one-hour sales call into a six-hour marathon.

Deleting activities

The only time you should ever consider deleting an activity from your schedule is when you inadvertently schedule it for the wrong account. To delete an activity, follow these steps:

1. **Right-click the activity within the Pending tab.**

2. **From the menu that appears, choose Delete and confirm by clicking the Yes button.**

3. **Find the correct account.**

4. **Schedule it all over again.**

You're probably inclined to delete an appointment when your client calls you and cancels your appointment. Resist the urge. Instead, complete the appointment and make a notation in the activity notepad that your client canceled, or alternatively, use a Result Code to indicate that the client cancelled the appointment. That way, you create a historical trail of events that documents every appointment you've made and the action taken. The following story is a perfect example of the importance of completing an activity rather than deleting it.

An insurance agent (I'll call him Moe) was having a hard time with a troublesome customer. Moe had scheduled an appointment at 2:00 p.m. with the customer to renew a policy, but the customer called Moe and told him not to come . . . ever.

So Moe deleted the appointment in GoldMine. At 2:30 p.m. on the appointment day, the client called Moe's boss and complained that Moe had once again not shown up for an appointment. Moe's boss checked the account's Pending and History tabs and found no evidence that Moe had ever scheduled the appointment because Moe had deleted the appointment. Assuming that Moe had just blown off another appointment, the boss fired him.

Ignoring activities

You don't have to do anything to ignore an activity. But if you choose to ignore an activity, it stays on your Calendar until you act on it. If you set the preferences to auto-forward uncompleted activities (see Chapter 9) to the next day, soon you'll have hundreds of activities scheduled for yourself. Coming into the office and finding a few thousand tasks on your schedule is pretty discouraging. And if you've set an Alarm for an activity, the Alarm annoyingly continues to nag at you until you have no choice but to do something constructive, such as completing it.

The Best Way to Complete an Activity

When you run out of all the other options and can no longer delegate or reschedule an activity, it's time to actually complete it. After all, you were supposed to do that in the first place. Although I use the word "complete" in different ways, let there be no mistake here: *Completing an activity* means accomplishing the intended task (such as going to the meeting or making the phone call) and then taking it off your schedule by actually completing it in GoldMine.

You can complete an activity from the Calendar, the Activity list, or the Pending tab. In this section, I explain the time and the place to use each method. The first two methods allow you to review all your daily activities and dispose of them appropriately. The Pending tab method forces you to go from one account to another. I like to use the Calendar method for completing most of my activities, but it's all just a matter of personal preference.

For at least the last few versions of GoldMine, you've been able to associate an activity with an Opportunity or a Project. Now, with Version 8, you can also associate an activity with a Case. To do so, no matter what technique you use to actually complete your activity, select the appropriate Case from the Complete an Activity dialog box.

Completing from the Calendar

To complete an activity from the Calendar, you must have the Calendar window in front of you. (Open the Calendar by clicking the Calendar button in the Navigation Pane.) I prefer to complete activities from the weekly Calendar view (click the Week tab on the main Calendar window), but the daily view also works well for this exercise.

To complete an activity from the Calendar, follow these steps:

1. **Right-click the activity on the Calendar and select Complete.**

   The Complete an Activity dialog box appears, as shown in Figure 11-2.

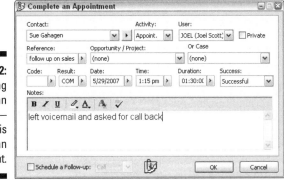

Figure 11-2:
Completing an activity — in this case, an appointment.

2. **Fill in all the appropriate fields on this dialog box.**

   The most important fields to fill in are

   - **Result Code:** Usually, you use the COM code to indicate the activity is complete.

   - **The Activity notepad:** Enter notes about the appointment or the call here.

   - **The Duration field:** Use this field if you want GoldMine to track how much time you spend on particular activities or with a particular client.

3. **If you want to follow up on this activity with another activity for this client, select the Schedule a Follow-Up option at the lower left of the dialog box.**

   If you want to have the information from the activity notepad carried forward as you continue with related activities, you can do so by choosing Tools⇨Options⇨Schedule and then selecting Carry Over Completion Notes.

4. **When you're finished, click OK.**

   You may want to use the Follow-Up option if you have just come back from an initial sales call, for example, and you promised your prospect that you would come back in a week with a proposal. If you select the Schedule a Follow-Up option, you then select from the lookup list what type of action is next. When you have done this, GoldMine brings you to yet another scheduling dialog box so that you can start all over again scheduling another activity for this account.

As soon as you complete a scheduled activity, GoldMine automatically moves it from the Pending tab to the History tab, where all the completed activities for each account are stored.

Completing from the Activity list

If you're more list oriented than graphically inclined, you may prefer to complete your activities from the Activity list. You can access the Activity list by clicking the Activities button from the Navigation Pane.

You can display the Activity list with many different options:

   ✔ **The type of activities to be displayed.** For example, you may be interested in seeing only appointments, or perhaps just phone calls. Just select the appropriate type of activity from the context-sensitive pane just above the Navigation Pane on the left of the screen. Figure 11-3 shows that Appointments have been selected.

✔ **The range of dates to be displayed.** Click the Show button, as shown in Figure 11-3. A submenu appears, allowing you to change the range of dates for the Activity list display.

Within the Activity list Actions is the Roll-over option. If you use this option improperly, you can easily transfer all your pending activities to another user. Because no way exists to get these activities back without also getting all of that user's regular activities, you could come to grief with this option.

Completing from the Pending tab

Complete an activity from the Pending tab if you want to focus on one particular account and if you're trying to dispose of some of the scheduled activities for that account.

After you highlight the Pending tab, you immediately see all the scheduled activities associated with that account. To complete any particular activity, you need only right-click the activity. As you can see in Figure 11-4, you get a shortcut menu. One of the choices is Complete, and you should choose that one.

Figure 11-3: Changing what you see in the Activity list.

Figure 11-4:
Completing
activities
right from
the Pending
tab.

Selecting the Complete choice leads you directly to the same Complete an Activity dialog box that the other two methods also arrive at. From there, you can fill in a Result Code, add some notes, and immediately go into Follow-Up mode.

Completing your activities, no matter which of the three methods you employ, transfers that pending activity directly to the History tab.

Chapter 12

Sales Forecasting

· ·

· ·

Sales forecasting is a basic tool that has been used by salespeople and sales teams forever. The idea is to have quotas, forecasts, and completed sales and to analyze each of these at every stage. By entering your expectations into GoldMine, you can then compare your forecast against reality as time goes by. Within GoldMine, you can also view statistical graphs and print reports to see how you and your team are progressing.

A forecasted sale is really just a special case of a scheduled activity. Basically, you assign a sale to a user (usually yourself) and estimate when you think you will close it. If you consistently perform this routine for every realistic prospective sale, you can use GoldMine to compile all sorts of sales forecasting graphs and reports. These analyses can relate to one individual salesperson or to an entire group of them.

You may already have a formal or an informal sales quota. GoldMine allows your manager to set up a formal quota system (sorry) and then allows you and the manager to check your progress against that quota. Even without a quota, the sales forecasting analysis will be very useful to you and to management.

Setting up Quotas

Setting up challenging but realistic quotas for yourself and your team is a basic ingredient of success. It applies to all facets of life and is what the monthly, quarterly, or annual quotas are all about.

Around the Thanksgiving holiday each year, I sit down and assign myself and my team goals for the coming year. I break our goals down into bite-size monthly sales numbers, trying to set the goals to be challenging enough to be exciting but realistic enough so that no one gets frustrated. Goals and quotas are also an important part of business planning: Someone else's annual budget is based on your quota.

To assign a quota, follow these steps:

1. **From the main menu, choose Go To⇨Analysis⇨Quota Analysis.**

   The Quota Analysis dialog box appears, as shown in Figure 12-1.

2. **Click the New button at the bottom of the dialog box.**

   The Assign New Quota dialog box appears, as shown in Figure 12-2. From here, you can custom build weekly, monthly, quarterly, or even recurring quotas for yourself or for other users.

3. **Enter the dates for the beginning and the end of the particular quota period.**

   You can do so most easily by clicking the arrow to the right of each date field. That brings up the calendar. You can make the time periods as long or as short as you like — but always in accordance with the accepted practice within your company's sales organization.

4. **Enter an amount in the Quota field and, optionally, enter some Notes in the blank area of the dialog box.**

5. **When you're finished, click OK.**

   The screen shown in Figure 12-3 appears, in which you can see not only the quotas for successive periods but also how your completed sales figures compare with those quotas.

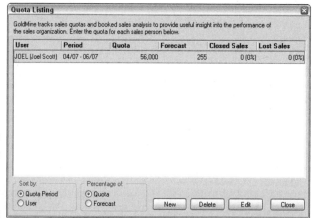

Figure 12-1:
Beginning to
set up a
quota.

Figure 12-2:
Assigning a
new quota.

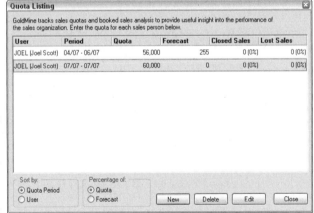

Figure 12-3:
Reviewing
all your
quota
periods.

Don't be surprised by the dates displayed in the Period column of the Quota Listing dialog box. The date range is shown in the MM/YY format, which is why you see only the month and year in Figure 12-3, even though I had actually entered the range as 07/01/07 through 07/31/07.

Entering Your Forecasts

First, let me state that not everyone enters forecasts for every possible sale. As a group, your organization should decide what kinds of deals merit inclusion in the sales forecasts. Often, very small sales, or those that are transactional (happen very quickly, perhaps with just one phone call), or those with very low probabilities just aren't included.

You can enter forecasts for those sales that are appropriate for forecasting by following these steps:

1. **Locate the account to which you intend to sell your product.**

   You can go directly into the Schedule a Forecasted Sale dialog box without locating the account first, but I prefer this more consistent approach.

2. **From the Global Toolbar, click the Sale button.**

   GoldMine brings you to the Schedule a Forecasted Sale dialog box, as shown in Figure 12-4.

3. **Fill in the Contact field.**

   This field defaults to the primary contact for the account. *If you are not positioned on the right account*, you can do so by clicking the magnifying glass to the right of the Contact field.

4. **Assign this sale to an Opportunity or Project in the second field (see Chapter 23 for more about opportunities and projects).**

   You probably won't need to use this field for most sales forecasts. Opportunities are relevant only to your largest and most complex deals.

5. **In the Product field, enter the product line you intend to sell to this account.**

   If you have a small and consistent set of products you typically sell, it is useful to use the lookup list associated with the Product field. I discuss Lookup lists in Chapter 26.

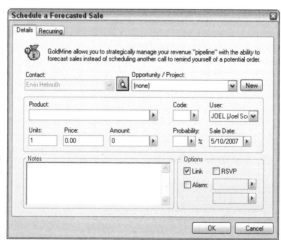

Figure 12-4:
Forecasting
a potential
sale.

6. **In the Units field, enter how many of these products you expect to sell. You can use decimals to sell fractional quantities.**

7. **Enter the price of the individual product into the Price field.**

   As soon as you fill in the Price field, GoldMine automatically calculates to the total amount of your projected sale. Items such as sales tax and shipping are usually not included here.

8. **In the Probability field, enter the probability that you will actually complete the sale.**

   This field is always an interesting exercise. Your choices are integers between 0 and 100. Neither of those two numbers is actually appropriate. If you sale has a zero probability, you shouldn't be wasting your time predicting it. In fact, just go on to the next deal and forget about it. A probability of 100 indicates that you already have at least a signed deal. If that's the case, this sale is complete and should not be in your forecast anymore (unless it was a recurring sale).

9. **In the Anticipated Sale Date field, enter what you feel is a likely date for the completion of the sale.**

   This field is also a fun item. Most of the time, this date is the result of a guessing game. If you enter a date that's not too far away, your forecast report looks good for the short term. Your sales manager will be pleased. At least, she'll be pleased until that date comes and goes and the deal isn't done. I assume that you've been doing this kind of forecasting one way or another for a long time now. Pick a date in whatever way seems to work for you and is consistent with your organization's guidelines.

10. **Select the Alarm check box if you want to be reminded of this sale.**

    I usually don't use this alarm. Instead, I regularly check my pending sales activities and do whatever follow-up seems best. Chapter 10 discusses how to check on pending activities such as sales.

11. **When you finish entering your forecast data, click OK to register this sales forecast.**

Sales forecasting is easy, requiring only six or seven entries and, as a result, you may never need to complete another forecast report again.

Click the Recurring tab on the Schedule a Forecasted Sale dialog box to enter multiple sales simultaneously. For example, if you sell an insurance policy that requires 36 monthly payments for the next three years, you can describe this sale as shown in Figure 12-5. In this way, you need enter the sale only once, not 36 times. This works only if each component is identical to the others.

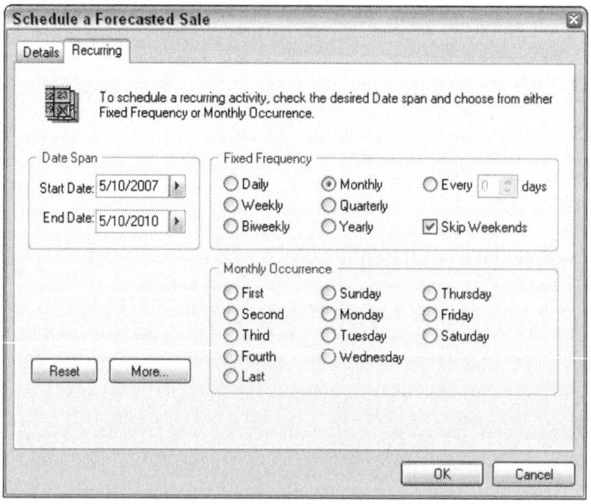

Figure 12-5: Recurring sales are repetitive sales that are exactly the same each time.

Viewing Your Sales Pipeline

If you or a manager previously entered a quota, you can readily compare your current situation with this guideline. You can see the sales projections in tabular format or in graphical format. Neither of these allows you to see individual sales, but you can see those from the Forecasts tab of the Activity list, which is discussed in the "Viewing individual items in the forecast" section, later in this chapter.

Analyzing sales in tabular format

Tabular format is the simplest way of looking at your sales projections. In this format, you can see weekly and monthly subtotals and totals. Start with this method before going on to the graphical format that requires a few more specifications before you actually see any results:

1. **From the main menu, choose Go To⇨Analysis⇨Forecast Analysis.**

   The Forecasted Sales Analysis dialog box appears, as shown in Figure 12-6.

2. **In the lower-left corner, click the Select User(s) button to select whichever user or users you want to analyze.**

From the Select Users dialog box, you can select individual users or groups. If you used the Code field when entering forecasts, you can isolate your analyses around the codes here as well. After you select users and codes, the analysis dialog box returns, but you won't see anything different yet.

3. **Click the Analyze button at the bottom of the dialog box to see some totals.**

   You should almost immediately see statistics for the current four-week period, for the next four months, and everything beyond, too, as shown in Figure 12-7.

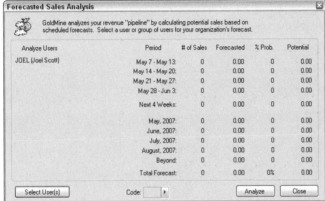

Figure 12-6: The Forecasted Sales Analysis dialog box.

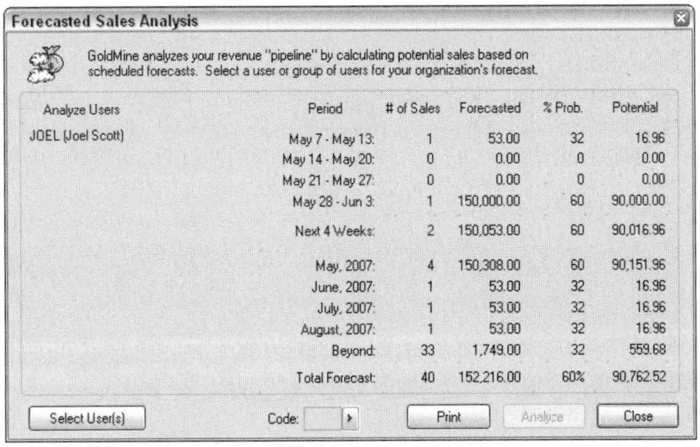

Figure 12-7: Click the Analyze button to see sales forecast statistics.

Most of these numbers are obvious, except for the column labeled Potential. Potential is a computed number and is the product of the total forecasted amount and the average probability. In other words, the potential sale amount is the amount you will probably sell in each time period.

Analyzing sales in graphical format

Sometimes a graph is worth a thousand tables. You can view your sales using graphs by following these steps:

1. **From the main menu, choose Go To⇨Analysis⇨Graphical Analysis.**

   The Graphical Analysis Options dialog box appears. The dialog box is divided into five sections:

   - Graph Type
   - Users
   - Activities
   - Time Span
   - Options

   This dialog box has a lot more options than the tabular analysis dialog box; however, it's not really hard to get through.

2. **In the Graph Type section, select Scheduled and Totals and choose whether you want to see the data as bars or lines — feel free to experiment.**

3. **Select one or more users whose forecasts you want to see. To select multiple users, double-click each user, one at a time, until all those users appear in the Selected Users panel. If you have defined User Groups previously, you can also choose one or more User Groups or even All Users.**

4. **In the Activities section, select Sales.**

5. **Select either the weekly or monthly Time Span.**

6. **Click the Graphs button to see a graphical analysis of your sales.**

   GoldMine may take a few seconds to cook up your graph, but you should shortly see a neat graph of your future. Figure 12-8 shows an example of a sales analysis graph.

7. **Click the Close button at the top right to exit this dialog box.**

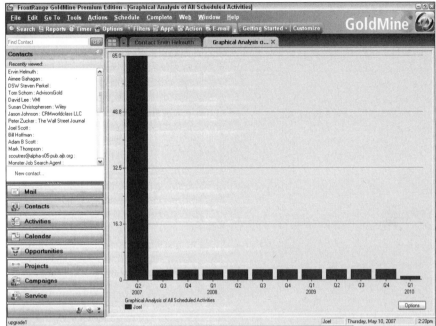

Figure 12-8:
A typical
sales
analysis in
graphical
format.

Viewing individual items in the forecast

Both the tabular and the graphical methods of examining your forecast give you summary information only. To see each pending sale, follow these steps:

1. **From the Navigation Bar on the left, choose Activities. Then, from the Current List just above the Navigation Bar, choose Forecasts.**

   Immediately, you see the browse window detailing the individual forecasted sales, as shown in Figure 12-9. You can change the user if you want. Just as important, you can click on any of the headings, such as %Prob and Forecast, to sort the display any way you want.

2. **To drill down on the details for each potential sale, double-click a sale.**

   The particular account for that sale appears. The forecasted sale itself is in the Pending tab for that account. You can examine the sale in the Pending tab by double-clicking the sale. Or easier still, right-click the highlighted sale (while still in the Activity listing) and choose Zoom or Edit to view the details. In either case (Zoom or Edit) you will see all the details. However, by using Edit, you can make changes, whereas the Zoom function allows you only to view or delete the forecasted sale.

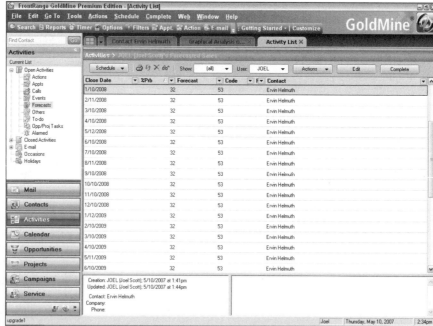

Figure 12-9:
The Activity
list shows
individual
forecasted
sales.

Forecast reports

GoldMine comes with an extensive series of standard reports, some of which relate to sales forecasting. You can review these reports by first accessing the report section. Clicking the Reports button on the Standard Toolbar takes you directly to the Reports dialog box.

Refer to Chapter 22 for more details on reporting, but for now, select the category of reports called Analysis Reports, as shown in Figure 12-8. Many predefined reports are included in the drop-down list within the field called "Report." One typical example is shown in Figure 12-10.

Viewing a group forecast

Although reports are often helpful, most of your analysis will probably be done by reviewing forecast details onscreen. You can do so for an individual's sales or for a group's sales. In the Forecasted Sales Analysis dialog box, notice a button in the lower-left corner that allows you to select users. Click this button and another dialog box appears that lets you select either individual users or groups of users.

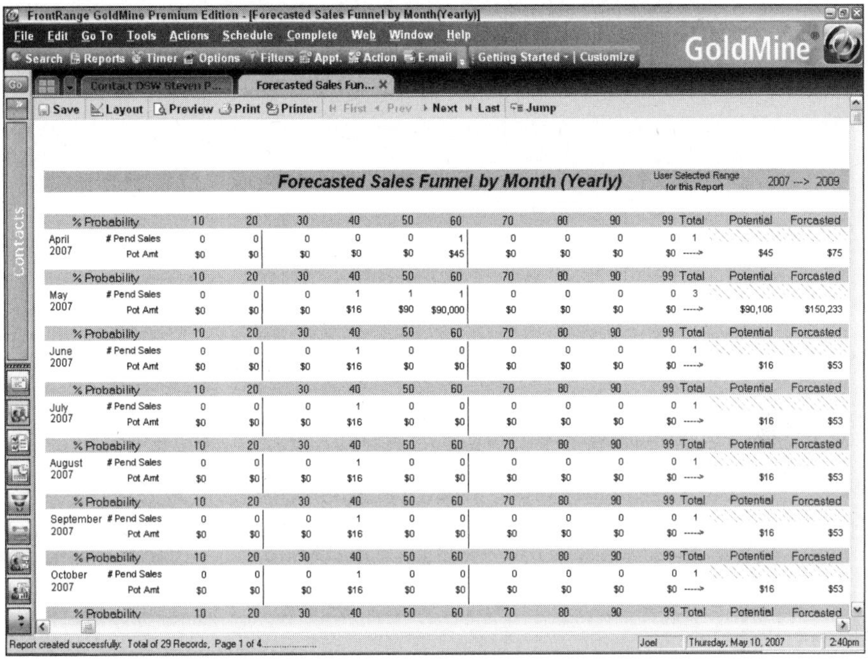

Figure 12-10:
A standard
sales
forecast
report.

Selecting a group of users is particularly useful if, for example, you're a sales manager and you want to see how all your people are doing according to their quotas or forecasts. As long as you have defined each of these salespeople as belonging to a specific group, you can easily perform this analysis in a moment.

Double-clicking any User or any group of Users listed just below will automatically move those people into the list of selected Users. After you have done this, click OK, and then click the Analyze button on the Forecasted Sales Analysis dialog box.

Completing Your Forecasts

One way or another, win, lose, or draw, you eventually need to complete your forecasted sales. You attack this from the individual account's Pending tab, from your Calendar, or from the Activity list. I usually start at the individual account's Pending tab. Highlighting the particular forecasted sale and right-clicking brings you to an option to complete the sale, as shown in Figure 12-11.

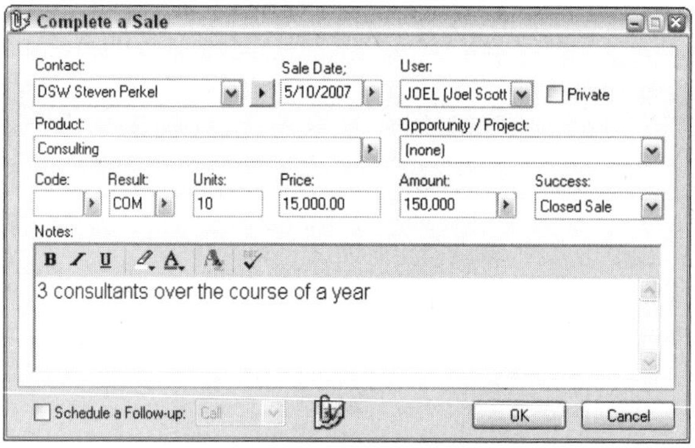

Figure 12-11:
Completing
a sale.

Several key elements are available for you to consider as you complete the sale. The first is the Private option on the upper-right part of the Complete a Sale dialog box. You can select this if you never want anyone to know what you sold. The Privacy button is particularly useful *(not)* if you expect a commission for the sale. To be truthful, I can't think of too many reasons to ever select this.

Further down the Complete a Sale dialog box are the Code and Result fields. I use the Code field to further describe the type of sale. For example, I might want to separate software and hardware sales for reporting purposes. The Result field allows the exact status of the deal to be further categorized. For example, you may lose a sale for many different reasons. Perhaps the client abandoned the project (ABA), or you lost it to a competitor because your management wouldn't budge on the price (PRI). Make up your own lookup lists for these two fields. Refer to Chapter 26 for help with lookup lists.

On the right side of the dialog box in Figure 12-11 is the Success field. You have two choices for this field: You either closed the sale or you lost it. Your selection governs how this sale is reported on the Statistical Analysis and Quota Analysis dialog boxes discussed earlier in this chapter. Any time you enter Closed in the Success field, GoldMine interprets this as a good thing — particularly in the Statistical Analysis area. As painful as entering Lost might be, it will be even more uncomfortable when you can't figure out why you are so far over quota even though it was a terrible month!

Part IV
Marketing and Support

The 5th Wave   By Rich Tennant

"The new technology has really helped me get organized. I keep my project reports under the PC, budgets under my laptop, and memos under my pager."

In this part . . .

Leads are the lifeblood of every organization. Without them, no new business is likely. In this part, you learn how GoldMine manages those leads and how marketing can stimulate the acquisition of leads. One way to get leads is to pester your vendors (all GoldMine dealers use this methodology). Another way is to use some technology to put your name out there. I like a combination of the two techniques.

The Service Management Center is brand new to GoldMine. It's meant to handle simple customer issues, allowing you to track each issue from the time it's first presented until it's resolved.

Chapter 13

Managing Your Leads

. . . .

. . . .

*E*very salesperson wants leads. I can't tell you here how to actually get leads, but I can tell you what to do after you do get them.

Importing Leads into GoldMine

Leads come from many sources. If you purchase lists, they hopefully come to you in a spreadsheet or in some electronic form that allows you to use GoldMine's Import Utility. The Import Utility accepts the following formats:

- ✔ DBF
- ✔ ASCII
- ✔ SDF
- ✔ SQL
- ✔ XML

You can also import from several versions of ACT and Outlook, but these are not usually sources of leads. You can see from the preceding list that Excel is not listed. If you have an Excel file to import, you save it as a .DBF file.

To begin an import, from the main menu, choose File⇨Import and Export⇨Import Contact Records, as shown in Figure 13-1. Doing so opens GoldMine's Import Wizard, which leads you through the entire process.

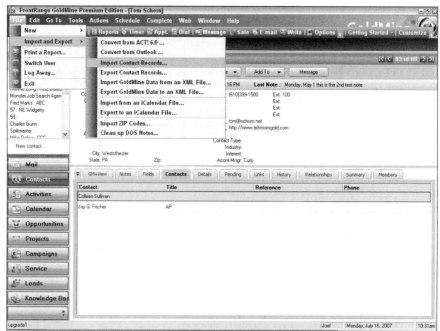

Figure 13-1:
Beginning to
import from
a variety of
file types.

As with all the wizards in GoldMine, this one just "walks" you through all the steps. Making sure that your incoming data is clean and consistent and matches the format and the size of the corresponding GoldMine fields is always a good idea. Figure 13-2 shows you the first real screen of the Import Wizard.

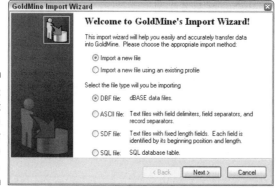

Figure 13-2:
The first
step in
getting your
data into
GoldMine.

More often than not, when importing data from multiple sources, you encounter an issue with duplicate records. This can easily happen when two sales-people are both working the same account. The duplicate records will likely have conflicting information. If you are in the situation of needing to import data from multiple sources, you are well served to consider using either GoldBox or Inaport. You can find more details on these two utilities in Chapter 30.

Follow the wizard along until it's done. When your new records are in GoldMine, you want to begin assigning these leads and monitoring their progress toward your eventual goal: closing the deals.

Assigning Leads to Users

Unless you have a completely automated lead follow-up system, every lead — and every account, for that matter — needs to be assigned to a real user. As obvious as that sounds, I have only rarely seen this to be the case within the thousands of databases our clients maintain.

The first thing to avoid is the infamous "House" account. House accounts are those accounts assigned to the company. This type of account happens when no one is quite sure whom to assign an account to, or it happens when terri-tories get reorganized or when salespeople leave the company. In reality, this guy "House" rarely makes any calls and never does even the least bit of pro-active sales.

Second, you should make sure that every lead is being handled by a real, live person and not by someone who used to work at your company six years ago. That means you have to stay on top of your logic for assigning leads.

Using ZIP codes

The United States has many ZIP codes. In fact, it has more than 79,000 ZIP codes, and that's considering only the first 5 digits. Canada has even more. The point is that basing your assignment of leads on ZIP codes forces you to maintain a very large database of codes, which occasionally change. In addition, in some states, ZIP codes are not arranged in any geographically sensible manner. In general, ZIP codes are a poor choice for determining whose lead it is.

Using telephone area codes

Telephone area codes are slightly more manageable. There are only hundreds as opposed to tens of thousands. And, in general, telephone area codes relate pretty well to geography and, to some degree, to population areas. However, as cell phones and Internet phones become more and more prevalent, they present a problem. My Internet phone number does not care where I am. It follows me from Connecticut to North Carolina should I decide to move my company.

Using geography

If you can assign accounts by state, you will have an easy time of it. But, of course, giving someone Alaska may not be quite the equivalent of California. I'm not sure about Hawaii. So, you may need to subdivide some of your larger states. You may be able to use a combination of state and the first digit or two of the ZIP code or, maybe, the telephone area codes. In general, this has been one of the more successful methodologies rather than just relying on ZIP codes or area codes alone.

In all three of these cases, you can make good use of GoldMine LOOKUP.INI file to automatically assign leads. See Chapter 26 for more details on the LOOKUP.INI file.

Other methodologies

Of course, you have other ways to divvy up leads. You can use a round-robin approach, which is similar to eenie-meenie-meinee-moe. And, that's fair but may not result in the most logic or productive pairing of sales people with accounts. You can do a weighted version of this approach, with your most productive sales people getting a few "extra" leads. Or, you can do a proximity calculation and assign the lead to whichever salesperson is geographically closest. Each of these "other" methodologies requires some amount of external programming because GoldMine does not have a built-in system to handle these approaches.

Or, you can forget geography altogether and assign leads based on that lead's product interest and each salesperson's expertise. This is a good method in an age when many sales are done over the phone and over the Web, and face-to-face meetings are less common.

Analyzing Your Leads

Out of the box, GoldMine already has quite a bit of analysis built in. By default, GoldMine assumes that you are using the Source field to track where each lead came from. Why would you use any other field?

To begin analyzing your lead data, choose Go To⇨Analysis⇨Leads Analysis, which opens the screen shown in Figure 13-3.

In Figure 13-4, you see a tabular display of all your leads. The very first item in the table shows 47 leads, but nothing in the Source field. This happens when no one enters the Source of the lead and is typically the most common result of manual entry of leads. An automated system, such as Web Import (see Chapter 29), resolves this problem.

Figure 13-3:
Finding the
Leads
Analysis
area.

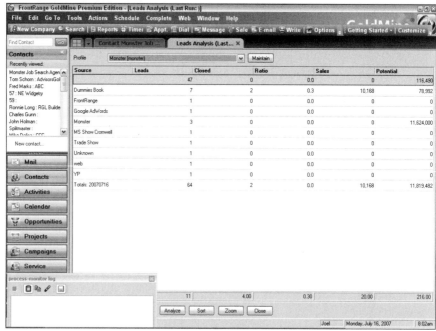

Figure 13-4:
Displaying
general
stats on all
your leads.

You can drill down and get a lot more detail on each line item by highlighting that line and double-clicking. This is the same as the Zoom option and opens the screen shown in Figure 13-5.

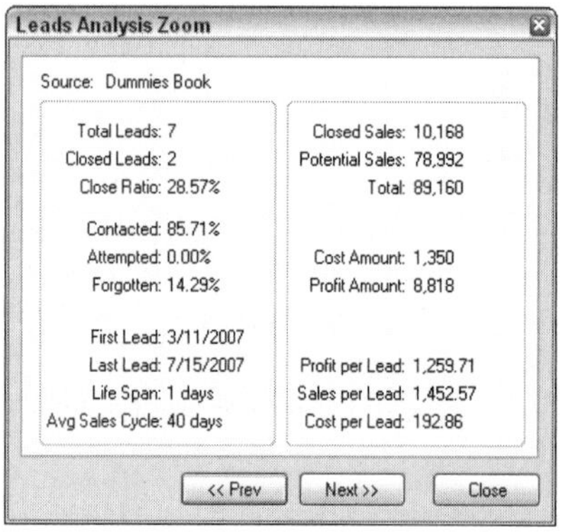

Figure 13-5:
Zooming in
to find out
more detail
on each
lead source.

Using the Previous and Next buttons shown in Figure 13-5, you can scroll through the statistics for each of your lead sources. Please be aware that, at least as of the early builds of Version 8, some of the math displayed in these screens is a bit suspect.

Although you see the leads analysis based on the Source field by default, you can also do the same analysis based on who is in charge of the account. By selecting the Analyze button at the bottom of the screen in Figure 13-4, you can specify sorting by other fields, for example by the Account Manager field, as shown in Figure 13-6.

Figure 13-6:
Analyzing
which team
members are
performing
the best.

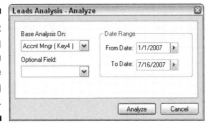

Using Automated Processes

Automating the entry of new records in general and leads in particular avoids the syndrome shown in Figure 13-4 — the Empty Source Field Syndrome. Forcing Valid Input for the Source field also goes a long way toward solving this problem.

One of the first business processes you develop should be to automate the assignment of leads and actually schedule some activities. I discuss Automated Processes in Chapter 27.

Although I cannot design your specific Automated Process here (everyone's is a little different), following are the basic components to consider:

1. **Assign each new record to a Track.**

2. **Make sure the Source field is filled in.**

   Even entering "Unknown" is better than just leaving the field blank.

3. **Assign a salesperson based on one of the methodologies discussed previously.**

   If you use some variant of one of those methods, make sure that your Automated assignment process can handle it.

4. **Have GoldMine automatically send out correspondence to the prospect, whether by mail, fax, or e-mail.**

5. **Schedule the salesperson for a follow-up activity.**

6. **Start a drip campaign, which is just a steady stream of correspondence and contacts until you can declare victory or defeat.**

   Do not give up before you've made at least six touches or have been asked to stop.

Chapter 14

Managing Your Marketing

- -

- -

*N*ot many people associate marketing with GoldMine. In fact, GoldMine seems to have gotten a bad rap when it comes to marketing. In the past seven or eight years, some of GoldMine's competitors came out with modules they labeled "marketing." GoldMine didn't have a module called "marketing," so the perception existed that GoldMine didn't do marketing.

Now, GoldMine has a module — and you can see it in the Navigation Pane — called Campaigns. Within this area is actually the same marketing functionality that has been in GoldMine for a long, long time. Now it's a little better organized, and you can use it to organize simple marketing campaigns.

In my office, we've used GoldMine to do our marketing for years, and we've developed some techniques to truly automate it and make it sing. This chapter discusses some of those ideas and techniques.

Using the Campaign Manager

You can use the Campaign Manager (CM) to create multiple marketing campaigns and assemble a series of simple steps inside each campaign. The CM is the right tool for a campaign that consists of some combination of importing data and then following up via e-mail, postal mail, or phone calls. A trade show is a typical scenario appropriate for the CM.

To create a new campaign for the trade show you just attended, follow these steps:

1. **Click the Campaigns button from the Navigation Pane.**

   GoldMine displays the Campaign Management Center, as shown in Figure 14-1.

2. **Click the New Campaign icon from the local menu and enter a unique campaign name into the Campaign Name field, shown in Figure 14-2.**

   Be sure to be very specific with your naming. Using just "Hartford Auto Show" is probably not good enough if you intend to go back year after year to this show, because you will want to track the results from each year's show. Click Next to go to the next step.

3. **Select the records in GoldMine that will be part of this campaign.**

   If the records already exist in GoldMine, and if they are part of either a filter or a group, you can select that filter or group from the list shown in Figure 14-3. But, if you are building this campaign from scratch, click the New button to create a new filter or group.

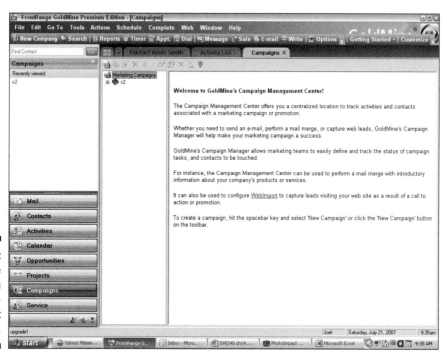

Figure 14-1:
Starting the
Campaign
Manage-
ment
Center.

Figure 14-2:
Naming a
Campaign.

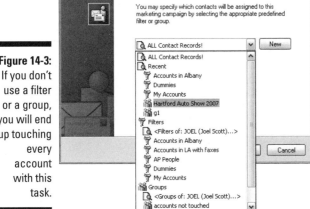

Figure 14-3:
If you don't
use a filter
or a group,
you will end
up touching
every
account
with this
task.

In deciding whether to use a filter or a group, consider whether you will be adding additional records later. A trade show, for example, is a one-time event and you are not likely to add more records later, so using a group makes more sense.

4. Click the New button and then Group from the drop-down list.

Enter the name for your new group and click OK. GoldMine now guides you through a detour to define your group. When you're done with this detour, GoldMine returns you to actually building your campaign and the screen shown in Figure 14-4.

After the campaign design is concluded, the tasks you define will be shown as Open, Completed, and Contacts.

Figure 14-4:
GoldMine
constructs
the tasks
that you
choose to
place in a
campaign.

5. **Begin building the individual tasks that comprise your campaign by clicking the New Task button (refer to Figure 14-4).**

The New button actually specifies a new task. For example, you may have purchased a list or just returned from that trade show. Select Import Data from the drop-down list. Doing so displays the screen in Figure 14-5.

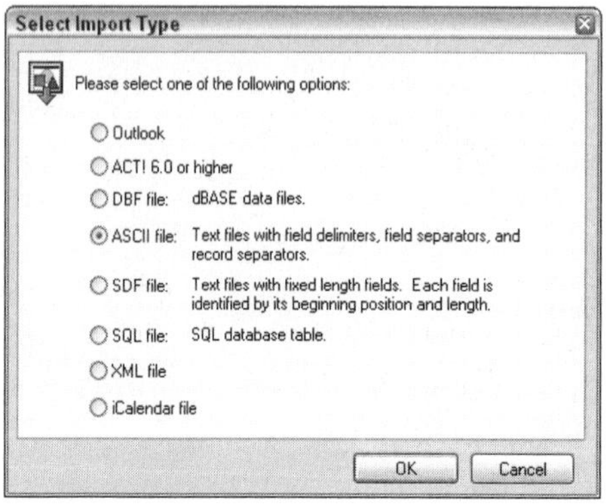

Figure 14-5:
GoldMine
now
provides
tools to
import data
from many
different
sources.

6. **Click the format your data is in and then click the OK button.**

Keep building new tasks until you have specified all the general steps in your Campaign. When you're done adding tasks to the campaign, your Campaign Manager looks like the one shown in Figure 14-6.

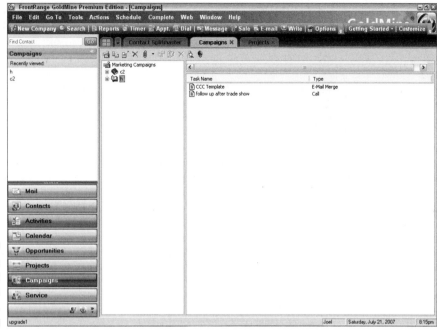

You need to understand that no behind-the-scenes process runs these campaigns. You are responsible for initiating each task, and here's how.

After you have set up one or more campaigns, go back to the Campaign Management Center. As shown in Figure 14-7, you can expand each of the campaigns in the left panel to see each of the tasks.

To initiate the next task you want performed, right-click that task and then select Complete Task from the drop-down list of choices (see Figure 14-8). The Campaign Wizard guides you through the necessary steps and then changes the task from Open to Completed.

The Campaign Manager is a good tool for simple campaigns. In reality, you find no new functionality here; the Campaign Manager merely assembles the already existing components of marketing into one place. To design a more sophisticated system, you are probably better off using the tools independently of the Campaign Manager.

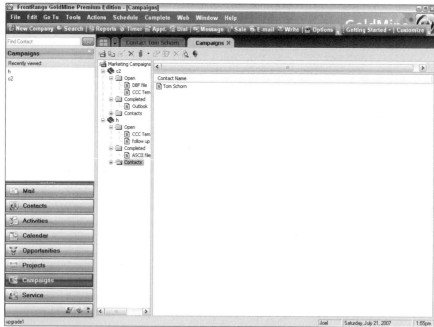

Figure 14-7:
The
expanded
list of tasks
for each
campaign.

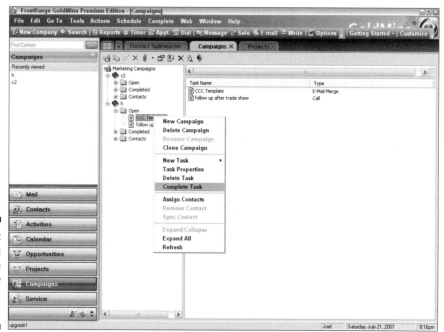

Figure 14-8:
Telling
GoldMine to
actually
execute a
task.

Using the Essential Fields for Marketing with GoldMine

Most Marketing managers will admit that they do not market the same way to every prospect or customer. Marketing mavens collect information that helps them target their marketing. GoldMine has enough tools to handle a good marketing program, but collecting some demographic information and storing that in GoldMine is essential.

Some of the fields discussed in the following sections come with GoldMine right out of the box. Others, such as Priority, Interest, and Products, must be created before you can use them. Your GoldMine administrator or your dealer can assist with that.

Source

The Source field is discussed in detail in Chapter 13, but needs to be reiterated here. You should use the Source field to track very specifically how this prospect or customer came to you. You should not use the Source field for anything else, and despite the fact that you can theoretically have multiple entries in the Source field, resist the urge to do so. Having anything other than the one primary way that this prospect heard of you will render any analysis of your marketing useless. The Source field has a lookup list and it should be set to accept only "valid input."

Priority

No Priority field comes with GoldMine, so you must create it if you want to use this concept. You use Priority to rate the importance of each account. You could use a simple "1,2,3. . ." or "A,B,C. . . " system. That rating drives your marketing. A-level accounts (or prospects) should be touched more often than C-level accounts.

You may want to calculate each account's Priority, and you can do this based on other fields you add to GoldMine. In my own system, we track custom fields such as

- Marquee Account
- Referral Account
- Geographic Location

- ✔ Attitude
- ✔ Payment Terms
- ✔ Gross Revenue
- ✔ Profit Potential

Each field gets a score and is a component of the calculation of that account's Priority. Based on the Priority field, an Automated Process determines how frequently to schedule phone calls and appointments.

Products

The system needs to know which of your products or services each account has already purchased. You can store this information in a single field, possibly allowing for multiple entries in the field, or in the Details tab if more information is needed. The Automated Process is easier to set up if Products are stored in a single field.

Interest

The Interest field should store those products or services that the account has expressed an interest in, or should be interested in.

Merge codes

Every e-mail address has an associated Merge Code (see Figure 14-9). The Merge Code is an essential component of any e-mail marketing campaign. You use this field to regulate who gets e-mail from you. As an example, you might set the Merge Code field to Z to prevent e-mail from going to a particular address. This is particularly important when a customer requests to be taken off your mailing list. You have a legal obligation to stop e-mailing at that point, and the Merge Code field allows you to comply.

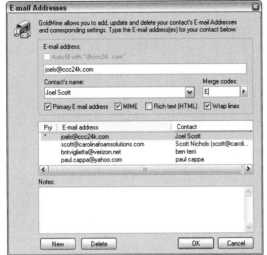

Figure 14-9:
Using
the Merge
Code field to
control who
gets e-mails
from you.

Chapter 15

Handling Cases

. . . .

In This Chapter

▶ Setting up your cases

▶ Making use of templates

▶ Handling your cases

▶ Using the Knowledge Base with cases

. . . .

*T*he Service Center is new in GoldMine Premium. It's fully integrated with the companies and contacts in the rest of GoldMine, not to mention with GoldMine's Knowledge Base. And, while you are reading about GoldMine 8, be aware that the Service Center portion of the program is more like Version 1.0 or, maybe, 2.0. A good beginning with lots of potential.

If your organization needs to track customer-related issues such as complaints, questions, or RMAs, GoldMine Premium might be just your ticket. FrontRange already has another product that manages service related cases. It's called HEAT, and it goes well beyond what GoldMine Premium currently does or is likely to ever do.

You can configure some of the fields in the Service Center, as I discuss in the first section of this chapter. Also in this chapter, I explore the basic capabilities of GoldMine's Service Center and how you can make use of them.

Configuring Your Case Setup

Each record within the Service Center is called a "Case" and each Case has a unique Case number. Other systems sometimes call these Ticket numbers. Actually, the Case number is not a number at all, but it's really a multi-part sequence of numbers and digits. If you already have a numbering system, you may be able to configure GoldMine's Case numbering system to match your existing system.

Figure 15-1 shows a typical Service Center screen. I intentionally dragged the main screen a little to the left to obscure some of the Navigation Pane. Without doing this you might miss the Customize button in the upper-right corner of the main work area. Clicking this button makes the screen shown in Figure 15-2 appear.

The first thing to do with the screen in Figure 15-2 is to click the button to the right of the Case Number Mask field. Doings so opens the screen shown in Figure 15-3, where you can configure the format of the Case Number field.

For either the prefix or the suffix (or both) you can elect to use a date stamp. GoldMine calls it a timestamp, but come on, it has only a date in it, and no time. Using the timestamp feature in either the prefix or the suffix certainly makes sense. That way, just by looking at a case number, you can tell when it was created.

The Identity Seed field provides a starting point for a unique numbering scheme. The Identity Format field controls how many digits are in that middle part of the case number. Use enough digits to handle at least the number of cases you anticipate in a typical year.

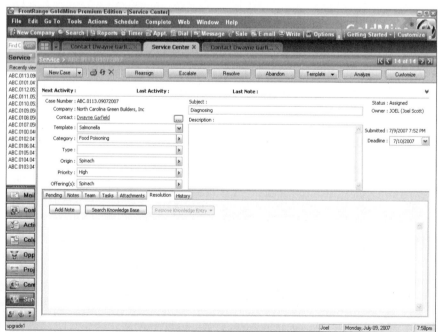

Figure 15-1:
A typical
Service
Center
screen.

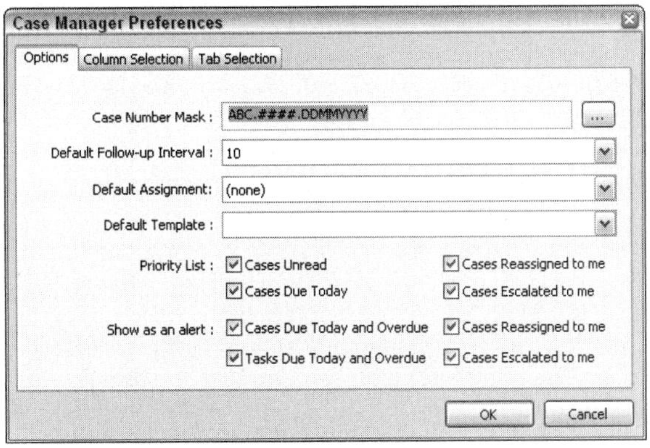

Case Manager Preferences

Options | Column Selection | Tab Selection

Case Number Mask : ABC.####.DDMMYYYY

Default Follow-up Interval : 10

Default Assignment: (none)

Default Template :

Priority List : ☑ Cases Unread   ☑ Cases Reassigned to me
     ☑ Cases Due Today   ☑ Cases Escalated to me

Show as an alert : ☑ Cases Due Today and Overdue   ☑ Cases Reassigned to me
     ☑ Tasks Due Today and Overdue   ☑ Cases Escalated to me

OK   Cancel

Figure 15-2:
Configuring
the Service
Center.

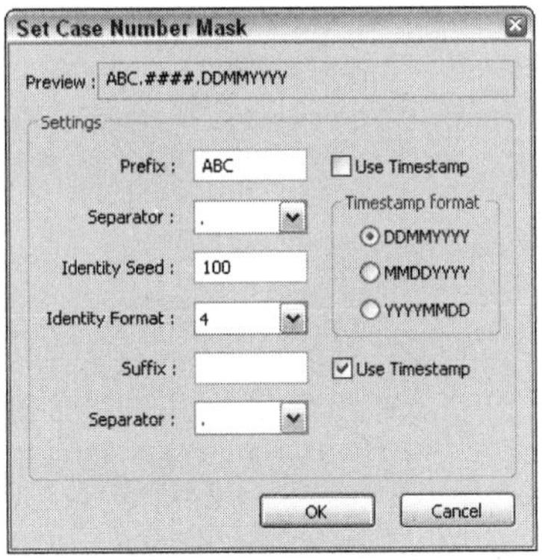

Set Case Number Mask

Preview : ABC.####.DDMMYYYY

Settings

Prefix : ABC   ☐ Use Timestamp

Separator : .   Timestamp format
     ◉ DDMMYYYY

Identity Seed : 100   ○ MMDDYYYY

Identity Format : 4   ○ YYYYMMDD

Suffix :   ☑ Use Timestamp

Separator : .

OK   Cancel

Figure 15-3:
Formatting
your case
number.

Put some thought into the format you will use, because you don't want to change the format after you already have a few hundred cases on file. When you're done with the screen in Figure 15-3, click OK to return to the screen in Figure 15-2.

At this time, you cannot add additional fields to the Service Center screen, and you can't change the field labels. With any luck, such enhancements will show up in later releases.

Using Templates

Many cases are similar, and to avoid entering the same old information time and after time, you can create one or more templates that fill in the fields in the upper area of the Service screen.

To create a new template, simply click the Template button in the Service Center toolbar and then select Manage Templates. Next click the New button on the Manage Templates screen. The screen shown in Figure 15-4 appears, in which you name your new template and fill in the default values for each of the fields shown.

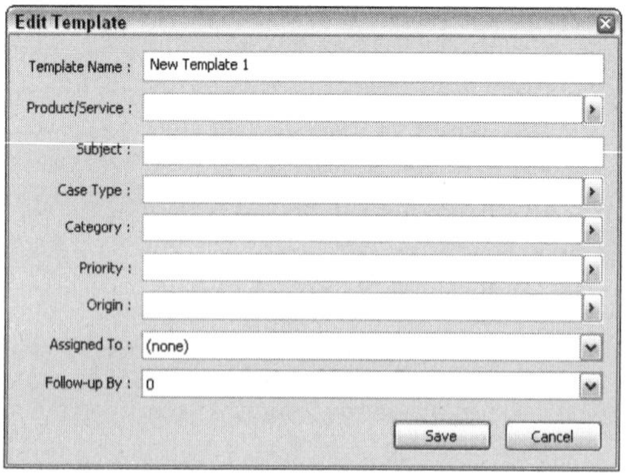

Figure 15-4:
Creating a
new
template
with default
values.

Edit Template

Template Name :	New Template 1
Product/Service :	
Subject :	
Case Type :	
Category :	
Priority :	
Origin :	
Assigned To :	(none)
Follow-up By :	0

Save   Cancel

Handling Cases

By "handling" cases, I mean assigning them to the right person, escalating issues as needed, and then, finally, putting them to bed, either successfully or not.

Assigning cases

When you configure your Service Center (refer to Figure 15-2), you can assign a default assignee. This is the poor soul in your organization who needs to deal with every gnarly issue that any customer or prospect ever calls in with. Chances are, you will want to manually override this selection, at least occasionally. You may, in fact, want to create a virtual user (someone who doesn't actually exist) called "Service Manager" and automatically assign all cases to her. Then you can reassign cases to the appropriate person.

Reassigning cases

The Service Center toolbar contains a button called Reassign. Clicking this button opens the screen in Figure 15-5.

Figure 15-5:
Reassigning
a case.

So, if you are not just automatically assigning every case to one individual, part of your process should be to reassign each case to the appropriate person. Make sure to include any special instructions, and be aware that text you enter in the Message field does not word wrap — at least not in the June 2007 release. When you click the Reassign button, GoldMine sends that user your message and assigns the case to him or her. It also changes the status to "Reassigned."

If you expect to do this kind of reassignment regularly, make sure that you have opted for an automatic alert for reassigned (and escalated while you're at it) cases. Refer to Figure 15-2 for a view of these settings.

Escalating cases

If your customer calls and complains that you aren't paying enough attention to his or her issue, you can escalate the case. To escalate it, simply select the Escalate button from the toolbar. The screen in Figure 15-6 appears.

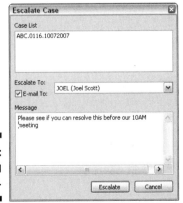

Figure 15-6:
Escalating
a case.

When you escalate a case, the message you enter is e-mailed to the assigned user, and the status of the case changes from Assigned to Escalated. Also, if you've set your alerts properly (refer to Figure 15-2), the assignee receives both an e-mail and an alert. However, nothing much else happens. The priority isn't changed, nor is the deadline. So, you may want to manually change those two fields if you are really serious about resolving the issue faster. You may also want to notify someone higher up in the food chain. Again, that would be done manually.

Resolving or abandoning cases

Ultimately, you want to resolve each case. This basically means that you are completing the assignment and, probably, entering some notes. To officially resolve a case, click the Resolve button on the Service Center toolbar. The screen shown in Figure 15-7 opens. You should enter some notes and, perhaps, link to a file in the Knowledge Base; then, click the Resolve button at the bottom of the Resolve Case screen.

Typically, resolving a case means that you have successfully dealt with it. Sometimes you may need to just abandon a case by no fault of your own. For example, if the next step in the process is for the customer to call you back with more information, and she never does, you may need to just abandon it, as shown in Figure 15-8.

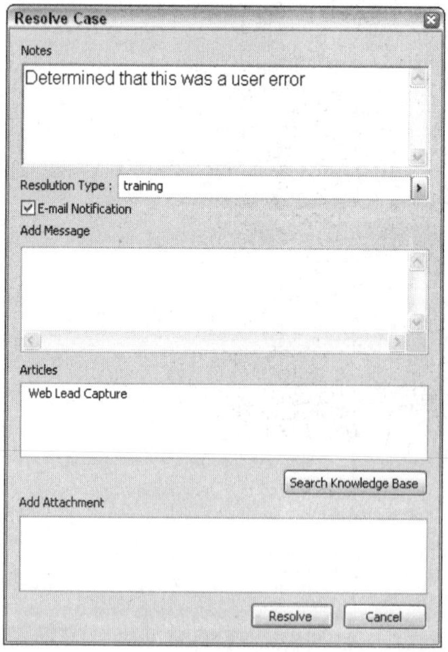

Figure 15-7:
Resolving
a case.

Figure 15-8:
Sometimes
you just
have to
give up.

Analyzing cases

The Service Center comes with some built-in analysis that you can access by clicking the Analyze button on the Service Center toolbar. When you do so, GoldMine opens the screen shown in Figure 15-9.

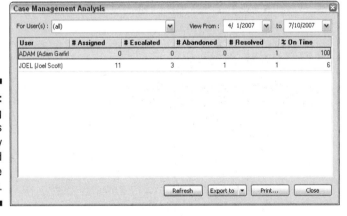

Figure 15-9:
Analyzing
who has
actually
provided
some
service.

In the analysis screen, you can select one or more users as well as the time-frame you want analyzed. As you can see from Figure 15-9, I have personally resolved only a very small percentage of the cases assigned to me. The solution may be for me to learn how to use the Reassign button better, or just do my work.

Using Your Knowledge Base

The Knowledge Base in the Service Center is the same Knowledge Base as in the rest of GoldMine. I discuss the Knowledge Base in much greater detail in Chapter 20. In this section, I cover how you should use the Knowledge Base in conjunction with the Service Center.

In the simplest sense, when setting up the Service Center (or GoldMine in general, for that matter) you should stock the Knowledge Base with every type of organizational expertise you have. When someone on the customer service staff — and, please consider someone who is in his second day with your company and is now manning the hot-line — needs to sound like an expert, the Knowledge Base is what might come to his rescue.

When you go to resolve a case, and find yourself on the phone with a customer, you can quickly search the Knowledge Base for all the relevant information you need. The figures that follow show the sequence of screens for locating information on how GoldMine interacts with the Internet. This, of course, is just a typical example. You might be more interested in finding out how to diagnose salmonella food poisoning or how to build a solar collector.

Clicking the Resolve button from the toolbar opens the screen shown in Figure 15-10. You can enter some notes in the upper pane and then click the Search Knowledge Base button to reach the screen shown in Figure 15-11.

Figure 15-10:
The Resolving Case screen from which you Search the Knowledge Base for the topic of interest.

Figure 15-11:
Searching
for
information
about the
Internet.

In Figure 15-11, I have simply entered the word Internet. The next step is to click the Search button, which immediately makes the window in Figure 15-12 appear. There, I have highlighted the entry for Internet E-mail. Doing so displays the text that applies to this topic.

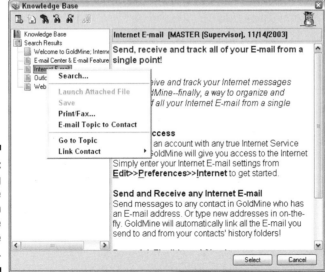

Figure 15-12:
E-mailing
the
information
from the
Knowledge
Base.

By right-clicking the Internet E-mail listing in the Knowledge Base Search area, you get the option to e-mail this information to the relevant contact. This option enables the rookie customer service person both to verbally explain the solution to the customer and easily send an e-mail with the solution.

As long as your customer support needs are relatively simple, GoldMine Premium's Service Center will serve you well. If you outgrow it, you can always upgrade to TeleSupport Help Desk, HEAT, or some other competitive product.

Part V
Managing Documents

By Rich Tennant

RICHTENNANT

"Sure, at first it sounded great – an intuitive network adapter that helps people write memos by finishing their thoughts for them."

In this part . . .

*I*f you like to send out letters — the old-fashioned kind — you'll really like GoldMine's interface with Microsoft Word. You can create and maintain a series of template documents that not only have HTML artwork but can also include dates from records in GoldMine.

GoldMine's e-mail system, which has been around since the early 1990s, is a great way to easily track all your incoming and outgoing e-mails. If you're an Outlook addict, you can use Outlook either in addition to or in conjunction with GoldMine's own e-mail system.

In this part, you also learn about linking documents of all types to records in GoldMine. This works with incoming and outgoing Word documents, e-mails, and any other kind of file you might imagine.

Chapter 16

Integrating with Word

· ·

· ·

Back in the day, GoldMine integrated with several word processing systems. Now that all but one of those systems has essentially bitten the dust, GoldMine can still claim a very tight integration with Microsoft Word.

You can use this integration to create Word templates that you can then use as mail merge documents. You can send these documents to clients on a one-off basis or as part of a marketing campaign via mail merge.

In this chapter, I discuss what works with what, and how to create a simple Word template and use it in a mail merge.

Understanding What Versions Work Together

GoldMine Premium officially works with Word 2003 (after you've installed Service Pack 2) and with Word 2007. Figure 16-1 shows a chart from FrontRange's Compatibility Matrix. This is part of a larger compatibility document published by FrontRange. The entire document is available at www.ccc24k.com.

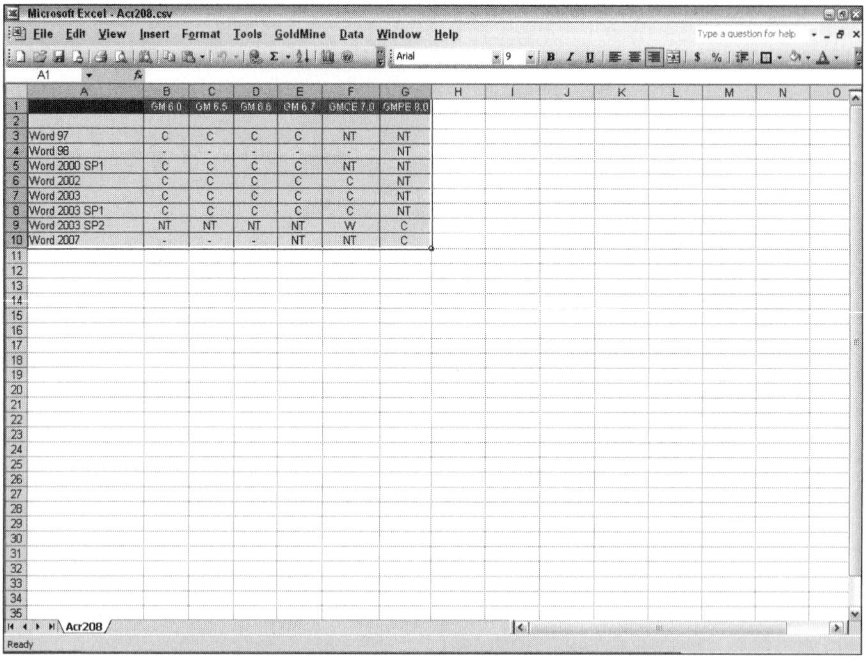

	A	B	C	D	E	F	G	H	I	J	K	L	M	N	O
1		GM 6.0	GM 6.5	GM 6.6	GM 6.7	GMCE 7.0	GMPE 8.0								
2															
3	Word 97	C	C	C	C	NT	NT								
4	Word 98	-	-	-	-	-	NT								
5	Word 2000 SP1	C	C	C	C	NT	NT								
6	Word 2002	C	C	C	C	C	NT								
7	Word 2003	C	C	C	C	C	NT								
8	Word 2003 SP1	C	C	C	C	C	NT								
9	Word 2003 SP2	NT	NT	NT	NT	W	C								
10	Word 2007	-	-	-	NT	NT	C								

Figure 16-1:
Using various versions of GoldMine with each version of Word. C=Certified; NT=Not Tested and not officially supported.

Creating Templates

You can easily create custom Word templates containing a combination of pictures, data from GoldMine fields, and standard and custom text.

After the link is created between GoldMine and Word, you have an extra tab in Word called, interestingly enough, "GoldMine." Clicking this tab, as shown in Figure 16-2, displays a drop-down list of choices.

To create a simple company letterhead that you can use for correspondence, follow these steps:

1. **Open Word with a new, blank document and press Return to create a couple of blank lines.**

2. **From Word's main menu, choose Insert⇨Picture⇨From File.**

   Browse to a copy of your company logo (assuming that you have such a thing; if not, adding your logo is optional, anyway). Select the logo and Word will position it where your cursor was positioned in the document. Add a blank line below the picture.

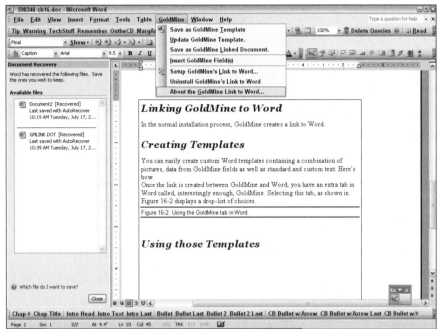

Figure 16-2:
Using the
GoldMine
tab in Word.

3. **From Word's main menu, choose Insert⇨Date and Time and then select whatever date format appeals to you.**

   Word inserts that below your logo. You probably want to click the Enter key once or twice to add blank lines below the date.

4. **From Word's main menu, choose GoldMine⇨Insert GoldMine Field(s).**

   Word brings you to a drop-down list of all the available fields, as shown in Figure 16-3. Those selections starting with an ampersand are actually combinations of fields. I recommend that you select &FullAddress. If the currently active GoldMine record has a complete set of contact information, you immediately see that information displayed in the template you are building.

   Always use a record with all the address fields filled in for your template. You can even create a test record with the names of each field so that you will know what the &FullAddress or other available fields are inserting into the template.

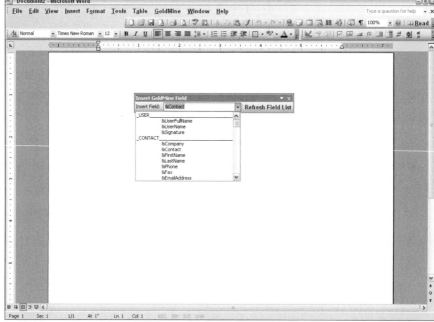

Figure 16-3:
Some of the available fields from GoldMine that you can use in your template.

5. **Add a salutation line below the address by selecting &Contact.**

   You probably want to append a colon after this insertion so the colon appears after the Contact name in your document.

6. **Enter a few blank lines (just a few) to allow room for custom text that you will compose each time.**

   If your text is longer than the two or three blank lines you've created, Word will expand your document to deal with it.

7. **Add some closing text and, better yet, add a picture of your scanned signature.**

8. **To save this new and valuable template, click the GoldMine tab again and then choose Save as GoldMine Template.**

   It is very important that you do NOT save this document by choosing Word⇨File⇨Save As!

The preceding procedure adds your new template to GoldMine's Document Management Center, and it is immediately available for your use.

Using Your Templates

GoldMine's Document Management Center houses all your templates, whether they are public templates or owned specifically by you or some other user. You get to the Document Management Center from the main menu by choosing Go To⇨Document Templates. Doing so opens the screen shown in Figure 16-4.

From the screen in Figure 16-4, you begin the process of merging the contact information from one or more records in GoldMine with any of the templates in the Document Management Center. Here are the basic steps:

1. **In the left pane, double-click the template you want to use.**

   GoldMine responds with the screen shown in Figure 16-5, which enables you to select either the primary contact or one of the secondary contacts. Pick one. GoldMine merges the contact information into the template you selected and displays the result on the screen.

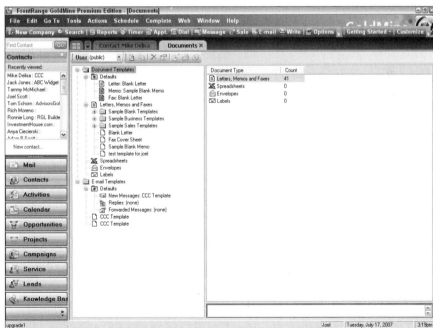

Figure 16-4:
The Document Management Center.

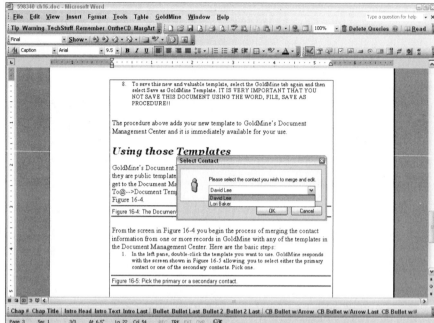

2. Click the local print icon.

GoldMine displays the dialog box shown in Figure 16-6. Although you can stick with the one contact you selected in Step 1, you can alternatively select either a filter or group.

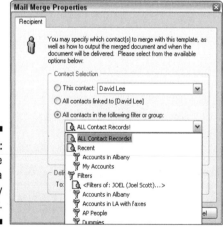

GoldMine presents you with the option to print all the documents. If you select No in Figure 16-7, you can add text to the documents before printing. Otherwise, GoldMine sends your documents to the printer and logs this activity in each accounts History tab.

Figure 16-7:
Deciding
whether
to print
or edit the
documents.

3. **After you've given GoldMine permission to print, that process begins and you should go hunting for stamps and envelopes.**

Templates can be public or owned by one user. If you can't locate the template you have in mind, check to see whether you have the correct user specified in the Document Management Center.

Chapter 17

Sending and Receiving E-Mail

In This Chapter

▶ Configuring the e-mail system

▶ Sending and receiving e-mail with GoldMine

*I*f you are one of those people who thinks e-mail is now just the current fad, then you can skip this chapter entirely. Papyrus, quills, and the abacus could make a comeback, and then you'll be in seventh heaven. (I still have one of my slide rules just in case.)

If you're thoroughly addicted to Outlook and just don't want to be bothered learning to use GoldMine's built-in e-mail client, even though GoldMine's is easier, faster, and better integrated, you might also consider skipping this chapter. You can go directly to Chapter 18, where I discuss all the pros and cons of being an Outlook addict.

Despite the plague of spam, e-mail is still one of the best communications tools ever developed. It's fast, easy, and basically free. All these things appeal to me, and apparently to many others as well.

The entire Document Management System, of which e-mail is a part, has been continually enhanced since the late 1990s. In particular, FrontRange recognizes that many, many people use Outlook as their e-mail client. Rather than fight that trend, the GoldMine/Outlook interface continues to become more and more robust. If you or others at your company are dedicated to using Outlook for e-mail, you can find more details in the next chapter.

In addition, e-mail features full HTML capability, so you can read and create rich-content e-mails.

In this chapter, you find out how to set up your GoldMine system to handle all your e-mail requirements, how to send an individual e-mail, how to send broadcast e-mails, and how to receive and catalog incoming e-mails.

Configuring Your E-Mail System

Before you can use GoldMine's e-mail system, you must first set up an Internet account, and you must configure GoldMine to use that account. To access the Internet, you must have an account with an Internet service provider (ISP). This ISP must provide true Internet mail access. AOL, for example, does not provide true Internet mail access. There are many regional, national, and international providers with good, competitive service.

Entering your ISP's account information

When you sign up with an ISP, you are given account information that you need to configure your GoldMine interface. You do so within GoldMine's User Preferences dialog box. Please refer to Chapter 3 for more information on setting up user preferences.

The QuickStart Wizard guides you through the setup of your e-mail account in GoldMine. If you are already beyond the initial installation and still need to configure your e-mail, follow these instructions:

1. **Choose Tools➪Options from the main menu.**

   The User Options dialog box appears.

2. **Click the E-Mail tab, as shown in Figure 17-1.**

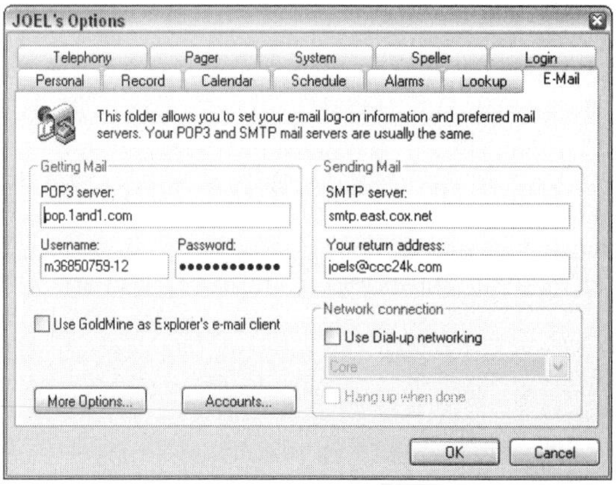

Figure 17-1: Set up your e-mail preferences.

3. **Enter the appropriate information, using the following explanations as a guide:**

   • **POP3 Server:** The name of the server that holds your incoming e-mail, and can be entered either as something like mail.something.com or as the actual IP address, which might be something like 207.187.163.57. In either case, your ISP provides this information.

- **Username:** You set up your user name with your ISP.

- **Password:** You also set this up with your ISP, and when you type it in, it appears on the User Preferences dialog box as a series of asterisks for security purposes.

- **SMTP Server:** The name of the server that processes your outgoing e-mail. It may or may not be the same as your POP3 server address. I use my actual IP address for both these fields.

- **Your Return Address:** Your actual e-mail address that probably appears on your business cards or that you tell people.

- **Network Connection:** The last field on the Internet tab of the User Preferences dialog box is for your network connection. If you do not have a dedicated connection through a router, or something like that, you do not need to select this option. If, on the other hand, you want GoldMine to dial in and make the connection for you each time you start the program, select the Use Dial-up Networking option. If you do select this option, you may also want to have GoldMine hang up for you when you are done. If so, then select the Hang Up When Done option.

4. **To set more options, such as composing, retrieval, and additional account information, click the More Options button in the lower-left portion of the E-Mail tab.**

   Clicking this displays the dialog box shown in Figure 17-2. This dialog box allows you to tailor how you compose, retrieve, view, and customize your e-mail messages.

5. **Click OK when you're finished.**

Figure 17-2:
Setting up
more e-mail
options.

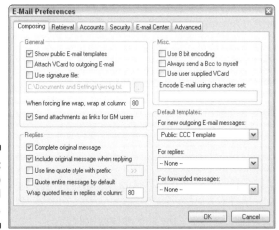

Setting options for composing your messages

This section deals with the most significant settings within the Internet Preferences dialog box in GoldMine. Each of these settings is discussed in the following sections. The new rules and wizards are set up within the E-mail Center itself and are discussed in the "Sending E-Mail Messages" section, later in this chapter.

Attaching a VCard to outgoing messages

You can have GoldMine attach your *VCard* (a .vcf file) to each of your outgoing e-mail messages. A VCard contains information similar to that of a contact record, such as the entries you made in your Personal tab, or other information that you enter outside of GoldMine. If the receiving system has VCard capabilities, the system will decipher the .vcf file to import this information. If the e-mail recipients use GoldMine to retrieve e-mail, they can use your VCard information to create a contact record in GoldMine, if a record does not already exist for you in their databases.

I don't use this option myself because many of my non-GoldMine-using recipients can't make use of it and virtually all my GoldMine-using e-mail buddies already have a record for me in their databases. I don't really care to receive .vcf files from anyone, either, because I don't want to store them on my hard drive, anyway.

Creating an e-mail signature file

If you would like to create an e-mail template with a touch of class, you should consider GoldMine's signature file capability. Without investing in any other HTML tools, you can still create an impressive and artistic signature that is automatically included in every one of your outgoing GoldMine e-mails.

Now, I need to define what I mean by a *signature file*. Many people think that a signature file contains an actual signature. The truth is, a signature file might include an actual signature, but it might not. Often, a signature file just contains personal and company contact information. And maybe a company logo or a descriptive phrase.

If you want your e-mails to actually contain your personal signature, you can do this, but you will need to scan a copy of your signature into a file. If you do this, you might just as well do it in color. Then, when you include this signature, it can look as though you signed the e-mail with a blue pen.

To create your own HTML signature file, including your signature, follow these steps:

1. **Start a brand new e-mail to someone (anyone, actually).**

   A few steps down, you'll add some simple text and a couple of graphics to the still empty window where you usually type the text of the e-mail.

2. **Add a couple of blank lines so that your final document will have room for you to start typing a message**

3. **Type "Respectfully yours" and then add a couple more blank lines for your signature.**

4. **Type your name, title, company name, company Web site, phone number, and e-mail address — each on separate lines.**

5. **Now comes the neat part: Position your cursor on the blank line between "Respectfully yours" and your name.**

6. **Click the Insert Picture icon, as shown in Figure 17-3, and then browse to select the file in which you saved your scanned signature.**

   After you've filled in the Picture Source field, click OK. You may need to resize your signature.

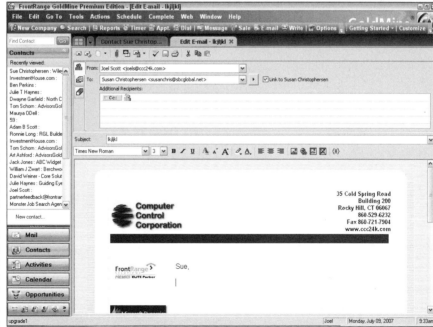

Figure 17-3:
The insert a picture and HTML icons you need to use to insert pictures into your template.

7. **Click the HTML icon.**

   You will immediately see that GoldMine has turned your text into HTML code. This code is what you want to save in your signature file.

8. **Cut and paste the code you've just generated into Notepad or Word and save it as a** `.txt` **file.**

9. **Tell GoldMine that you want it to always use this signature file by choosing Edit⇨Preferences⇨Internet⇨More Options.**

   Make sure that Use Signature File is selected; it's the third option on the screen. Click the Browse button just below to link GoldMine to the signature file you just created. You can see an example of the finished product in Figure 17-4.

Violà! You're in business and looking really professional! You can add a company logo and a slick catch phrase later.

I get far too many e-mail requests from people who don't even bother to tell me who they are. All I get is an e-mail message saying, "Please send me pricing," or "Send literature on Client Retention." I am happy to do this, but only if I know with whom I am corresponding. Proper etiquette dictates that you provide this information; using a good signature file is the easiest, most consistent way to do so.

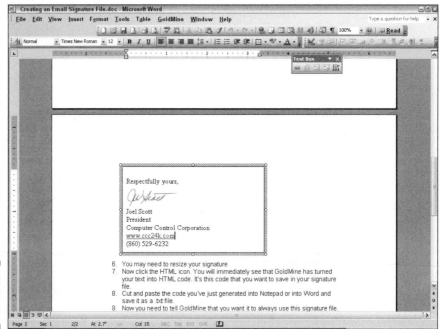

Figure 17-4:
The finished product!

Additional options for composing e-mails

Within the Composing tab of the E-Mail Preferences dialog box (refer to Figure 17-2), you can make some additional choices, as explained in the following list:

- ✔ **When Forcing Line Wrap, Wrap at Column X:** Specifies the character at which GoldMine wraps the text to the next line. By default, GoldMine wraps to the next line at the 80th character in a line.

- ✔ **Complete Original Message:** Places the original message in the History tab when you either reply to or forward a message. If you do not want to designate the original message as a completed activity when you respond, leave the check box corresponding to this option blank.

- ✔ **Use Line Quote Style with Prefix:** Specifies the characters that GoldMine uses to identify lines quoted from the original message when you copy those lines into your reply. By default, GoldMine uses >>.

- ✔ **Quote Entire Message by Default:** Specifies that GoldMine copies the entire text of the original message in your reply, using the characters entered in the Use Line Quote Style with Prefix option. This is a good option to select if you want each e-mail you send to contain a thread of the previous messages from a correspondent.

- ✔ **Wrap Quoted Lines in Replies at Column X:** Specifies the character at which GoldMine wraps to the next line of quoted text. You can use this option to create an indented block for text quoted from the original message. By default, GoldMine wraps to the next line at the 80th character in a quoted line.

- ✔ **Default Templates:** Select an existing e-mail template from the corresponding drop-down list that appears when you work with one or more of the following message types:

  - New outgoing e-mail messages

  - Replies

  - Forwarded messages

  To apply no default template to any or all of the messages, select None.

When you finish defining settings, either click another tab to continue defining options or click OK to close the Internet Preferences dialog box.

Retrieving e-mail from the Internet

You can define a variety of options for retrieving Internet e-mail messages. These options, as shown in Figure 17-5, can specify the location of attachments, scan intervals, and the criteria that GoldMine uses to select messages for retrieval.

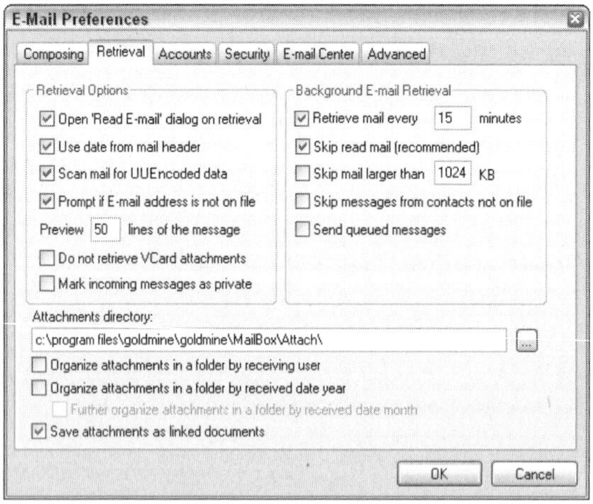

Figure 17-5:
Choosing
your e-mail
retrieval
options.

To define criteria for e-mail retrieval, follow these steps:

1. **Choose Tools➪Options, click the E-Mail tab on the dialog box that appears and then click the More Options button.**

2. **Click the Retrieval tab and choose from the following options:**

   - **Delete Retrieved Mail from Server:** Removes messages from the Internet mail server upon retrieval.

   - **Open 'Read E-mail' Dialog on Retrieval:** Retrieves e-mail and opens the Read E-mail dialog box, displaying the first retrieved message.

   - **Use Date from Mail Header:** Sets the date of incoming mail to the date sent, as indicated in the header information of the message. Selecting this option ensures that your e-mail is posted in true chronological order on your calendar.

     If you don't retrieve e-mail frequently, however, you may want to leave the check box corresponding to this option blank. For example, with this option selected, a mail message sent four days prior to retrieval is posted in the calendar with the four-day-old date.

   - **Scan Mail for UUEncoded Data:** Sets GoldMine to scan the Internet mail server for any e-mail messages that contain UUEncoded attachments. Selecting this option does not affect retrieval of MIME-encoded files.

   - **Prompt If E-mail Address Is Not on File:** Sets GoldMine to display the Attach E-mail to Contact dialog box upon retrieving an unlinked e-mail message, from which you can select options for linking the message.

- **Preview X Lines of the Message:** Specifies the number of lines of text that GoldMine retrieves with the message for display in the lower pane of the E-mail Center window. By default, GoldMine retrieves the first 15 lines.

- **Retrieve Mail Every X Minutes:** GoldMine automatically connects with your POP3 mail server to check for new mail at the interval as specified in minutes. For example, if you want to retrieve waiting Internet e-mail every two hours, type 120 in this field. The default value of 15 sets GoldMine to scan for and retrieve waiting e-mail every 15 minutes. You must select this option to define any options listed in the Rules section.

  To retrieve e-mail for the account, you must select the Auto-retrieve option from the Account tab of the Internet Preferences dialog box. If you do not select the Auto-retrieve option but select the Retrieve Mail Every X Minutes and Send Queued Messages options, GoldMine sends queued mail only.

- **Skip Read Mail (Recommended):** Bypasses displaying any e-mail messages that you have already read if you have not selected the Delete Retrieved Mail from Server option. This option is available only if you select the Retrieve Mail Automatically Every X Minutes option.

- **Skip Mail Larger Than X KB:** Retrieves only Internet E-mail messages that are equal to or smaller than the kilobyte (KB) value in this field. By default, GoldMine skips messages that are 1,024 kilobytes or larger. This option is available only if you select the Retrieve Mail Automatically Every X Minutes option.

- **Skip Messages from Contacts Not on File:** Retrieves e-mail only from those contacts who have Internet e-mail address entries in their detail records. This option is available only if you select the Retrieve Mail Automatically Every X Minutes option. This might help reduce incoming spam, but you might also miss something important from some new prospect.

- **Send Queued Messages:** Sends all queued messages when automatically retrieving mail — see the description previously in this list for the Retrieve Mail Automatically Every X Minutes option. The Send Queued Messages option is available only if you select the Retrieve Mail Automatically Every X Minutes option.

- **Attachments Directory:** Designates the destination for retrieved e-mail attachments. Type the entire path information. To search for the destination, select the Browse button, which displays the Browse for Folder dialog box.

3. **When you're done defining retrieval settings, either click another tab to continue defining options or click OK to close the E-Mail Preferences dialog box.**

Sending E-Mail Messages

GoldMine has a unified e-mail system, enabling you to use the same E-mail Center for both internal (other users on your GoldMine system) and external (Internet mail) correspondence. In addition, you can send an e-mail message to an outsider who uses, say, AOL, and send a copy to your sales manager, another GoldMine user on your team. I refer to this type of e-mail as "dual e-mail."

To create or edit an e-mail message to a primary contact, you can simply position your cursor on the E-mail field label on the main screen. In GoldMine, this field label is similar to a hyperlink. Clicking it displays the Create E-mail window, as shown in Figure 17-6.

Figure 17-6:
Create or edit an e-mail message using an HTML template.

Addressing a message

GoldMine assumes that you intend to send an external e-mail to the primary contact of the record that is currently active. You can easily redirect this message, however, if you want to send this e-mail to one of the secondary contacts at this account. Click the down arrow to the right of the recipient in the To field. You then get a list of all the other contacts at this account for which you have an e-mail address. Selecting another contact replaces the default recipient, as shown in Figure 17-7.

You can expand the scope of your recipient list by clicking the right arrow button. You have a total of five options, as follows:

- ✔ **To: Contact:** You can use this option to redirect your e-mail to any person at any account in your GoldMine database.

- ✔ **To: Manual Recipient:** You can use this option to redirect your e-mail to someone who may not even be in your database, as long as you know his or her e-mail address and are willing to type it in.

- ✔ **To: GoldMine User or Group:** This choice allows you to send the message to another GoldMine user on your team, or even to an entire group of users, for example, everyone in your Minneapolis office. (See the "Sending messages to a group" section, later in this chapter.)

Figure 17-7: Choosing additional recipients to e-mail.

✔ **To: Distribution List:** You can build a distribution list of recipients. This is similar to a group and allows you include an almost random list of people who should get regular messages from you.

✔ **To: Outlook (MAPI) Recipient:** This is part of the interface to Microsoft Outlook, and allows you to redirect your e-mail output to someone in your Outlook address book.

You can further expand the recipient list by clicking the CC (carbon copy) symbol just below the primary recipient's name. The menu that appears (shown in Figure 17-8) allows you several more options:

✔ **To:** You can manually enter an e-mail address that may not exist in your database.

✔ **CC** *(carbon copy):* You can select one or more additional primary or secondary contacts to receive this message.

✔ **BCC** *(blind carbon copy):* You can select one or more people to send this message to, but the primary recipient will not know you have sent it to anyone else. For example, you might use this to notify someone of a problem and to simultaneously inform his or her supervisor.

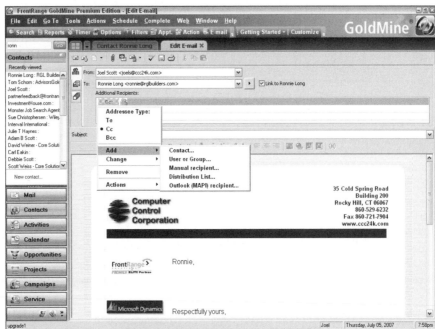

Figure 17-8:
Expanding
your
recipient
list.

Composing the subject and body of a message

The subject appears as a header so that your recipient has some idea what this message is about. Below that, of course, is the area in which you compose your actual message. Simply type your message in there.

Many people, aware of viruses and other suspicious things, won't read or even download messages that don't have a recognizable Subject field. If you want your messages properly dealt with, make the subject succinct and appropriate.

Completing a message

After you address and compose your message, you can check your spelling, attach a file or files, or print your message before you send or save it. You select these options by clicking the icons on the Create E-mail window's local toolbar, as shown in Figure 17-9. The icons are as follows:

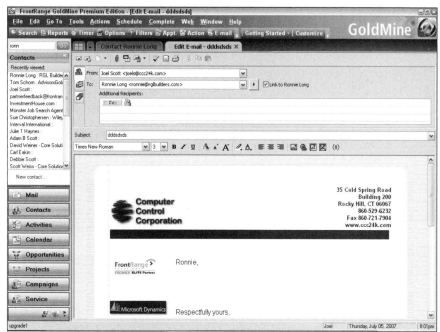

Figure 17-9:
Click an icon for more tasks.

✔ **Send:** Immediately sends your e-mail message.

✔ **Queue:** Puts the message into a queue with other messages for later transmission. This might be useful, for example, if you are composing e-mails in an airplane and intend to send a batch of them later.

✔ **Save as Draft:** Saves the message if you need to work on it later, before you send it.

✔ **Attach Files:** Attaches one or more files of any type to your e-mail.

✔ **Encrypt:** Puts a password on your message and enables you to add 32- or 128-bit encryption. If you use GoldMine's encryption, only another user with GoldMine (and only in the United States, believe it or not) can read it.

✔ **Check Spelling:** Runs the spell checker on your message. This is good if you can't spell and your recipient can. While you're composing, or when you're done composing a message, you can click the Check Spelling icon to avoid embarrassing yourself.

✔ **Save as File:** Saves the message as a file on your system in addition to sending it.

✔ **Print:** Prints the message.

✔ **Cut, Copy, and Paste:** The standard tools to manipulate your data within your document or from/to another document.

Also notice the Link check box, which is already selected by default. This selection automatically creates a link between this e-mail and the active account. In this way, a record of this e-mail appears in the History and, if there is an attached document, in the Links tab of the main record.

Sending messages to a group

One of the more powerful features of the e-mail system is its ability to automatically send an e-mail message to each member of an active group of accounts. This should be one of the cornerstones of your marketing program. Not only can you use this to send an initial blast to prospects, but more important, you can use this as part of a client retention system. You should be regularly corresponding with all your clients, making sure that your name gets in front of them as often as possible. This applies equally well to simple e-mail messages and to e-mail templates.

The first step in sending e-mails to a select set of accounts is to activate either a filter or a group. See Chapter 8 for details on this. After you have activated your filter or group, you can send the e-mail message to each of them quite easily. The following is a step-by-step outline for sending a boiler-plate e-mail to a group of people after you activate a filter or group:

Bear in mind that in this version you don't have to activate the filter or group. You can choose at the time you decide to whom the email will be sent.

1. **Click Go To⇨Document Templates.**

   The Document Management Center appears.

2. **Right-click on an e-mail template such as the Hello template that comes with GoldMine and select Merge from the shortcut menu, as shown in Figure 17-10.**

   The Mail Merge Properties dialog box, shown in Figure 17-11, appears.

   You can now decide to send your e-mail just to the primary contact for this one active record (if this is all you wanted to do, there are easier ways) or all the secondary contacts for this record, or to a filter or group that you have already set up.

Figure 17-10:
Choosing
an e-mail
template.

3. **Choose either the Send Now option or the Queue for Later Delivery option and then click OK.**

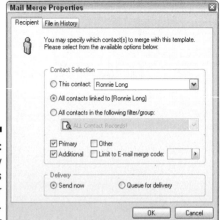

After you have completed these steps, your e-mail message is on the way to all your recipients (assuming that you didn't just put the message into the queue for later transmission), and the message can be registered in the History tab of each account to whom you sent the e-mail.

Getting Your Mail

In the simplest sense, you can use the GoldMine E-mail Center to retrieve your messages, read them, and then either save them or delete them. From the E-mail Center window, you can perform all the usual and simple e-mail functions, but you can also go a step farther and define rule conditions and actions. For example, you can tell GoldMine what to do with your e-mails while you are on vacation, or what to do if the subject line contains the word *complaint*. You can set all this up using the E-mail Rules Wizard.

I just wanna get my e-mail, already

Life in the e-mail fast lane is really not as complex as all the foregoing implies. After your options are set, retrieving your e-mail is very easy. The E-mail Center icon is on the main screen. Just click the Mail button in the Navigation Pane to open the E-mail Center window, connect to the Internet (if you're not already connected), and retrieve your e-mail. The E-mail Center window is shown in Figure 17-12.

You may have more than one e-mail message waiting for you. GoldMine begins retrieving, and you can see each e-mail message coming in, along with the sender's name, the subject, the size of the message, and the date it was sent to you. As soon as GoldMine is done retrieving these headings for you, you can begin looking at each message.

With your user preferences, you can set a relatively small default amount of text to come in with these headings. This text is displayed in the lower panel of the E-mail Center window so that you can get a little better idea of the topic of the e-mail. To see the full text of the message, double-click the particular From or Subject listing you want. GoldMine then retrieves any remaining text or attached files. At this point, you have a variety of options, ranging from reading the message, viewing the attached files, forwarding the message to another person, replying, or saving the e-mail for future reference.

Defining rule conditions

Using the E-mail Rules Wizard, you can define one or more conditions for GoldMine to evaluate when retrieving online messages. If a message meets the conditions, GoldMine then applies the action(s) that you define in the E-mail Rules Wizard.

Defining these conditions means that you can actually automate the processing of your incoming e-mails. Examples of the use of such automation includes having GoldMine redirect incoming messages with particular headings to someone else, or send a return message indicating that you are on vacation and won't be reading your messages until you return to the office.

To define a new condition or to edit an existing condition, follow these steps:

1. **Click the E-mail button on the Navigation Pane.**

2. **From the E-mail Center, click the Actions button and then set up E-mail rules.** The E-mail Rules Center appears.

3. **Right-click in the left panel of the E-mail Rules Center and choose the New icon, which is the leftmost local icon.**

   The E-mail Rules Wizard appears, as shown in Figure 17-13.

Figure 17-13:
Use the
E-mail
Rules
Wizard
to define
e-mail rules.

The E-mail Rule Wizard gives you the following options to choose from:

- ✔ **Mail Field:** Click to select the e-mail field that you want GoldMine to search for a specified value. For example, if you want GoldMine to look for a specified value that appears as the title of the e-mail, select Subject.

- ✔ **Logical Condition:** Click to select a condition, such as Begins With. By default, GoldMine displays Equal To.

- ✔ **Value:** Type the value for which you want GoldMine to search when evaluating the field that you selected in Mail Field.

When you're done setting up your new rule, click OK to enter the condition in the Browse part of the Condition dialog box. To add another condition, click the New button. To change a selected condition, click the Edit button. When you're done adding or editing rules, you can specify how GoldMine should apply the rules by selecting either the All Of option or the Any Of option.

When you're done, click the Next button. The E-mail Rule Wizard: Action dialog box appears. The actions you specify are executed only when the conditions you just defined are met.

Defining rule actions

After you have defined any condition that you want GoldMine to check for in incoming messages, you can define the action or actions for GoldMine to apply upon finding a message that meets the condition. Click the New button. The E-mail Rule: Action dialog box appears, containing the following options:

- ✔ **Action on Mail:** Click to select the operation that you want GoldMine to perform upon detecting a message with any specified condition, such as the Move to Inbox option or the Delete Attachments option.

- ✔ **Value:** Provides additional information necessary for GoldMine to complete the operation. For example, if you selected the Move to Inbox option in the Action on Mail field, you can click to display a drop-down list from which you can select the subfolder of your Inbox where you want GoldMine to place the messages that meet any of the conditions.

  The Value field is available only when needed to complete the action. For example, if you select the Delete Attachments option in the Action on Mail field, GoldMine needs no further information to process this request, so the Value field is not available.

Click OK to enter the rule in the Browse section of the Action dialog box. To add another action, click the New button. To change a selected action, click the Edit button.

When you're finished, click the Finish button. GoldMine adds the rule to the selected rule set. The name of the rule appears in the left pane under the rule set. Any selected conditions and actions of the rule set appear in the right pane.

If you actually want your rules to work, you need to make sure that you've told GoldMine to auto-retrieve your mail. You do this within your e-mail options settings. And, of course, you need to leave your GoldMine system running with an active Internet connection while you're away.

Chapter 18

Using Outlook

In This Chapter

▶ Knowing what versions work with what

▶ Discovering all the Outlook integration options

▶ Using GISMO with GoldMine

*F*irst, I have to go on record reminding you that GoldMine has its own e-mail client. That's my favorite way to send and receive e-mail and, for the life of me, I don't understand why anyone would actually want to complicate life by adding Outlook to the mix.

Okay, I do understand it a little. Many people were familiar with Outlook long before they started using GoldMine and just don't want to learn a new system. Still, I just can't see this as a good enough reason to insist on using Outlook.

Because I have been losing this argument for seven or eight years now, it's time to include a chapter on how to use Outlook with GoldMine in case you insist on doing so.

What Versions Work Together

If you are looking for the simplest approach — just transferring records back and forth from Outlook to GoldMine — then the chart in Figure 18-1 applies. In this chart, C means the application has been fully tested and is supported; NT means the application has not been tested and is not supported.

Figure 18-1:
Using versions of Outlook with GoldMine.

Microsoft Outlook (For Synchronization with GoldMine)

	GM 6.0	GM 6.5	GM 6.6	GM 6.7	GMCE 7.0	GMPE 8.0	iGM 6.0 / 6.1	iGM 6.6
MS Outlook 97	-	-	-	-	-	-	-	-
MS Outlook 98	C	C	C	C	-	-	-	C
MS Outlook 2000 SP1	C	C	C	C	-	-	-	C
MS Outlook 2002	C	C	C	C	C	NT	-	C
MS Outlook 2003	C	C	C	C	C	C	-	C
MS Outlook 2007	NT	NT	NT	NT	NT	N	NT	NT
MS Outlook Express	-	-	-	-	-	-	-	-

If you are using GISMO, which is the most popular of the three methods, the chart in Figure 18-2 applies.

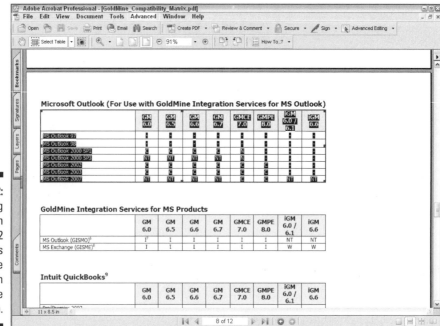

Figure 18-2:
Everything from Outlook 2002 and up is compatible with GoldMine Premium.

The Three Options for Outlook

Depending on the level of sophistication of your network and, of course, on your requirements, there are three ways to connect GoldMine and Outlook. This chapter focuses on the second method, GISMO, but at least knowing about the other two is useful.

Importing and Exporting

GoldMine gives you the ability to simply export data from GoldMine into Outlook. This is most appropriate as a one-time activity to populate Outlook with your contact information from GoldMine or vice versa: send your Outlook address book to GoldMine.

GISMO

GISMO, which is an acronym for GoldMine Integration Services for Microsoft Outlook, is included (sort of) with GoldMine 8. It's actually not on the CD you get with your initial order, but you can download it via NetUpdate for free after you've got GoldMine installed. Go figure.

With GISMO, you can

- ✔ Link both sent and received e-mails to a GoldMine contact
- ✔ Create a new contact and link the incoming e-mail to it
- ✔ Launch contacts in GoldMine
- ✔ Automatically link all the messages received from a particular e-mail address to its corresponding GoldMine contact
- ✔ Access GoldMine contacts from the Outlook address book

GISME

GISME, short for GoldMine Integration Services for Microsoft Exchange Server, is the most sophisticated of the integrations between GoldMine and Outlook. It requires a Microsoft Exchange Server and gives your GISME users access to shared calendar information.

GISME is not included with GoldMine Premium and needs to be purchased separately. It also requires some in-depth technical expertise to properly implement.

Using GISMO

If you are already familiar with Outlook, then using GISMO shouldn't stress you very much at all.

Before jumping in and processing your e-mail for the first time in GISMO, you should set your preferences. To do so, choose Tools⇨Options and then click the GoldMine Link tab. The screen shown in Figure 18-3 appears; this figure shows the way I have my preferences set.

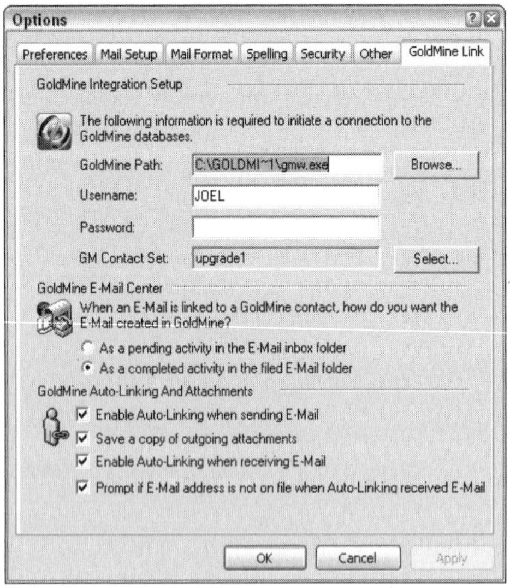

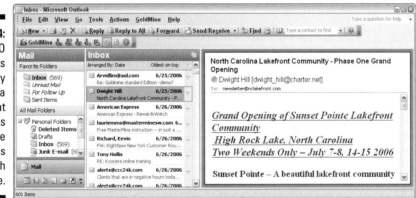

Figure 18-3:
Setting your
e-mail
processing
preferences.

When you "create the e-mail as a completed activity in GoldMine," you are really saying you want the e-mail logged in the History tab rather than the Pending tab. I also recommend choosing all the auto-linking options, thus having Outlook/GoldMine do as much of the work for you as possible. After you save your settings by clicking OK on the screen shown in Figure 18-3, you can move on to processing some e-mail.

You can see in Figure 18-4 that GISMO just adds an additional toolbar to Outlook.

Figure 18-4:
GISMO
expands
Outlook by
adding a
toolbar that
handles
all the
interactions
with
GoldMine.

Receiving e-mails in Outlook

The local toolbar in Figure 18-3 gives you all the tools you need. From left to right, here's what the buttons do and when to use them.

- **Launch Contact Record in GoldMine:** This button is important if GoldMine isn't open. Selecting this button opens GoldMine with the appropriate contact record open (assuming that record exists). Of course, because you will always have GoldMine open, you shouldn't need to use this button very often, or at all.

- **Link Message to GoldMine Contact:** This automatically links the email message without forcing you to leave Outlook. In fact, you won't even see the GoldMine record, although if the record does not exist in GoldMine, you will be asked whether you want to create the new record.

- **Create a New GoldMine Contact and Link Message:** If you already know that the record doesn't exist in GoldMine, this is a good option.

- **Link All messages from This Sender:** If you have multiple e-mails from the same person, this option saves them all in one step.

- **Unlink This Message from GoldMine:** If you suddenly realize that you just linked a confidential message to a contact record and have exposed it to every user, you may want to unlink it with this option.

- **Re-link This message to GoldMine Contact:** If the message has become unglued, this option links the message to the contact you select.

- **Auto-link All Messages to GoldMine Contact when Receiving E-Mails:** This is what makes GISMO do the most work for you, although actually reading your e-mails before having the system just store them for you is probably better.

- **File This Message in GoldMine:** This option saves the e-mail in GoldMine but keeps you in Outlook.

- **GoldMine Integration Service for Microsoft Outlook Help:** This is the place to go for immediate, context-sensitive help.

GISMO determines where the e-mail gets attached by the e-mail address on the record. Don't attempt to attach e-mails to a record that come from someone who is not part of the record unless you totally understand the LINK/UNLINK concept in GoldMine.

Sending e-mails from Outlook

When you send an e-mail via Outlook, it is automatically linked to the GoldMine record that contains that e-mail address. You have nothing manual to do. However, you can avoid a lot of manual address entry into Outlook by adding your GoldMine Address Book to Outlook before using Outlook to send e-mails to contacts in GoldMine.

For Outlook 2000 users, the GoldMine Address Book is not available if your Outlook is in "Internet Only" mode. To add your GoldMine Address Book to Outlook, follow the steps below:

1. **In Outlook, choose Tools⇨E-mail Accounts.**

   The E-mail Accounts wizard appears.

2. **Under Directory, select Add a new directory or address book.**

3. **Click Next.**

   The Directory or Address Book Type dialog box appears.

4. **Select Additional Address Books.**

5. **Click Next.**

   The Other Address Book Types dialog box appears.

6. **Select the GoldMine Address Book.**

7. **Click Next.**

   The GoldMine Integration Services for Microsoft Outlook information dialog box appears.

8. **If the GoldMine Path text box is empty or incorrect, click Browse to locate the correct** gmw.exe **file.**

9. **Type your GoldMine Username and Password.**

10. **Click Select and then OK.**

11. **Click OK to verify changes are applied the next time Outlook is run.**

12. **Click OK to save changes.**

13. **Exit and re-open Outlook.**

Chapter 19

Linking Documents

. . . .

In This Chapter

▶ Linking word-processing files and e-mails automatically

▶ Linking files and folders

▶ Accessing your linked documents

. . . .

Document links are a very powerful feature in GoldMine that allows you to store any type of file with the contact record. Using document links, along with the contact record, or even the service record, you can store forms relating to the contact, incoming facsimiles, voice-mail messages, or contract documents created with a word processor. When you need to view or edit the linked file, GoldMine automatically loads both the application and the file in one operation.

In this chapter, I explain what types of documents and files you can link to contact records, demonstrate how to link documents and files, and show you how to view your linked files. You also discover how to launch the application that runs your linked file so that you can view the linked file quickly and easily.

Exploring the Links Tab

The Links tab maintains the connections from the clients' records to their linked documents. When you click the Links tab, shown in Figure 19-1, GoldMine displays each of that contact's linked documents. The link to each document shows the name of a file and the name of the application used to edit or display the file.

The Links tab contains the following information:

 ✔ **Document:** Descriptive title of a document or folder that's linked to the contact.

 ✔ **Type:** Document type that must match a registered application in the Windows Registration Database.

✔ **File:** Filename and path of the linked file.

✔ **Date:** Date the file was linked to GoldMine. This date may be different from the date the file was created or last modified. You can see the document's most recent modification date in Windows Explorer.

✔ **Owner:** Owner of the document or file, which is typically the user name of the GoldMine user who created the document.

Each column can be sorted by clicking on the column header. Click again and GoldMine sorts the opposite way. You can change the order in which the columns appear by dragging and dropping the column headers.

If you right-click a blank area in the Links tab, a shortcut menu enables you to choose from the following options:

✔ **Launch:** Launches and loads the highlighted file and its application. This option is the same as double-clicking the linked document entry in the Links display.

✔ **Move:** Moves the highlighted file to a different location.

✔ **E-Mail Document:** Enables you to e-mail the highlighted file to a contact, GoldMine User, User Group, Manual Recipient, or Outlook contact.

- ✔ **Find:** Enables you to search the data associated with the link to the document. This is used most often to locate documents with particular words or phrases in their filename.

- ✔ **Output To:** Enables you to send the list of files under the Links tab to a printer, Word, Excel, or the Windows Clipboard. This list includes all the information found under the Links tab (Document, Type, File, Date, and Owner) but not the information found in the actual files.

- ✔ **New:** Creates a new link.

- ✔ **Delete:** Deletes the highlighted link. The actual file is not deleted.

- ✔ **Edit:** Displays the Linked Document dialog box, in which you can edit the highlighted link.

- ✔ **Group:** By choosing Group, you can click a column header and drag that header into the gray bar above the column headers. That action then groups your links by whatever header you choose.

- ✔ **Summary:** Doesn't currently appear to do anything.

- ✔ **Filter:** Works in a way similar to Groups except that you click the down arrow next to the column header that you want to sort by. For example, you may want to see only Word document files. In that case, you select Microsoft Word Document from the file type list, thereby activating a filter for the Links tab of the entire contact set. As you go to other records, only .doc files show.

The needle in the haystack

In my years of being in business B.G. (Before GoldMine), I wrote many letters and proposals. I would often mail a 15-page proposal and then wait for the inevitable signed contract to arrive. I now suspect that the arrival of those signed contracts probably could have been expedited and made a more regular occurrence if I had followed up with a phone call. But without GoldMine to remind me to make the calls, it almost never happened — I relied on the innate beauty of the proposal to pull me through.

An equally serious problem typically arose about six months after I mailed a proposal — a phone call from the prospective client. I would pick up the phone and hear something like, "Hi, this is Charlie at Universal. I want to go over that proposal you just sent me." My first problem was trying to remember who Charlie was. If I did remember him, I was still left with another issue: What did I do with that proposal? Is it in the pile on my desk, in the pile on the floor, or (I hope not) in the circular file? "Charlie, I'll call you right back."

GoldMine's ability to keep track of documents and files cured my disorganization. Well, maybe not all of it, but I'm much better off now. Whether it's a 15-page proposal, a spreadsheet, an e-mail, a fax, or a photo of the kids, GoldMine can link the file to the appropriate contact record. Locating any document that relates to the client becomes a snap, so you won't have to call a client back after ransacking your office to find a proposal.

Linking Files Automatically

Some of the more common file types, such as word-processing documents and e-mails, link themselves automatically to records. Certain fax programs also link automatically. Most other files require you to manually connect them to the client record. (See "Manually Linking Files and Folders" later in this chapter for more information.) In this section, you discover how GoldMine automatically links files to a contact record.

Linking word-processing documents

Out of the box, GoldMine comes with links to various versions of Microsoft Word. If you match the proper version of GoldMine with the correct linking file and the correct version of Word, you can automatically link every document you create to the Links tab. This process is actually easier than it sounds.

When Word is initially installed, you must also install its links to GoldMine. See Chapter 16 regarding setting up the Word link. If you don't install it, GoldMine can't create mail merge documents for you.

After the connection is made, creating Word documents starting from GoldMine is easy, and linking them after they're created is even easier. During the linking procedure, Word creates several blank template documents, one of which is BLANK.DOT. You can see it in the list of mail merge documents. You access these documents by choosing Go To↷Document Templates from GoldMine's main menu. This takes you to the Document Management Center window, as shown in Figure 19-2.

When you select Letter: Blank Letter, GoldMine shows you a Word template document that starts creating a letter for you by filling in the salutation portion of a typical letter you might write. You can fill in the actual text of the letter and then save this letter using the Save As command. Make sure that you don't simply save the letter, because doing so overwrites the original template. After you save the letter, Word automatically sends the file information back to GoldMine.

GoldMine takes all the file information and lists it within the Links tab of the active contact record for you. You don't need to do anything, assuming that you began this process from the Document Management Center window within GoldMine. If you didn't start from the Document Management Center window, Word doesn't send any linking information back to GoldMine, and you have to manually link the document.

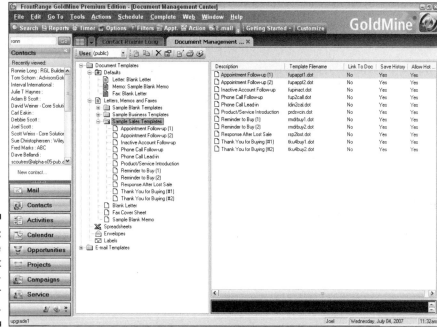

Figure 19-2:
The
Document
Manage-
ment Center
window.

Linking e-mails

I discuss the details of sending and receiving e-mails in Chapters 17 and 18, but basically, the GoldMine e-mail system is tightly integrated with contact records through the History tab, not the Links tab. It's as automated as the Word link, but the results are a little different.

Outgoing e-mails

To automatically attach an outgoing e-mail to a contact record, you must complete the following steps:

1. **Find the record with which you're associating the e-mail and display it on-screen.**

   That record becomes the active record.

2. **From the main menu, choose Go To and then Document Templates.**

   The Document Management Center appears.

3. **Click the Create a New Mail Message icon on the local toolbar.**

4. **Compose the e-mail message and send it by clicking the Send icon on the local toolbar.**

These outgoing e-mails, whether they have attached documents or not, are automatically recorded in the History tab, *not* in the Links tab! If these outgoing e-mails have attachments, you can access them by double-clicking the e-mail message on the History tab.

Incoming e-mails

Incoming e-mails are automatically registered in the History tab, too. Any incoming files attached to e-mails are recorded in the Links tab. The e-mail system allows you a good bit of control over exactly which records are associated with particular e-mails. Please refer to Chapter 17 for more details on controlling incoming e-mails.

Linking faxes

You must have a third-party program in order to fax at all. Of the commonly used ones, only one automatically records what it has done in the Links tab. FaxRush (a.k.a. OmniRush) is the most tightly integrated fax system. When properly configured, OmniRush automatically links all outgoing and incoming fax activity for you.

WinFax and ZetaFax, which also integrate with GoldMine and with Word, are not quite so tightly integrated as to automatically record what they have done in your GoldMine records. It is up to you to manually link or record those files that these applications have sent or received.

Manually Linking Files and Folders

You can manually link virtually any file to GoldMine. You can create document links by using either the local (shortcut) menu on the Links tab of the contact record or by dragging and dropping the file with an application that supports file dragging, such as Windows Explorer.

Using the Links shortcut menu

To manually link a file using the local (shortcut) menu, follow these steps:

1. **Click the Links tab on the contact record (the main GoldMine screen).**
2. **Right-click the mouse anywhere in the display area below the tab.**

    The Links shortcut menu appears, as shown in Figure 19-3.
3. **Select New from the menu.**

    The Linked Document dialog box appears, as shown in Figure 19-4.

Figure 19-3:
The Links
shortcut
menu.

Figure 19-4:
The Linked
Document
dialog box.

4. **Enter a name in the Document Name text box that will make sense to you six months from now.**

5. **Enter a user name in the Document Owner text box if it is someone other than you.**

   Consider using Public as the Document Owner to make this file available to everyone on your team.

6. **Record the exact filename of the file using the Browse button at the bottom of the Linked Document dialog box.**

7. **Select the Allow File to Synchronize check box if you want this file included in a transfer set.**

8. **Click OK when you are finished, and your file is linked.**

Using drag-and-drop

Using the drag-and-drop method is the quickest way to link a document to GoldMine:

1. **Click the document name in the application that supports drag-and-drop (such as Windows Explorer) to highlight it.**

2. **Hold down the left mouse button, drag the file icon to the currently open record (you don't even need to have the Links tab selected), and release the mouse button.**

   GoldMine displays the Linked Document dialog box.

3. **Type the linked document name in the Document Name field.**

In just three moves, you completely link almost any kind of file or document. In no case have you moved the document itself. You merely established a pointer from GoldMine to the document.

Accessing Linked Documents

When a document file is linked with GoldMine, you can launch directly into the application and load the linked file with one operation. This means that you can easily start Word or Excel and immediately display the linked file. To do this, click the Links tab to access the list of linked files, and then double-click a file.

If you select a Word document, for example, GoldMine starts up Word (if it isn't already running in the background) and loads the document you have requested. It does the same for Excel spreadsheets, or for that matter, for any program that allows file access.

By linking all your client-related documents to the appropriate contact record, you're assured that you can always find those documents when you need them.

If you work on a network, always store your documents on a server accessible to all who may ever need to reference those documents. Even if others won't need to reference those documents, chances are that only your file servers are being regularly backed up. And you probably want all your documents backed up. The take-home lesson is to save your documents in a standard, agreed-upon location that's accessible to your team and that's backed up regularly.

Part VI
Organizing and Distributing Information

The 5th Wave   By Rich Tennant

"I find it so obnoxious when people use their cellular phone in public that I'm making notes about it on my HPC for a future opinion piece."

In this part . . .

The Knowledge Base is an intranet. It houses and organizes files and documents that are used in your daily operations and directly integrates with the new Service Center.

Managers worth their salt love graphs and statistics. Sometimes, it's hard to make decisions without them. GoldMine provides a nice array of graphs, stats, and built-in reports. In addition, GoldMine provides the tools to customize all these reports or to create new ones. You can also use some third-party tools to get even more sophisticated.

Complex sales require more complex tools to keep track of what's going on. That's the Opportunity Manager. When you successfully close a deal that you've been tracking in the Opportunity Manager, you can use all that information in the Project Manager to make sure that you come through with everything you've promised.

The Relationships feature is the new Organizational Chart. This is the perfect tool to see very graphically how each person relates to others and how different accounts relate to each other.

Chapter 20

The Knowledge Base

In This Chapter

▶ Navigating through the Knowledge Base

▶ Creating new Knowledge Base sections

▶ Editing in the Knowledge Base

▶ Notifying your staff of important changes to the Knowledge Base

*T*he Knowledge Base is like an encyclopedia that you can develop for use by your staff as well as for distributing information to clients and prospects. In previous versions of GoldMine, the Knowledge Base was called the InfoCenter. You can use the Knowledge Base to catalog your company's rules and regulations, make them available to every employee, and notify staff of any changes to the rules and regulations. You can also stock the Knowledge Base with product catalogs and price lists for easy maintenance and distribution. And now with GoldMine 8, the Knowledge Base is integrated with the new Service Center.

The Knowledge Base divides its information between two sections:

✔ **Knowledge Base:** Contains general information relevant to staff and clients alike, such as company rules and product prices.

✔ **Personal Base:** Contains information pertinent to an individual user, such as family birthdays and anniversaries.

The Knowledge Base and the Personal Base are structurally the same and operate in the same way. Whereas only users with Master rights can control access to the Knowledge Base, determining reading and writing access for individual users, individuals can set up their own sections in their Personal Base. The Personal Base is designed for use by an individual, and the only way to access a Personal Base is to log on with the same user name as the user who originally created that particular Personal Base. Also, whereas the Knowledge Base is integrated with the Service Center, your Personal Base is not.

This chapter explains how to navigate through the Knowledge Base to find relevant information and how to create and post new entries.

Navigating the Knowledge Base

You can easily access the Knowledge Base from the main menu by choosing Go To⇨Knowledge Base. The Knowledge Base window, shown in Figure 20-1, appears.

As you can see in Figure 20-1, the Knowledge Base window contains two tabs: the Knowledge Base and the Personal Base. The Knowledge Base and the Personal Base tabs are functionally the same, so this chapter focuses just on the Knowledge Base.

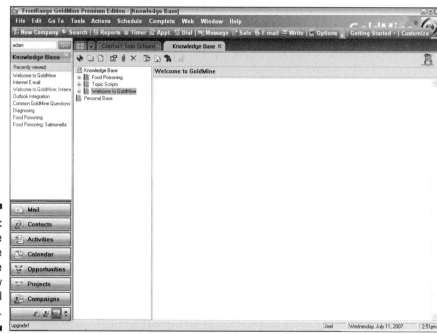

Figure 20-1:
The
Knowledge
Base
window
with initial
books.

Understanding how the Knowledge Base is organized

The left pane in Figure 20-1, which by default shows the Knowledge Base tab when you open the Knowledge Base, categorizes all the information in the Knowledge Base into books, sections, and topics. A *book* is the most general grouping. Each book contains one or more sections. *Sections*, in turn, may contain one or more *topics*, or may themselves house information directly. If sections contain topics, then topics are where data is actually stored.

Below the Knowledge Base section (refer to Figure 20-1) is the Personal Base section. Again, the Personal Base is structurally identical to the Knowledge Base; the only difference being the access rights.

When you first install GoldMine, two books exist — Topic Scripts and Welcome to GoldMine. Each of these books is further divided into sections. You can see this structure simply by double-clicking one of the book icons, as shown in Figure 20-2. As soon as you open a book, the icon changes from a closed book symbol to an open book symbol.

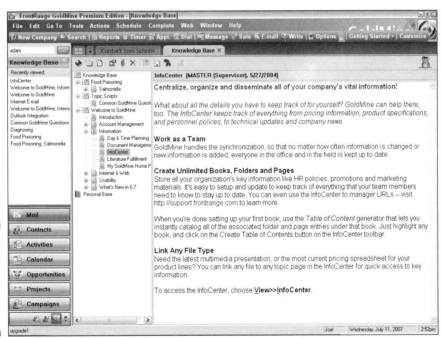

Figure 20-2: Section and topic detail in the Knowledge Base.

Searching the Knowledge Base

As you begin expanding your Knowledge Base, finding any particular item within the Knowledge Base can become challenging. Fortunately, a search tool exists that can help. The Search icon on the local Knowledge Base toolbar allows you to search for keywords or phrases that may be in some folder or topic in the Knowledge Base. Clicking this icon brings you to the Search dialog box, as shown in Figure 20-3.

Figure 20-3:
Enter a term
you want
to search
for in the
Knowledge
Base
Search
dialog box.

In the Search For field, you can either type the keyword or phrase you want to search for, or you can select a previously searched-for item from the drop-down list.

In the Search Scope section, you can specify the range of entries that you want GoldMine to search. You have the following choices:

- ✔ **Knowledge Base:** Searches through every book, section, and topic in the Knowledge Base for the term you entered in the Search For field. This is often a good choice unless you have so much material in your Knowledge Base that a full search takes a long time.

- ✔ **Welcome to GoldMine:** This is a context-sensitive choice and searches just the book, folder, or topic you currently have highlighted in the left pane of the Knowledge Base window. In the example shown in Figure 20-3, Welcome to GoldMine is highlighted, so the option shows up as Welcome to GoldMine.

- ✔ **Last Pages Found:** Searches only the pages that were identified by the last search you performed. This function allows you to drill down to find further detail.

The following options allow you to determine how closely a phrase must be matched during the search:

✔ **Match Whole Words Only:** Considers the term in the Search For field as a unit, so an exact match must be made to the entire value. In other words, if you enter "Joe" as the term you want to look for, and "Joel" exists in one of the topics, then "Joel" won't show up as a match.

✔ **Match Case:** The exact upper- and lowercase letters must match between your phrase and those phrases found in the Knowledge Base. If you turn on this option, "Sun" will not match with "sun."

In the Search Area section, you can identify which areas of the Knowledge Base to search for potential matches. Your choices are

✔ **Keywords**

✔ **Topic Name**

✔ **Folder Name**

✔ **File Names** (of attached files)

✔ **Topic Text**

After you specify your search criteria, you can begin the search by clicking the Search button at the bottom of the Search dialog box. Figure 20-4 shows the results of a search for any book, folder, or topic containing the word *e-mail*. To continue searching for a second, third, or further match, click the Search Next icon, which continuously moves through the text looking for additional matches.

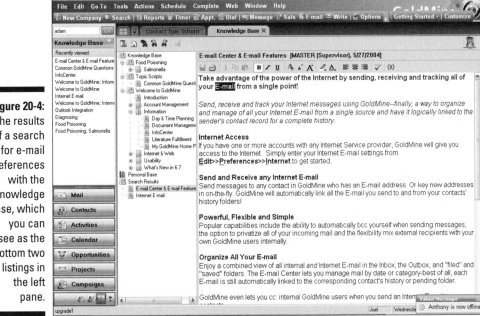

Figure 20-4: The results of a search for e-mail references with the Knowledge Base, which you can see as the bottom two listings in the left pane.

Creating New Knowledge Base Books, Folders, and Topics

You can set up a virtually unlimited range of material in your Knowledge Base. I have found it particularly useful for housing my company's employee handbook. Other useful topics include such things as product catalogs, price lists, and competitive information. Now that the Knowledge Base is integrated with the Service Center, you should consider stocking the Knowledge Base with product information that will be helpful to your customer service people and to your customers.

Creating a Knowledge Base book

The following procedure illustrates how to create a new book in the Knowledge Base. The procedure for creating books, folders, and topics is the same in both the Knowledge Base and the Personal Base, except that you don't need to be concerned with access rights in the Personal Base.

1. **From the Knowledge Base local menu, click the New Book icon (the leftmost icon).**

   A temporary name, New Book, appears within brackets.

2. **Type over <New Book> with the actual title of the new book you are creating and press Enter to save your new title.**

   If you're creating a handbook of company rules, you might call it something clever like *Company Rules*.

After you have a new book, you can add folders and topic pages. You can create a folder or a topic page by following these steps:

1. **Highlight the book in the left pane of the Knowledge Base and then right-click it.**

2. **Choose New from the shortcut menu.**

   Choose book, folder, or page. Figure 20-5 illustrates this.

3. **Enter your new text in the right pane.**

4. **When you're done typing, click the leftmost local icon (Save) to save this new text in the Knowledge Base.**

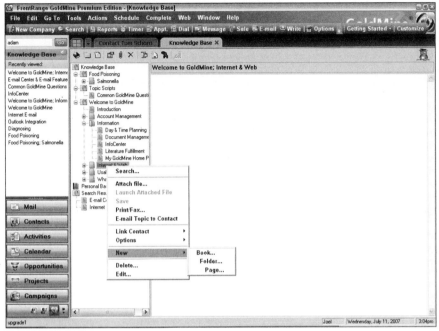

Figure 20-5:
Starting a
new folder
or page.

After you create a topic page, you have three methods of getting information into it. You can

- ✓ Type the information directly into the right pane of the Knowledge Base.
- ✓ Paste a document from another source, such as your word processor.
- ✓ Attach an existing file of any type, such as a text file, data file, picture, and so on.

Here's a clever idea. Because the Knowledge Base can house virtually any kind of file, including a WAV file, you can record someone talking about a solution to a particular problem. And, in fact, you can make these recordings in multiple languages. Because the Knowledge Base is now integrated with the Service Center, a recording can then be sent to a non-English speaking customer!

Editing entries in your Knowledge Base

Editing a topic in the Knowledge Base is easy. Highlight the folder or topic page in the left pane of the Knowledge Base. In the right pane, you see the actual text, to which you can make necessary edits.

Notifying Your Staff of Important Changes to the Knowledge Base — or Not

Back in the days of the InfoCenter, a What's New feature existed that allowed you to have each user automatically notified when you entered a new and important entry into the InfoCenter. Sadly, that feature has not found its way into the Knowledge Base. So, to make sure that all your staff members know about the new parking rules or the vacation schedule, you now need to send an e-mail to each group of users who ought to know. Oops.

Chapter 21

Graphical and Statistical Analysis

. . . .

In This Chapter

▶ Displaying account statistics

▶ Analyzing statistics

▶ Looking up the leads analysis

▶ Going over the statistical analysis

▶ Foreseeing with the forecast analysis

▶ Drawing up the graphical analysis

▶ Using quota and sales analysis

. . . .

*G*oldMine has a substantial amount of graphical and statistical analysis capability built into it. Using this analysis capability, you can focus on one individual account, a group of accounts, on a GoldMine user, or on a group of users.

If you're a sole practitioner using GoldMine by yourself, you can use these analysis tools to monitor your performance and to keep yourself on target. Resist the urge to check your stats only when you think you're doing well. Use the tool the same way a manager might. Check consistently, and make mid-course corrections whenever needed.

If you're a manager, resist the urge to use the analysis tools in a Big Brother type of way. Use them to help your staff achieve goals. Your team probably wants to achieve its goals as much as you do. Don't ask, "When are you going to close that deal?" Instead, you should ask, "What can I do to help you with this opportunity?"

In this chapter, you find out how to get those statistics to help you chart your course.

Displaying Account Statistics

Using GoldMine, you can track a variety of up-to-date statistics for any contact in your database. To access this statistical data, follow these steps:

1. **Open a contact record and then click the History tab.**

2. **Right-click in the display area and choose Options from the shortcut menu.**

3. **Choose Analyze from the next menu that appears.**

   The Contact Record Statistics dialog box, shown in Figure 21-1, appears, giving you information such as the amount of time you're dedicating to the contact and the amount of sales generated by the account.

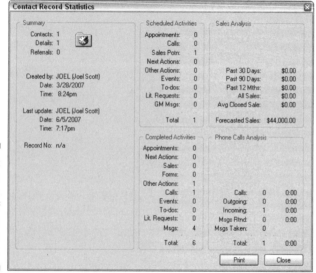

Figure 21-1:
GoldMine
displays
tons of
statistics in
this dialog
box.

The Contact Record Statistics dialog box displays important information about the contact, grouped into the following categories:

- ✔ **Summary:** Displays the number of additional contact records, detail records, and referral records; information about the creation and updates to the record.

- ✔ **Scheduled Activities:** Shows the number of appointments, calls, forecasted sales, next actions, and other actions currently scheduled for the account.

- ✔ **Completed Activities:** Lists the number of appointments, sales, forms, and other actions that have been completed for the account.

- ✔ **Sales Analysis:** Displays the total dollar amount spent by this account over the past 30 days, 90 days, and 12 months; the total amount the account has purchased; the average sale amount; and how much is currently forecasted for the account.

- ✔ **Phone Calls Analysis:** Shows a breakdown, by number and total duration, for each type of phone call to and from this account.

Lying with Statistics

The Statistical Analysis of Completed Activities dialog box displays completed activity information for an individual user, a group of users, or on a system-wide basis. Analyzing completed activities can provide useful insight into your performance or into the performance of others in your organization.

You can access the Statistical Analysis of Completed Activities dialog box, as shown in Figure 21-2, from the main menu by choosing Go To⇨Analysis⇨Statistical Analysis.

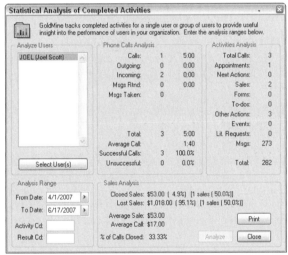

Figure 21-2:
Viewing
completed
activities.

The Statistical Analysis of Completed Activities dialog box contains the following options:

✔ **Select User(s):** Click the Select User(s) button to display the Select Users dialog box, from which you can pick GoldMine users for activity analysis. The list box above the button displays the users who will be included in the analysis; your user name is displayed by default.

✔ **From Date:** Sets the first date of the period to be included in the analysis.

✔ **To Date:** Sets the last date of the period to be included in the analysis.

✔ **Activity Cd:** Enter an activity code into this field, and GoldMine includes in the analysis only those completed activities that have the activity code you specify. When the field is left blank, GoldMine includes all completed activities.

If you code your activities as billable versus nonbillable, you could enter the activity code for billable activities here and get an analysis of these activities only.

✔ **Result Cd:** Enter a result code into this field, and GoldMine includes in the analysis only those completed activities you specify by the result code. When the field is left blank, GoldMine includes all completed activities.

✔ **Phone Calls Analysis:** Shows the total number of completed telephone calls of the specified type in the history file. Call-backs, outgoing calls, incoming calls, and returned messages are listed, as well as the total duration of calls in each category. GoldMine displays the average duration of calls below the total line for this section. Successful Calls shows the number and percentage of calls with a satisfactory outcome, whereas Unsuccessful calls are those calls that were not answered at all.

Unsuccessful outcomes (such as *lost the sale* or *they told me to buzz off*) should be recorded through the result code. When you mark a call as Unsuccessful, GoldMine labels that call Attempted in the Summary tab, as opposed to Last Contact. You might want to consider using Unsuccessful to indicate that you failed to connect with the person related to the scheduled activity.

✔ **Activities Analysis:** Lists the total number of completed activities in the history file, including to-do actions, sales, received messages, appointments, and other actions.

✔ **Sales Analysis:** Displays the completed sales statistics. Closed Sales shows the total number of closed sales activities in the history file. The totals are displayed on the right. Look at % of Calls Closed to compare the number of completed sales as a percentage of completed call activities. The average sales value per completed call activity is also displayed.

✔ **Analyze:** Recalculates the totals in the display. Until you click this button, your analysis window remains blank. After clicking the Analyze button once, the Print button appears, which enables you to print this window.

After you select Analyze, GoldMine presents you with a Print button that allows you to print out the results of this statistical analysis. This print option also applies to the forecast analysis, discussed in the next section.

Using the Forecast Analysis

The forecast analysis is different than the sales analysis. Although sales analysis contains information on quotas, forecasted sales, and completed sales, the forecast analysis focuses on just those opportunities that have not yet closed.

To access the Forecasted Sales Analysis dialog box, as shown in Figure 21-3, choose Go To➪Analysis➪Forecast Analysis. This dialog box provides the following information about projected sales or cash flows for individuals, groups of individuals, or the entire organization:

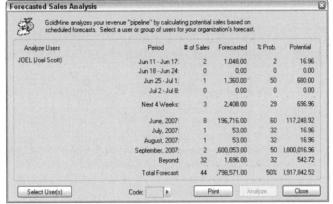

Figure 21-3:
Analyzing
your sales
forecast.

✔ **Analyze Users:** Lists the users who will be included in the analysis; your user name is selected by default. To add or change the analyzed users, click the Select User(s) button.

✔ **Period:** Shows forecasted sales statistics divided into several periods. The top portion of the analysis window shows forecasted sales statistics by week for the next four weeks. Total amounts for the four-week period are displayed below the weekly section.

Below the weekly section, forecasted sales for the next four months are broken down by month. The Beyond line includes all forecasted sales scheduled to close after the next four months. Grand totals for the lower section are displayed at the bottom of the screen.

✔ **# of Sales:** Displays the total number of forecasted sales activities scheduled on the calendar for the period.

✔ **Forecasted:** Presents the total dollar amount of sales scheduled on the calendar for the period.

✔ **% Prob.:** Unveils the average probability that a sale will close in this period. This value is calculated by averaging the values entered in the Probability field for all the Forecasted Sales activities scheduled in the period.

✔ **Potential:** Lists the expected value (or weighted value) of sales that will be closed in this period. This value is determined by multiplying the total forecasted sales amount (Forecasted) by the average close probability (% Prob.).

✔ **Select User(s):** Click this button to display the Select Users dialog box, from which you can select GoldMine users for activity analysis.

✔ **Code:** Displays forecasted sales that have the entered activity code. You can use wild cards to select multiple activity codes. By default, this field is blank, and the resulting analysis includes all activity codes.

✔ **Analyze:** Click this button to calculate the totals in the display.

Using Graphical Analysis

If you prefer graphs to columns of numbers, then graphical analysis is for you. The GoldMine graphical analysis tool generates summary graphs of user activity data based on a variety of criteria. You can display your data as a bar graph or a line graph. GoldMine can represent all activity for a defined period of time, or one of several defined types of activity. Graphs can also represent total activities, a comparison of all users, or selected users.

To generate a graph, from the main menu choose Go To⇨Analysis⇨Graphical Analysis. The Graphical Analysis Options dialog box appears, as shown in Figure 21-4.

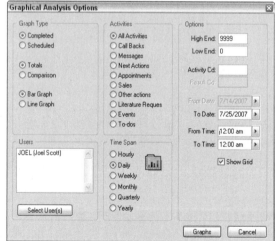

Figure 21-4: Choose how your graph will look in the Graphical Analysis Options dialog box.

The Graphical Analysis Options dialog box contains options that determine the time range and activities to be included in the graph:

✔ **Completed:** Displays completed activities in the graph.

✔ **Scheduled:** Shows scheduled activities in the graph.

✔ **Totals:** Charts together activity data for all specified users on the graph.

✔ **Comparison:** Graphs activity data for individual users as specified.

✔ **Bar Graph:** Generates a bar graph. Bar graphs are generally used to compare different periods or users.

✔ **Line Graph:** Creates a line graph. Line graphs are generally used to show trends over time.

✔ **Select User(s):** Click the Select User(s) button to access a list of users. If the Comparison option is selected under Graph Type and more than one user is selected, data for these users will be displayed on one graph with color-coded entries to differentiate between users.

✔ **All Activities:** Displays scheduled or completed data for all activity types in the graph.

✔ **Call Backs:** Generates a graph for either completed or scheduled call backs, depending on whether Completed or Scheduled is selected under Graph Type.

✔ **Messages:** Churns out a graph for either completed or scheduled messages, depending on whether Completed or Scheduled is selected under Graph Type.

✔ **Next Actions:** Creates a graph for either completed or scheduled next actions, depending on whether Completed or Scheduled is selected under Graph Type.

✔ **Appointments:** Generates a graph for either completed or scheduled appointments, depending on whether Completed or Scheduled is selected under Graph Type.

✔ **Sales:** Shows a graph for either completed or scheduled sales, depending on whether Completed or Scheduled is selected under Graph Type.

✔ **Others:** Displays a graph for either completed or scheduled other actions, depending on whether Completed or Scheduled is selected under Graph Type.

✔ **Time Span:** Allows you to specify a time range for your graph. Selecting the Hourly option provides a full day's worth of hourly data, starting at the beginning of the time period specified. The Daily option gives you about 10 days of data. The Weekly option provides about three months of data graphically.

✔ **High End:** Type a numeric value that corresponds to the uppermost number you want displayed on the vertical axis of the graph. For example, if experience shows that users rarely schedule more than 30 appointments per week, entering 30 in the High End field generates a graph with a vertical axis that ends at 30. The default, zero (0), allows GoldMine to generate the high-end value based on included data.

✔ **Low End:** Type a numeric value that corresponds to the smallest number you want displayed on the vertical axis of the graph. For example, if experience shows that users have never scheduled fewer than five call backs per week, entering 5 in the Low End field generates a graph with a vertical axis that starts at 5. The default is zero (0).

✔ **Activity Cd:** Generates the graph from activity records with the specified activity code. You can use wild cards to select multiple activity codes. By default, this field is blank, and the generated graph includes all activity codes.

✔ **Result Cd:** Type a result code to be used as the basis for graph data. Only activity records with this result code will be included in the graph. You can use wild cards to select multiple result codes. The default value for this field is blank, and all result codes will show up in the generated graph. This field is available only if you select Completed for Graph Type.

✔ **From Date:** Enter the beginning date from which data will be graphed. The default is the current date. This field is available only for a graph of completed activities; the ending date for scheduled activity graphs is always the current date.

✔ **To Date:** Enter the ending date to which data will be graphed. The default is the current date. This field is available only for a graph of scheduled activities; the beginning date for completed activity graphs is always the current date.

✔ **From Time:** Place the beginning time of a range you want to include in the graph. The default is 12:00 a.m. When combined with the default To Time entry of 12:00 a.m., the graph will display data for a 24-hour period. This field is not available when generating hourly graphs for completed activities.

✔ **To Time:** Place the ending time of a range you want to include in the graph. The default is 12:00 a.m. When combined with the default From Time entry of 12:00 a.m., the graph will display data for a 24-hour period. This field is not available when generating hourly graphs for scheduled activities.

✔ **Show Grid:** Displays lines that represent the horizontal axis of the graph (default). To generate a graph without this grid, remove the check from the check box.

✔ **Graphs:** Click the Graphs button, and GoldMine generates a bar graph or line graph based on your selections in the Graphical Analysis Options dialog box.

Using Leads Analysis

If you ever wondered what that Source field on the main screen is really for, read on; you find out in this section.

GoldMine enables you to track valuable information on the current status of sales efforts and on the effectiveness of various advertising and promotional efforts in generating inquiries and sales. Employed in this way, GoldMine becomes a strategic asset. GoldMine can provide timely and accurate information to help managers make better decisions on deploying their resources.

You can use the Source field to determine the profitability of individual marketing campaigns or groups of campaigns. GoldMine can report the total number of leads generated from each seminar, advertisement, or trade show from each Source value, the total sales volume generated from each Source value, and the potential sales pending from each Source value. You can then easily identify the most effective lead sources in terms of total leads or total sales volume generated.

Further, if you also know the cost of each lead, you can calculate the profit for each lead, easily locating the most profitable lead source. For example, if this lead source is an advertisement, you have an excellent tool that helps you determine whether to run that ad again.

When the analysis is complete, the Leads Analysis dialog box contains one record entry for each unique value found in the selected field in the contact database. These records appear in the Source column.

To generate a leads analysis, from the main menu choose Go To➪Analysis➪Leads Analysis. The Leads Analysis dialog box appears, as shown in Figure 21-5.

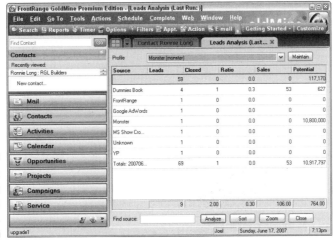

Figure 21-5:
The Leads
Analysis
dialog box.

The Leads Analysis dialog box contains the following fields, each of which controls a portion of the analysis you can get:

✔ **File Description:** Profile name of the currently open leads analysis file, followed by the filename (in parentheses). You can select a different leads analysis from the drop-down list.

- ✔ **Maintain:** Click the Maintain button to display the Open Leads Analysis File dialog box, from which you can add, modify, or delete a leads analysis. GoldMine does not automatically create Analysis files, so you need to use the Maintain function to create a new Analysis file for each different analysis you want.

- ✔ **Source:** Name of the lead source, such as LAN Magazine. This entry appears in the Source field of the contact record.

- ✔ **Leads:** Total number of accounts in the database with this value in the selected field.

- ✔ **Closed:** Total number of accounts with this source that have at least one purchase, as recognized by the presence of a sales activity record in the history file.

- ✔ **Ratio:** Percentage of closed sales based on number of leads.

- ✔ **Sales:** Total dollar amount of sales generated by this lead source. This value is calculated by summing up all sales activity history records linked to the accounts with this source.

- ✔ **Potential:** Total dollar amount of future sales activities scheduled on the Calendar. This value is calculated by summing up all the Forecasted Sales records linked to the accounts with this source.

The Leads Analysis dialog box also contains the following additional options:

- ✔ **Find Source:** Moves through the Source entries to position the list at the first record that starts with the specified letter. For example, type C to select the first Source that starts with the letter C, such as Comdex.

- ✔ **Analyze:** Click the Analyze button to regenerate the leads analysis information for the current leads analysis database. You must select the field on which to base the analysis and the range of dates to be scanned for calculation of statistics. If you don't click this button, no analysis is performed.

- ✔ **Sort:** Click the Sort button to display the Leads Analysis Sort Menu dialog box, from which you can select the ordering of the records in the Leads Analysis dialog box.

- ✔ **Zoom:** Click the Zoom button to see more detailed information about the highlighted leads analysis record in the Leads Analysis Zoom dialog box.

Setting Quotas and Measuring Performance against Them

The sales analysis section of GoldMine can be independent of setting quotas but is much more meaningful if quotas or guidelines are set up ahead of time.

Whether you are a one-person operation or a multinational conglomerate, you should always be setting performance goals, standards, and quotas. In my company, toward the end of each year, I sit down and develop a game plan for the coming year. That includes some strategic analysis and planning, detailing the expected expenses for my company, and then setting sales goals with the idea of bringing in sufficient revenue to handle all those expenses.

GoldMine's quota analysis is a big part of that effort. By setting each sales-person's goals (quotas) for each product line, you can decide whether your goals are reasonable and obtainable. Then, by comparing your forecasted and completed sales against that quota, you can make midstream adjustments as needed.

Assigning a quota

To assign a quota to a user, follow these steps:

1. **From the main menu, choose Go To ➪ Analysis ➪ Quota Analysis.**

   The Quota Listing dialog box appears, as shown in Figure 21-6.

2. **To develop a new quota, click the New button.**

   The Assign New Quota dialog box appears, as shown in Figure 21-7.

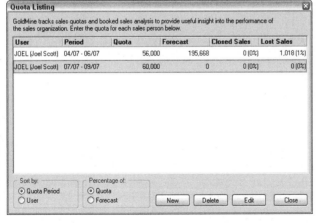

Figure 21-6:
Viewing your quota in the Quota Listing dialog box.

Quota Listing

GoldMine tracks sales quotas and booked sales analysis to provide useful insight into the performance of the sales organization. Enter the quota for each sales person below.

User	Period	Quota	Forecast	Closed Sales	Lost Sales
JOEL (Joel Scott)	04/07 - 06/07	56,000	195,668	0 (0%)	1,018 (1%)
JOEL (Joel Scott)	07/07 - 09/07	60,000	0	0 (0%)	0 (0%)

Sort by:
- ◉ Quota Period
- ○ User

Percentage of:
- ◉ Quota
- ○ Forecast

[New] [Delete] [Edit] [Close]

Figure 21-7:
Assign
quotas to a
user in the
Assign New
Quota dialog
box.

The dialog box for assigning a quota, contains the following information and options:

- **User:** By default, GoldMine displays the name of the currently logged-on user. To choose a different user, click the down arrow to the right of the User field. The name of the selected salesperson appears in the User column of the Quota Listing dialog box.

- **From Date:** Starting date of the quota period. By default, GoldMine displays the first day of the current month.

- **To Date:** Ending date of the quota period. By default, GoldMine displays the last day of the current month.

- **Quota:** Dollar amount of sales that the salesperson is expected to make during the quota period.

- **Forecast:** Displays the total dollar amount of forecasted sales scheduled on the calendar for the period. This entry changes as the salesperson schedules sales he expects to close during the quota period.

- **Closed Sales:** Displays the total dollar amount of sales completed successfully during the quota period. This entry changes as the salesperson completes sales during the quota period.

- **Lost Sales:** Displays the total dollar amount of sales that are completed as lost or unsuccessful during the quota period. An uncompleted sale is neither closed nor lost and remains in the Forecast field.

- **Goals & Objectives:** You can store up to 32,000 characters of information related to the quota.

3. **When you finish entering information, click OK to leave the Quota Profile dialog box.**

    Doing so adds the new or updated quota entry to the Quota Listing. To edit a previously defined quota, right-click the quota listing and choose Edit from the shortcut menu.

The Quota Profile dialog box has a Recurring tab, as shown in Figure 21-8. The recurring feature makes it easy to create quotas for daily, weekly, or monthly sales. You enter one period's quota and then immediately click the Recurring tab. From this tab, you specify the rate at which the quota should increase (or even decrease), as well as the period over which this should occur. Before version 6.0, you had to manually enter each month's quota. Now you can do many in one fell swoop.

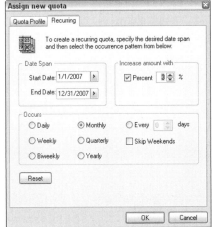

Figure 21-8:
The Recurring tab of the Assign New Quota dialog box.

Analyzing sales versus quota

As soon as your quotas are established and entered, you can check your progress against these quotas. For this process to work at all, you must be forecasting and completing all your sales (discussed in Chapter 12). Assuming that you are religiously doing this, go to the main menu and follow these steps:

1. **Choose Go To⇨Analysis⇨Sales Analysis to view the Sales Analysis dialog box, as shown in Figure 21-9.**

The Sales Analysis and the Select Users dialog boxes appear. Select at least one user's name in the Select Users dialog box.

2. **Select individual users, multiple users, or groups by highlighting an entry in either the User List or the Group List and double-clicking.**

3. **When you have chosen all the users you want, click OK.**

The Select Users dialog box disappears, leaving you with a blank Sales Analysis dialog box. It is blank because you have not yet asked it to do any analysis. Before asking for your analysis, make sure that the range of dates in the lower-left corner is correct. You may also want to enter a particular activity code or result code if you want to analyze just those types of sales. If you leave the Activity Code and Result Code fields empty, GoldMine uses all sales activity within the date range you picked.

4. **When you are satisfied with the dates and other codes, click the Analyze button.**

You then see the resulting analysis. Figure 21-10 shows an example. According to this example, I'm not doing too well at sales. (Not to worry; it's not real data).

Figure 21-9:
Select
which users
you want
to analyze
sales for.

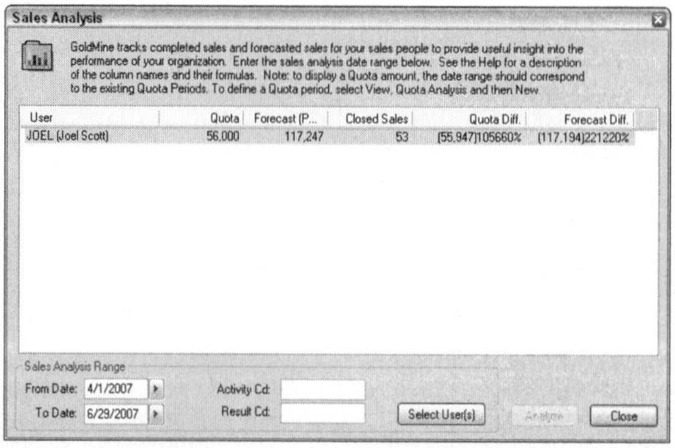

Figure 21-10:
Some
sample
forecast vs.
quota data.

Chapter 22

The Reporting System

· ·

· ·

*G*oldMine comes with 101 reports already developed for your immediate use. As of the June 2007 release, no Service-related reports are included. The 101 reports are divided into six report categories, so you can more easily find the one you are looking for. In this chapter, I show you how to generate, view, and print a GoldMine report.

Although GoldMine provides a report for almost every purpose, you may still need to modify an existing one or even create one from scratch. Thus, GoldMine provides the ability to revise any existing report or to develop new reports from scratch. In this chapter, you also discover how to build a customized report.

If the built-in report generator proves too limiting (and there's a good chance it might), a number of very good third-party, report-generating utilities exist that work directly with GoldMine files. I also discuss a few of these third-party utilities in this chapter.

Choosing a Report Category

GoldMine generates six different categories of reports. Each category enables you to construct a report containing specific information. The following list details the six report categories and the information each one contains:

✔ **Contact Reports:** Print contact and activity data to meet a variety of needs, such as phone lists and completed activity logs.

✔ **Calendar Printouts:** Print scheduled activity data in graphical formats, such as monthly calendars.

✔ **Service Reports:** None exist yet.

✔ **Analysis Reports:** Print statistical information similar to the analyses available from the View menu, such as phone-call statistics and quota analyses.

✔ **Labels and Envelopes:** Print selected data in formats that conform to various Avery label types and envelope dimensions.

✔ **Other Reports:** Present a variety of useful information, such as organizing information from your personal rotary file entries and a listing of available merge forms.

Generating a GoldMine Report

In this section, I show you how to generate a GoldMine report. To create your report, you must do the following:

✔ Select the type of report you want to create.

✔ Specify the order in which you want your data organized.

✔ Choose the actual data you want to include in your report.

Choosing the report type

From the Toolbar, choose the Reports button. This brings you to the Reports Center. The left panel has a folder called GoldMine Reports, which you can expand to show all the report categories, as shown in Figure 22-1. In this example, you see the Analysis reports that come with GoldMine. Select the report you want by clicking it.

The next step in creating a report is to select and sort the information each report requires. See the next section for more details.

Sorting and selecting data for your reports

Contrary to popular belief, sorting and selecting are not the same thing. *Sorting* a report means that the items on the report are alphabetized or, perhaps, listed numerically. *Selecting* involves specifying a subset of all your data — for example, only the accounts in California, or only those accounts that are on credit hold. You may very well need to select a portion of your database for your report and specify sorting criteria as well.

Sorting report data

When you prepare a report, typically you want to control the order in which data is shown; that is, you want to list data in a sequence that makes the information clear and meaningful. Sorting allows you to arrange data in a specified order by one or more fields. GoldMine provides up to three levels (primary, secondary, and tertiary) by which each report can be sorted. For example, if you select the Company field as the first sort field, all the records listed in the report will be ordered alphabetically by company name.

The Sorts option is available for only Contact Reports, Analysis Reports, Service Reports, Labels and Envelopes, and Other Reports. This option is not available for Calendar Printouts.

With many canned reports, if you change the sort field, the report does not work without many other changes. If you're a GoldMine rookie, I suggest that you *not* change the sort option on a canned report without training or a real knowledge of database report writing.

Because GoldMine allows three levels of sorting, you can also select a secondary sort order if the Company field is the same for two or more records. For example, if you select the Company field as the primary sort, and the secondary sort is the Last Name field, then the records will be ordered by company name in the report. However, when two records have the same company name, they will be further ordered alphabetically by last name.

When a field is selected for tertiary sort, the records are ordered by the third sort field only when the first- and second-level sort fields are identical. For example, if the first- and second-level sorts are the State and City fields, and the third-level sort is the Zip field, then records will be ordered by ZIP code only when two or more records share the same state and city.

Without a second- or third-level sort, records in the report are ordered by date and time of entry in the database when the first-level sort is the same over several records. Listing records by the order in which they were entered is known as the *natural order of records.*

When selecting the sort order for your report, keep in mind that GoldMine queries the database in the most efficient way. If you select a multilevel sort, or a single-level sort with a field that's not already indexed, GoldMine builds a report sort table. This additional step allows other users to access GoldMine data while the report prints, and it speeds the printing process.

To sort records in a GoldMine report, click the Sorts button on the Reports Menu dialog box. The Report Sorting dialog box appears, as shown in Figure 22-2, which shows the specific report highlighted in the right pane, the cursor pointing to the Sorts icon, and the resulting dialog box.

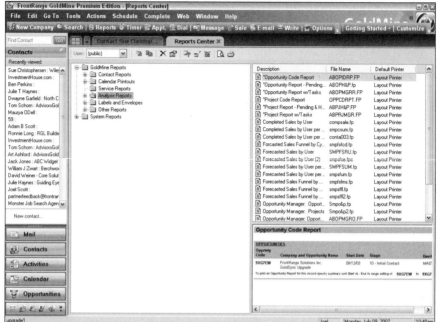

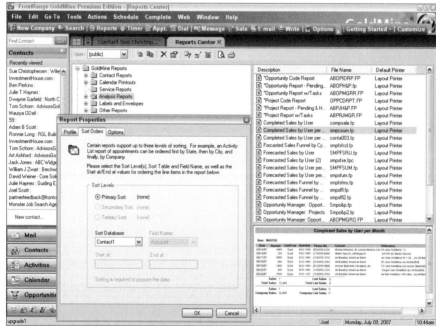

Use the following options to specify your sort:

- ✓ **Primary Sort:** Specifies the first set of parameters for ordering records. To complete the sort definition, select the Sort Database and Field Name by which you want GoldMine to order records in the report. To specify a range of records, specify a value in the Start At and/or End At fields.

  Every GoldMine report must have at least a primary sort defined to operate properly, even if no sorting is required. To preclude any sorting, set the Sort Database option to (none).

  If the Primary Sort option is defined as (none), the data preparation entry dims, indicating that GoldMine will sort records by the natural order of record entry.

- ✓ **Secondary Sort:** Specifies the second set of parameters for ordering records. To complete the sort definition, select the database and the field by which you want GoldMine to sort records. To specify a range of records, specify a value in the Start At and/or End At fields.

  You must define a first-level sort before you can define a second-level sort. If you want a report with only one sort level, define the first-level sort only.

- ✓ **Tertiary Sort:** Specifies the third set of parameters for ordering records. To complete the sort definition, select the database and the field by which you want GoldMine to sort records. To specify a range of records, specify a value in the Start At and/or End At fields.

  You must define a second-level sort before you can define a third-level sort. If you want a report with only two sort levels, define the first-level sort and the second-level sort only.

- ✓ **Sort Database:** Selects the contact database that contains the field on which records will be sorted for the selected sort level — that is, primary sort, secondary sort, or tertiary sort. The selected database appears to the right of the sort level.

  To display a list of contact databases, click the arrow to the right of the field.

- ✓ **Field Name:** Selects the field on which records will be sorted for the selected sort level. The selected field appears to the right of the sort level and the contact database name. To display a list of contact databases, click the arrow to the right of the field.

- ✓ **Start At:** Specifies the beginning value of a range that defines how the selected sort level will order records. If the Start At and the End At fields are blank, (all) appears to the right of the sort level database and field, and all records will be sorted in ascending order. For example, `Primary Sort: Contact1->Lastname (all)` indicates that the first-level sort will order all records by the Lastname field of the database in alphabetical order.

You can enter a value in the Start At field alone to define a range; that is, without entering a value in the End At field, to specify a beginning point from which you want GoldMine to select and order records. The resulting report will include and order records from the specified starting point to the implied end of the range. For example, if the Start At field contains 06/11/07, the report will order records by the selected field from June 11, 2007, to the current date.

✔ **End At:** Specifies the ending value of a range that defines how the selected sort level will order records. If the Start At and the End At fields are blank, (all) appears to the right of the sort level database and field, and all records will be sorted in ascending order.

You can use the End At field alone to define a range; that is, without entering a value in the Start At field, to specify an ending point to which you want GoldMine to select and order records. The resulting report will include and order records from the earliest or smallest value through the value entered in the End At field. For example, if the End At field contains M, the report will order records by the selected field from the beginning of the alphabet through records with field entries that start with M.

✔ **Save as Defaults:** Saves the sort settings for future printings. If you want to apply the sort settings to the currently generated report only, do not click this button.

Playing with report specifications can be hazardous to the health of the original report. You should not generally try any major modification unless you are sure you have a backup of your files. That's one thing that *cloning* is good for. To clone a report, just right-click the report you want to alter and choose Clone. Give it a new description and filename and you'll be okay if you mess up the original report.

When you finish choosing your sort options, click OK.

Selecting data for a Contact, a Service, an Analysis, or a Labels and Envelopes report

Five of the six report categories allow you to select further options before printing. After you choose how you want your data sorted, select the data you want to include in a Contact, an Analysis, Other Reports, or a Labels and Envelopes report. In the Reports Menu dialog box, highlight the report you want to set data options for and click the Options button. The Contact Record Options dialog box appears.

The Contact Report Options dialog box, shown in Figure 22-3, is divided into three sections. Each section contains options that you use to control which data appears in the report.

✔ **History Data:** This section enables you to include activity data from history records (completed activities), as well as the date, time, and user who created the history record, and any reference information associated with the record. Select one or more types of data by checking the appropriate boxes in the dialog box (see Figure 22-3). In other words, if you want appointments included in your report, check that option. You can check multiple activity types.

You can also select the individual user who created history records, or you can select all users. You can also specify a range of dates as well as an Activity (Actv) code and a Result code.

If an Actv code and a Result code have been entered, the two codes work as an AND condition to include events that have been assigned both to the specified Actv code and to the Result code. If no code is specified, GoldMine includes data with all activity codes.

✔ **Calendar Data:** The Calendar Data section, on the right side of the dialog box shown in Figure 22-3, allows you to select which kinds of scheduled activities to include in your report. You can check off as many activity types as you like, in the same way as you can in the History Data section.

The User and Date fields function in the same way here as in the History Data section. So does the Activity (Actv) field, but there is no Result field. That's because scheduled activities have not yet been completed, so they don't have a Result code associated with them.

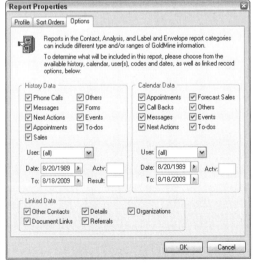

Figure 22-3:
The Contact
Report
Options
dialog box.

If no items are checked under Calendar Data or no data exists for any of the checked data types, GoldMine suppresses the scheduled activities from the report and continues with the next section for which data is available.

✔ **Linked Data:** The Linked Data section, at the bottom of the Contact Report Options dialog box, allows you to choose what types of additional data to include on the report. Each of these warrants a little further definition.

- **Other Contacts:** Includes data about individuals entered as additional contacts for the contact records, including additional contact name, title, telephone number, and any reference data associated with the additional contact.

- **Document Links:** Includes documents linked to the contact records and provides information about the document, such as the creating application, the user who created the document, and the path and filename of the document.

- **Details:** Includes detail information linked to the contact records, such as birthday, and provides data about the Detail record, any reference data associated with the Detail record, and the date it was created.

- **Referrals:** Includes referral information linked to the contact records, such as the source of the referral (of:), to whom the referral was made (to:), and any reference data associated with the referral.

- **Organizations:** Includes Org Chart information linked to the contact records.

Displaying and Printing Reports

The local toolbar in the Reports Center (refer to Figure 22-1) has a Print Report icon. From the dialog box this displays (see Figure 22-4) you can specify where to send your report output by using the radio buttons. Your choices are Window or Printer. In this case, selecting the Window option means that the report will be displayed on-screen.

If you're not sure about how much data will be printed, or if you're unsure of your own report specifications, you should generally send your output to the window first. After the report is displayed on-screen and you're satisfied with it, you can easily send it directly to your printer from the window display.

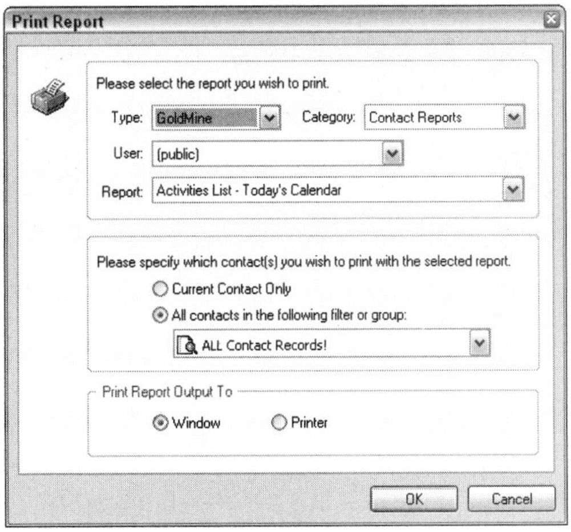

Figure 22-4:
Specifying
how and
where to
print your
report.

Sending a report to a printer

To print an entire report without previewing it on-screen, click the Printer radio button in the lower-right corner of the Reports Menu dialog box, and then click the Print button. The Printing in Progress status window appears, displaying information about the selected printer, the number of pages printed, and the number of records printed.

To stop printing at any time, click the Cancel button. Otherwise, the Printing in Progress status window closes when GoldMine finishes sending the report to the printer.

Sending a report to display on-screen

GoldMine can generate a report on-screen just as the report would look if printed on paper. To make a report appear on-screen, simply select the Output to Window radio button on the Print Report dialog box, and then click the Print button. GoldMine may chug for a little while as it sorts and selects, but your report shortly appears on-screen. From that window, you are given the option to look at the data and cancel out of the report, or print the report.

Modifying Existing Reports

The idea of a report is to have all the information you need, exactly the way you want to see it, not the way the programmers think you want to see it. GoldMine allows you to modify its already existing reports to meet your specific needs. However, this is another thing you may not want to try at home.

The best advice if you want to modify a report is to make sure you don't destroy the original, existing report. Make a clone, or copy, of the report you want to modify and rename it to ensure that you don't lose the original report as follows:

1. **Choose the Reports button from the Toolbar.**

   The Reports Center appears.

2. **Highlight the report you want to modify, right-click, and select Clone from the shortcut menu.**

   The Report Profile dialog box appears.

3. **Enter the report description, any notes you feel appropriate, and the report filename.**

   Make sure you give the cloned report a unique filename. If anyone else uses this same report filename, it will overwrite your report. Also review the User option. If this report is one that everyone should have access to, you can leave User as Public; if this report is for your eyes only, change it to your user name. If you do change a public report to one with another user name, be sure to select the correct user the next time you try to access that report.

4. **Click OK.**

   You now have a cloned copy that you can feel free to modify.

Structuring your report

Modifying reports is not usually a fun task for poets, but if you need to, then choose the Edit Report Layout icon from the Reports Center to display the selected report in its design layout. A typical report layout is shown in Figure 22-5. The field labels and the fields themselves are designated by a series of Xs.

The first section is the Page Header. Any field in the Page Header prints on the top of each page. The next section on a report is the Report Header, which contains the title of the report. The data contained in the report header prints only on the first page. The next section down is the sort headers, in which the break field is defined. *Break fields* group the data within the report and specify the database that is linked to a particular section of the report. You can only define break fields in a sort header. GoldMine limits the number of sort headers to nine. Information such as company, contact, address, and phone is contained in the sort header as well as the column labels for the Detail sections. The sort header prints only once per company. The Detail section is where the meat of the report displays. Working in conjunction with the sort header, this section displays all the information in the sort header based on the break field. The Page Footer is on the bottom of each page of the report. Included in this section are the date the report was printed and the page number. The date and page number are system fields that GoldMine automatically updates.

To modify the design of a report, from the Reports Menu dialog box, follow these steps:

1. **Select Contact Reports from the categories listing and highlight the Contact Wide Line Report — Landscape.**

2. **Click the Edit Report Layout icon from the Reports Center.**

   The programming involved in specifying this report appears in the window.

The Page Header contains the title of the report (refer to Figure 22-5). The Sort 1 header contains the company contact, address, phone, and text labels for the information that will be displayed in the Detail 1 section. If you want to see the actual field names instead of just Xs, right-click in any blank area of the report and choose Edit↪Show Field Names.

To view the filter and break field for the Sort 1 header, shown in Figure 22-6, double-click the dark bar labeled Sort 1 Header. The Sort 1 Header dialog box appears, and you can choose break field or the filter from the buttons at the bottom of the window. Click the Break Field button. In this report, it's set to "Contact1->Owner." No filter exists on the sort header or detail header in this report.

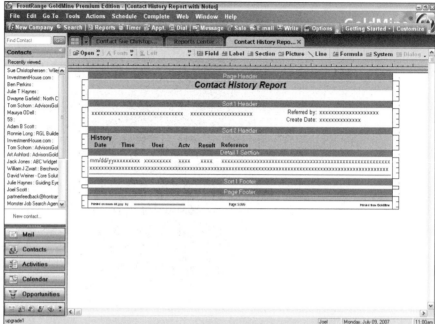

Figure 22-5:
A report layout window.

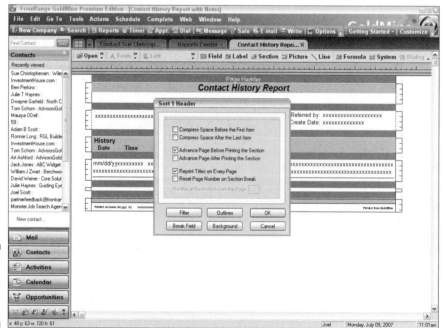

Figure 22-6:
Filters and break fields in a report.

Adding new fields

One of the most common modifications you may make to existing reports is to add a field that isn't already on the report. For example, you might want to include the Account Manager's name along with the account itself; for example, I want to add Key 4, Acct Mngr, under the company and address. Follow these steps to add a field to your report:

1. **Increase the size of the Detail 1 Section to accommodate the additional field by clicking the Detail 1 Section label and dragging down to make the section larger.**

   Two small black squares appear at the top and bottom of the section when you first click it. After you have dragged the section label to make it larger, you have room for some extra fields.

2. **In an empty area of the report, right-click and choose Insert⇨Data Field from the shortcut menu.**

   The Select a Field dialog box appears. The top drop-down list allows you to choose what database you want to add a field from. Choose the field from the database in the second drop-down list. To add Accnt Mngr, choose Contact1 from the top drop-down list, and then Accnt Mngr from the second drop-down list.

3. **Click OK.**

   Your mouse pointer changes into an outlined field that you can move.

4. **Move the cursor to where you want to place the field; in this case, under Company, and then click to place it there.**

   After you place the field, you can use the black squares that appear to resize the display of the field. You can move or change the size of the field at any time. You may want to indent the Accnt Mngr field under company for easier visual reference.

5. **To change the font of the field, right-click in the field and choose Edit⇨Fonts.**

   The Font dialog box appears. Pick out a font you like and make any other tweaks to the font's appearance; click OK when you're done.

In order to preview the changes, GoldMine asks whether you want to save the modifications you have made. If you choose Yes, a sample of the report with your changes appears. *If you choose No, you lose all changes you have.* To change back to the Layout view, simply click the Layout icon on the Reports toolbar.

Adding a label

Of course, what good is adding a field if you don't label it? To add the label for Accnt Mngr, you need to make the Sort 1 header larger. Click the Sort 1 header label and pull down the bottom black square. Notice that the shading doesn't increase with the size of the header.

1. **Click the Label button at the top of the window.**

   A rectangle appears in the window with dashed lines surrounding it. The word "Label" appears in this box.

   In order to distinguish between Company and Accnt Mngr, indent the field slightly under Company and click to place it.

2. **To define the label, double-click it to see the Text Field Parameters dialog box; in the text box, type** Accnt Mngr **and click OK.**

   The shading for the Sort 1 header is defined in the Company label. To increase the shading, you need to resize the Company label.

3. **Click the Company label and drag the bottom black square down until the label meets the top of the Detail 1 header.**

   The shading now encompasses the entire Sort 1 header. Notice, however, that Company has moved down and is centered in the header.

4. **To correct this problem, double-click the Company label, and in the Text Position section of the Text Field Parameters dialog box, select the Top option; click OK.**

   Company now aligns at the top of the header.

5. **To view the changes, click the Preview icon in the Reports toolbar.**

6. **Make sure to save your modifications by clicking OK.**

To get a better understanding of report design and modifications, choose different reports and go into each layout and see how they are set up. Look at the break fields, filters, and general layout of the report. Doing so can give you a good idea of how to make the modifications you desire.

Creating Custom Reports

Most of your reporting needs can be met by the reports that come with GoldMine or by making some minor modifications to them. However, you may find it necessary to create your own reports based on your company's specific needs.

To create a new report:

1. **Choose the Reports button from the toolbar.**

   The Reports Center appears.

2. **In the Report Description section and select the New Report icon.**

   The Report Profile dialog box appears.

3. **Fill in the Report description, make any notes you may want to add, and give the report a unique name; click OK.**

   You are returned to the Reports Menu dialog box.

4. **Highlight the new report in the Reports Menu dialog box and click the Layout icon.**

   GoldMine automatically gives you a Page Header, Sort 1 Header, Detail 1 Section, and Page Footer. Using the instructions from the example in the "Modifying Existing Reports" section, earlier in this chapter, you can add the labels in the Sort 1 header and fields in the Detail section.

If you want to add a filter to the entire report, click the Report Filter icon from the Reports local toolbar (in layout mode). This brings up the Record Selection Criteria dialog box, where you can build a filter for your report. See Chapter 8 for more information on filters.

Using Alternatives to the Built-in Reporting System

Because the GoldMine file structure is built on well-known and well-established SQL files, you can use many third-party utilities to create reports. I discuss some of the more common ones I have used in the following sections. Others are available. Basically, any report system that can handle SQL files can produce reports from your GoldMine data.

Excel

Almost everyone has a spreadsheet program, and most of us have Excel. Almost all the GoldMine data files are standard SQL files, which Excel can read directly. If Excel can read the file(s), then Excel can also manipulate the data for you.

By opening a GoldMine file with Excel, you can then reformat the data, perform all sorts of calculations, and generate graphs and charts. You can also use Excel to save these same files in some other format if you need access to the data from another program.

Do not open your GoldMine files with Excel or any other utility while GoldMine is being accessed by another user. And, most important, do not save the Excel files using the original name of the file. After you have made any changes to the data or the file structure with Excel, GoldMine will not be happy trying to use that file later. Even if it looks as though it is working, you will probably have destroyed GoldMine's ability to synchronize its data.

In order to successfully use Excel to manipulate your GoldMine data, you need some understanding of the GoldMine file structure, or you at least need to know what data is contained in which files. The GoldMine Reference Guide details all this information.

Access

Consider Microsoft Access to be Excel's big brother. You can use Access to do almost anything Excel can do. In addition, Access has much more reporting capability than does Excel. The downside is that you need to have some serious experience with Access before trying to do too much with GoldMine files.

Crystal Reports

Crystal 11 runtime licenses are included with GoldMine Premium. And, to tell it the way it really is, Crystal Reports is probably the reporting tool of choice with GoldMine. It's much stronger and better documented and more widely known than is the built in report writer that comes with GoldMine. Crystal is what our team uses for most reporting requirements. If you need to make more than a minor modification to an existing GoldMine report, or if your GoldMine report is running like molasses in January, you should consider using Crystal Reports instead.

Microsoft Reporting Services

For the first time, Microsoft Reporting Services is also included with GoldMine Premium. This is another good choice, particularly if you need to have reports automatically scheduled to run without human intervention.

Other report generators

Stonefield Query is a query builder and report writer with a simple wizard interface. Its wizard is easy to use and allows you some flexibility that Crystal Reports just doesn't have. MasterMine is another well-respected tool that generates Excel-based pivot tables from GoldMine data. For more about these options, see Chapter 30.

Chapter 23

Opportunity and Project Manager

· ·

In This Chapter

▶ Using the Opportunity and Project Manager

▶ How the Project Manager differs from the Opportunity Manager

· ·

*O*pportunity tracking is the next step up from just forecasting sales. It's actually a giant step up. You use the Opportunity Manager to track complex sales. A complex sale involves either an individual or a team trying to close a sale that may have more than one decision-maker on the other side. These sales might also include multiple products or services. Often these complex sales also have a long sales cycle compared to simpler sales.

Although the use of the Opportunity Manager is not directly related to the dollar value of a potential deal, very often the more complex sales are also the ones with greater-than-average value. It is probably not a coincidence that these larger deals also seem to attract the most competitors. The Opportunity Manager also allows you to track those competitors.

After you close a complex sale, it usually becomes a complex project. And GoldMine lets you easily turn that opportunity into a project. A project is the natural next step for an opportunity that you managed well. When you have a project to track, you can manage your team of workers, the timeline, and the money involved using Project Manager.

Initially, setting up the Opportunity or Project Manager (or both) is a lot of work. Many fields need to have lookup lists built. It's also a lot of work to monitor an opportunity or a project in detail. You should probably consider using these tools only for those opportunities and projects that really are complex or are very important. This caution notwithstanding, these tools are potentially valuable when used under the right circumstances.

In this chapter, you discover when and how to make use of the Opportunity/ Project Manager (O/PM).

The Opportunity/Project Manager

The Opportunity Manager and the Project Manager contain similar types of information, and thus their screens look similar. The first icon on either screen allows you to toggle back and forth from an Opportunity to a Project. Each of these tools contains two major sections. The upper section displays general information about a selected opportunity or project. The lower section consists of a series of tabs. To access either of these screens, from the main menu, choose either Go To➪Opportunities or Go To➪Projects. The Opportunity or Project Manager screen appears. The Opportunity screen is shown in Figure 23-1.

The Opportunity Manager and its functions

Chances are, if this is your first time anywhere near the Opportunity Manager, nothing has been entered. Selecting the first icon at the top of the Opportunity Manager screen displays the new Opportunity Manager Wizard (after confirming that you really want to run the wizard) as shown in Figure 23-2. This is a terrific way to start — you never forget your first time.

Figure 23-1:
The Opportunity screen that you will see the first time.

Figure 23-2:
Starting to
build a new
opportunity.

On the first wizard screen, as shown in Figure 23-2, you relate the new opportunity to a contact record and to a particular person at that company. You should use the Browse button to the right of the Company field to assist in locating the correct company. After doing so, click the Next button to move on to the screen shown in Figure 23-3.

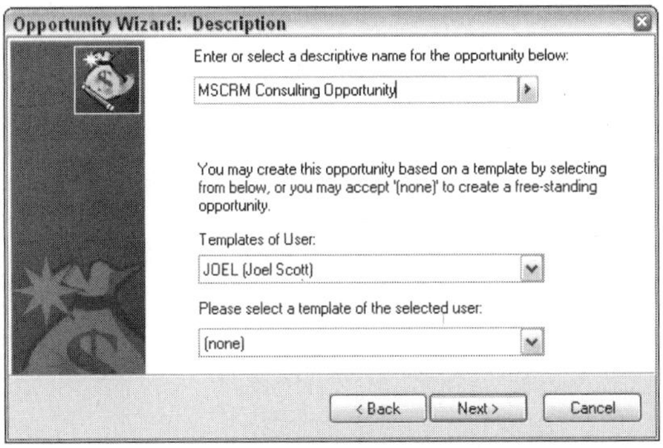

Figure 23-3:
Naming
your
opportunity.

In Figure 23-3 you enter a unique and descriptive name for this opportunity. Please remember that you may have multiple opportunities with the same customer, and you may have similar opportunities with completely different customers. So, you should select names that are descriptive enough to allow you and others on your team to recognize which opportunity this really is. Examples of reasonable names might be Designing Our Retention Workshop or Competitive Bid on Space Shuttle.

Creating a template is possible, but in this chapter I discuss opportunities from scratch. After you have named your opportunity, you can move on to the next screen.

Figure 23-4 shows the third wizard screen, enabling you to begin specifying the details of this opportunity.

Figure 23-4: Beginning to specify the opportunity's details on the Overview screen.

✔ **Manager:** You can designate a manager for the opportunity if you like, or you can accept the default manager, which is you (your user name).

✔ **Code:** You can classify your opportunities with a three-letter code from the lookup list associated with this field. You may want to consider using some departmental codes or product category codes.

✔ **Probability:** This field identifies the likelihood of successfully landing this opportunity. The Probability field comes with a preset lookup list that you will probably want to modify to your own situation and for your entire team's consistent use.

✔ **Stage:** Displays more detailed information related to the level, or stage, of the process. The entry is represented by a number and a descriptive reference, such as "10 - Initial Contact."

✔ **Source:** This field is taken by default from the Source field on the main screen of the contact record linked to this opportunity. You have the same lookup list available to you, but you can enter a new selection if you want.

✔ **Start Date:** This date relates to projects more than to opportunities, so you can pass this one by for opportunities.

✔ **Close By:** The date by which you expect to close this deal. By default, GoldMine sets it to be the current date, so take care to put in a more realistic date. If this date comes and goes without someone actually closing this deal, GoldMine sends you an alarm about it.

After you have finished with these fields, move on to the next screen, as shown in Figure 23-5. This screen allows you to set up the Opportunity Influencers.

Figure 23-5:
The
Influencer
screen.

Influencers and Contacts

Influencers are the people on the other side of the table who are involved in the ultimate decision-making process. They don't have to actually work for the prospect. They might be outside consultants, for example. After an opportunity becomes a project, these same people are referred to as *contacts,* which is the usual terminology throughout GoldMine.

The Role field is for the specific contribution that this influencer or contact is likely to make to the decision-making process.

The Response Mode field (in the Opportunity Manager only) specifies the perceived attitude of this person toward your product or service. By default, a few sample entries are already in the lookup list, such as Even Keel or Trouble. Feel free to make up your own. If you've had any formal sales training, you might recognize where the default terminology comes from.

Forecasted Sales

The next section allows you to divide the total opportunity into its component sales, assuming that you have more than one product or one stage of the sale. A typical example may be when selling a GoldMine consulting project that involves the software itself, a pilot or test phase, and then a full rollout to an entire sales force. Forecasting sales along with illustrations of the various screens is discussed in Chapter 12.

An opportunity must already exist before you can link a forecasted sale to it. In the normal course of business, you might just create a simple sales forecast without any initial intention of using the Opportunity Manager. Then, as the complexity of the potential sale begins to grow, you might decide to create an Opportunity Record. If this happens, you can edit the original sales forecast record and link it to the just recently created opportunity.

The forecasting screen that you will use within the Opportunity Manager is virtually identical to that of the general sales forecasting. Please see Chapter 12 for more details. You can, however, have multiple forecasts linked to one opportunity. In fact, this situation is fairly common in a complex sale.

Team

These are the people on your team with whom you are working to close this deal. You can even put someone from your prospect's team, or someone else from outside your own firm, on the team. Doing so is sometimes appropriate when you have someone from the other side acting as a coach. The first field, Type, shown in Figure 23-6, enables you to specify either a User, who is someone from your own team, or an Other Contact, who is anyone else in your database.

Figure 23-6:
Your sales
team.

In the Role field, you can enter each person's anticipated role in the opportunity or project. Examples are "write RFP response" or "Q/C testing."

Issues

In this section, shown in Figure 23-7, you keep track of any issues that come up that need to be addressed. As you pursue an opportunity, you may, for example, become aware of a pending price increase that will go into effect next month. Because this increase would conflict with the budget your prospect has already set up, it could be a serious problem and have an impact on your schedule for closing the deal.

> ✔ **Issue:** Enter a brief description of the issue your team must handle, or you can select a previously defined issue from the lookup list.

> ✔ **Status**: You can use this field's lookup list or create your own brief description.

> ✔ **Priority:** Specify a rank-order of this issue. You generally should assign numbers in ascending order so that the more important issues have smaller, or lower numbers.

> ✔ **Date:** You can set a date for this issue. You can either enter the date the issue became known, or you can indicate when the issue needs to be resolved. You must be consistent, however. I like to use the resolution date in this field.

> ✔ **User:** Assign a member of your team to this issue.

Competitors

The Competitors screen, shown in Figure 23-8, allows you to track companies and products with which you are competing for this opportunity. Competitors do not apply to Project Management, because after you close the deal, if you're lucky, you don't need to worry too much about competitors. If you're lucky.

> ✔ **Rating:** You can indicate just how strong a competitor you are dealing with. The standard ratings range from –5 to +5 and are a little out of order due to the vagaries of alphabetic order in lookup lists.

> ✔ **Status:** You can describe your prospect's attitude, as best you understand it, toward this competitor. You can use or modify the lookup list for this field. An example might be: If you were trying to upgrade a prospect from ACT! to GoldMine, but they already had 30 users who knew ACT!, you might describe them as "entrenched."

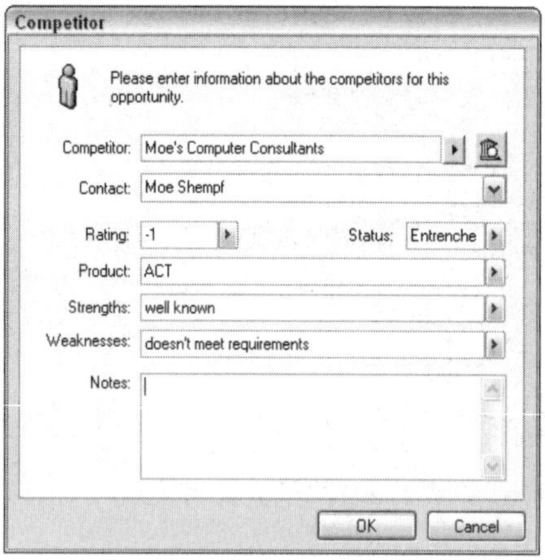

Figure 23-8:
The
Competitor
screen.

- ✔ **Product:** You enter the name, if there is one, of the product against which you are competing.

- ✔ **Strengths:** You can enter a brief description of the most attractive features of this competitor. Please note that this field refers more to your competitor than to that competitor's product, although you can use it either way.

- ✔ **Weaknesses:** The Weaknesses field is, of course, the exact opposite of the Strengths field.

Tracking details

Using the Details/Links screen, you can track custom information associated with the opportunity (or project). This section is a combination of the Detail tab and the Links tab associated with the main records. You can define an unlimited number of items. Each item has an associated Reference field that actually houses the data. In addition, you can link an external file (a Word document or an Excel spreadsheet, as examples) to each item.

The Finish Line

On the last screen of the Opportunity Manager Wizard, you finish your data entry with essentially the remaining parts of your sales forecast. That is, you enter the probability, total revenue, and potential close date for this deal. One of the slickest features of the Opportunity Manager is the graphical pipeline that shows where all the deals are. The Pipeline Funnel icon at the top of the Opportunity Manager produces this display, as shown in Figure 23-9.

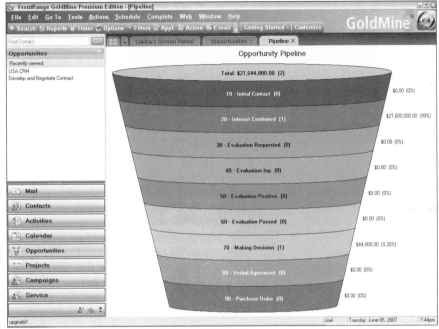

Figure 23-9:
A Pipeline
Funnel with
a couple of
significant
jobs in it.

Tasks

An opportunity (or a project) complex enough to merit tracking by the Opportunity Manager usually involves multiple tasks that start and end over differing time periods. Some tasks might overlap in time, or occur at different times, or be dependent upon the completion of prior tasks. In a complex sale, tracking these individual tasks is essential to successfully completing a sale. A completed set of Task specifications is illustrated in Figure 23-10.

To view or add tasks to an opportunity or to a project:

1. **Make sure you have the proper opportunity or project displayed and highlighted in the upper section of the Opportunity/Project Manager screen.**

2. **Click the Tasks tab.**

3. **To add a new task, right-click below the Tasks tab and select New from the local menu.**

4. **In the Reference field, enter a descriptive name for the task, such as "Survey for number of users."**

5. **Fill in the Status field from its lookup list.**

6. **In the Begin Date field, set the beginning date by either typing it in or by accessing the calendar with the right mouse button.**

7. **Enter the User who is responsible for this task or for the entire opportunity.**

8. **Use the Color field to designate the type of task.**

   These colors will then be displayed on the Gantt chart associated with the opportunity or project. I like to use the same color scheme as described in Chapter 9.

9. **In the Priority field, enter a ranking order for the task.**

   You can use numerals (1, 2, 3, and so on) or an alphabetical scheme (A, B, C, and so on). Just be consistent.

10. **In the %Done field, enter the percentage of the task that has been completed.**

    You will need to enter this information on an ongoing basis.

11. **Use the Notes field for any additional free-form information.**

12. **When you are done, click OK.**

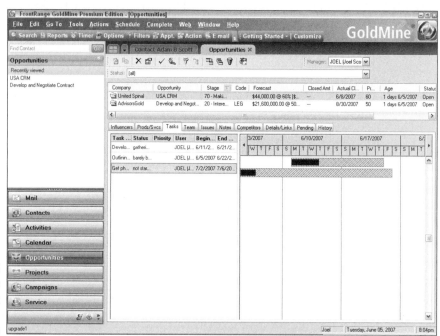

Figure 23-10:
Task
descriptions.

Pending

This tab may contain the scheduled activities relating to an opportunity or to a project. A complex opportunity or project usually involves many activities to be performed by various members of your team. Although you can add these activities from the Schedule main menu, you can view and manage each one from the Pending tab of the Opportunity or Project Manager (O/PM). You may also want to make use of the Gantt chart that GoldMine builds for you. This will graphically lay out everyone's tasks.

History

This tab contains all the activities that have been closed in pursuit of the opportunity. The History tab in the O/PM relates to the O/PM just as the Pending tab does. You can edit and close activities either from the main screen or from the History tab within the O/PM.

Closing and Converting Opportunities

When an opportunity closes, it becomes a project. You close an opportunity by right-clicking the opportunity and selecting Convert to Opportunity/Project from the menu that appears. You can also convert a project into an opportunity. Converting projects back into opportunities is a function of your Sales Prevention Team. With luck, you don't have such a team and won't need to do this.

Chapter 24

Managing Relationships

In This Chapter

▶ Creating relationships

▶ Activating sections

▶ Rolling up activities and documents

*T*hose familiar with previous versions of GoldMine and, specifically with the Organizational Chart, will recognize a lot of the Organizational Chart in the new Relationships tab. Basically, the Relationships tab is the Organizational Chart's bigger brother.

You use the Relationships tab to connect one GoldMine record with one or more other records. GoldMine builds a graphic display of these connections and allows you to not only see the connections but to use them as you might use a filter.

A typical Relationships tab display is shown in Figure 24-1. I call this a "chart" from now on in deference to its predecessor, the Org Chart.

In this chapter, I explain how to use the Relationships tab.

Figure 24-1:
A simple
Relation-
ships tab.

Building Relationships

Relationships are linked to each of the specified records. That is, the same chart is displayed within the Relationships tab for each of the companies or contacts within the chart. The relationship's name is taken from the Company field of the selected contact record. You can create up to five secondary levels under each organization and you can link contacts to any section.

You create a new relationship with the following steps.

1. **From the Relationships Tab, right-click and select Create a new Relationship.**

   The New Relationship Tree Options dialog box appears, as shown in Figure 24-2.

2. **Lookup another contact and create a Relationship.**

   This launches the Contact Search Center and lets you add a new Relationship to another Contact Record.

You may need to refresh the Relationships tab, move back and forth from one record back to the original before you can actually see the results of adding a new contact or company to your relationships.

Although you can add records to a chart one at a time, a more efficient way to build a chart is to use filters or groups. To do so, follow these steps:

1. **Activate an existing filter or group (see Chapter 8 for details on filters and groups).**

2. **Right-click a section within your existing Relationships tab.**

   A menu of choices appears.

3. **Select New Contact, which leads to yet another menu (see Figure 24-3).**

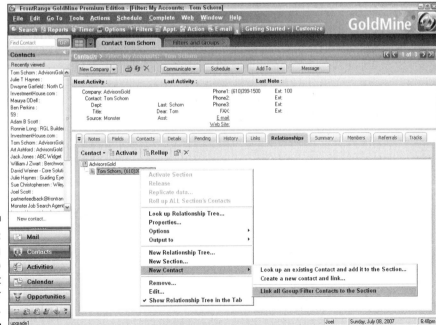

Figure 24-3:
Adding entries to the chart using a filter or a group.

4. **Select the last choice, which is Link all Group/Filter Contacts to the Section.**

   This will automatically add every record from the active filter (or group) to this section of your chart.

Even if using a filter adds a few too many records to your chart, it is way easier to remove them than it would be to individually add more than a few records.

Activating a Section

You can activate an entire relationship or just a section. This lets you quickly create a working group of related contacts. When you do this, GoldMine treats the activated section very much as it does a filter and allows you to scroll through all the records in the chart exactly as you can scroll through a series of records within an active filter or group.

In the Relationships tab, right-click an entry (either a relationship or a section) and then select Activate. (Depending on your selection, select either Activate Relationship or Activate Section.) To deactivate the group, click the Release button on the Relationships toolbar.

Doing a Rollup

I actually believe rollups are the most important feature of the Relationships tab. Rollups are important when you want to view, for example, all the history for all records within one section of the Relationships tab. A common request from users in the financial community is to see all the history for the members of a family in one consolidated view. This is actually called "householding."

Doing a rollup accomplishes this, and more. In fact, you get this consolidated view for pending and historical activities as well as for Contacts, Details, Referrals, Linked Documents, Members, Tracks, Opportunities and for Projects.

If you have a particularly large database, or if the section of the Relationships chart you are rolling up is large, you might need to go get a cup of coffee while you're waiting for your rollup to happen. You can expedite this by asking your

GoldMine Administrator to do some routine database maintenance first. To actually do a rollup, you must activate a section and then select the Rollup button in the Relationships tab. The information you see in the rollup applies to the section of the Relationships chart that you have currently highlighted.

Here's how you do it, step by step:

1. **Right-click the entire relationship or just a section of it and then select Activate Section (see Figure 24-4).**

2. **Select Rollup.**

   A caution appears, but if you did your maintenance recently, you might just as well go ahead. This is shown in Figure 24-5.

3. **Click the History tab (or any of the other supported tabs that you're interested in).**

   GoldMine displays all the history for all the members of the relationship section you selected, as shown in Figure 24-6.

Figure 24-4: Activating a section of a relationship.

Figure 24-5:
Selecting
the Rollup
option.

Figure 24-6:
The consoli-
dated
history for
all members
of the
section
selected.

4. **Right-click in the blank area of the History tab (Figure 24-6) to get a statistical analysis of the activities or output the history to a printer or to Excel, for example.**

5. **To release the rollup, click the Deactivate Rollup button, shown in Figure 24-7.**

Part VII

Customizing GoldMine

The 5th Wave   By Rich Tennant

"So, what kind of roaming capabilities does this thing have?"

In this part . . .

Part of the power of GoldMine, in fact since the beginning, has been your ability to expand the system by adding new fields and customizing labels. In this part, you learn how to do this as well as how to tailor lookup lists that are associated with many of GoldMine's fields.

Automated Processes is an underutilized and powerful tool that, when properly designed, has GoldMine doing as much grunt work as possible. A good Automated Process makes sure that nothing falls between the cracks because it schedules users to do things and sends out correspondence.

GM+Browser enhances the power of GM+View by creating an environment in which you can scroll through multiple GM+Views, all organized in one place.

The fact that you can fully integrate GoldMine with your Web site should be enough to convince you to truly enhance your Web site or create one if you don't already have one. Prospects and customers visiting your Web site can automatically have their records created or updated. When attached to a good Automated Process, this updating can make it look as though your sales and customer service teams are working 24/7.

Chapter 25

Creating New Labels and Fields

. . . .

In This Chapter

▶ Adding new fields to your database

▶ Organizing and creating field views

▶ Displaying new fields

▶ Changing field labels and data on the fly

▶ Modify an existing field

▶ Changing the face of GoldMine with Record Typing

. . . .

*O*ne of the most powerful aspects of GoldMine is its capability of con-
forming to your business. You can customize the labels for individual
fields so that they more closely fit your needs. You can create an almost
unlimited number of additional fields, and you can rearrange where many
existing fields appear on the screen. Record typing creates yet another
option for customizing your fields — you can completely change the fields
and appearance of your GoldMine screens depending on the data you enter
in just one of the fields.

Modifying fields and labels is relatively straightforward. All the tools you
need are included with GoldMine. But, very significant and powerful new features, such as Record Typing, have been added recently, giving you a reason
to maintain a relationship with a knowledgeable dealer.

This chapter helps you break into some of the secret tools of those dealers
so that you can do at least some of your own customization, rather than pay
someone else to do it.

Adding New Fields to Your Database

You can add hundreds of additional custom fields. Several steps are involved,
the first of which is, of course, deciding what fields you need and where they
will go. Next you add the new field(s) to the database structure. And finally
you rebuild the database, and position the field somewhere in the window so
that you can see and use it.

A somewhat new Screen Design utility presents an alternate method of adding new fields to your database. The older method, which I describe in this chapter, allows you to see your existing fields while adding new ones. I think this is a significant enough advantage that I recommend the older method and ignore the new one.

To begin adding fields to the database, from the main menu, choose Tools⇨ Configure⇨Custom Fields. The User Defined Fields dialog box appears, as shown in Figure 25-1.

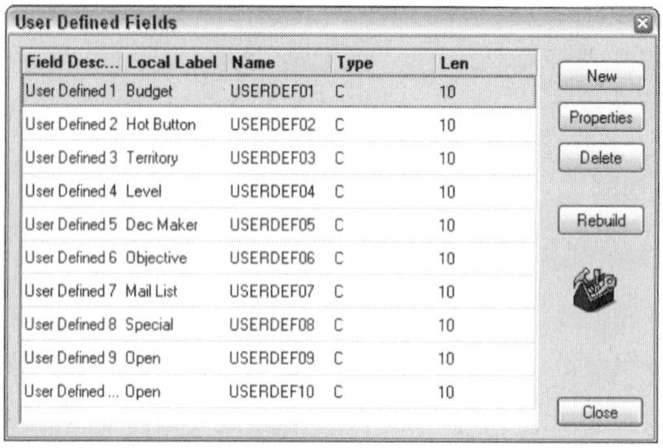

Figure 25-1:
Use this
dialog box
to define
custom
fields.

Field Desc...	Local Label	Name	Type	Len	
User Defined 1	Budget	USERDEF01	C	10	New
User Defined 2	Hot Button	USERDEF02	C	10	Properties
User Defined 3	Territory	USERDEF03	C	10	Delete
User Defined 4	Level	USERDEF04	C	10	
User Defined 5	Dec Maker	USERDEF05	C	10	Rebuild
User Defined 6	Objective	USERDEF06	C	10	
User Defined 7	Mail List	USERDEF07	C	10	
User Defined 8	Special	USERDEF08	C	10	
User Defined 9	Open	USERDEF09	C	10	
User Defined ...	Open	USERDEF10	C	10	Close

Select the New button and you can begin defining new fields, one at a time.

The User Defined Fields dialog box contains the following information:

- **Field Name:** Name that GoldMine uses to identify the field in the contact database.

- **Description:** Description of the field that typically describes the contents or purpose of the field; for example, Business Type.

- **Local Label:** Displays the default label that will ultimately appear on-screen.

- **Field Type:** Identification code for the data type of the field from one of the following values:
    - C — Character
    - N — Numeric
    - D — Date

- **Len:** Length of the field in number of characters. The length of the field determines how much data the field can hold, or the total number of characters that can be stored. For numeric fields, you must count the decimal point and the plus or minus sign, if you anticipate using one.

When adding a field type, you should know the types of fields and when you should use them. You can add three different field types:

✔ **Character fields (C)** can contain any keyboard character and are generally used to hold text. Although the maximum length you can define is 254 characters, a practical limit is imposed by the size of your screen. The largest field that can be displayed across the screen and without room for a field label on the same line is 76 characters. You can, of course, have a field larger than 76 characters, and you can scroll from right to left within the field.

✔ **Numeric fields (N)** have a maximum length of 16, including any plus or minus signs. You can have from 0–9 decimal places. This limitation should never be a problem if you design your numeric fields properly.

One of my clients in the financial services industry insisted that she needed 25-digit numeric fields. Some of her clients, she said, had very large accounts. The entire United States national debt is currently just under 8 trillion, which would take up 13 digits in a numeric field. She and I finally settled on 16 digits because that was all GoldMine can handle anyway.

Very few human beings can look at a number like 5132563436666 and have any appreciation for what it represents. If you need to keep a number in the billions or trillions or more, you should label it as such and keep the number itself to a reasonable length. Examples include the following:

Field Label	Data Field
Bank balance (billions)	498.5
Avogadro's number (10^{23})	6.023

✔ **Date fields** must contain a valid date only and always have a length of eight characters. Dates are represented in a MM/DD/YY format.

Creating a new field

To create a field and add it to your existing database, follow these steps:

1. **If you don't already have the User Defined Fields dialog box open, choose Tools⇔Configure⇔Custom Fields and then click the New button.**

   (Refer to Figure 25-1 to see the User Defined Fields dialog box.) After you click the New button, the User Defined Field Profile dialog box appears, as shown in Figure 25-2.

Figure 25-2:
The User
Defined
Field Profile
screen with
an example
of a custom
Anniversary
field.

2. **Enter the name of your new field.**

   The Field Name field itself already has a *U* as the first character. *U* stands for *user-defined* and must be the first character in all fields you build. All user-defined fields

   - Must begin with the letter *U*.

   - Can contain up to, but not more than, ten alphanumeric characters.

   - Must have unique field names.

3. **In the Description field, enter a short, plain-English phrase describing the contents or purpose of this field. Spaces are allowed.**

4. **Select what type of data the field will contain and the length of the field.**

   As mentioned previously, you have three choices of field type: character (C), numeric (N), and date (D), and you must select one of these options in this dialog box.

   If you're adding a field for a phone number, the field name should start with UPHONE. You can use either upper- or lowercase. Designating a user-defined field name with these first six characters forces GoldMine to format the data into typical phone-number format, with parentheses and dashes.

5. **When you're finished entering the information for a new data field, click OK.**

   You return to the User Defined Fields dialog box. (Refer to Figure 25-1.)

You can continue with this procedure, adding as many new fields as you need. After you finish adding all the new fields, you have one more step to complete before you can actually use these fields: You must *rebuild* your database. In fact, GoldMine has a reminder message that awaits should you forget the rebuild process. See the next section to find out how to rebuild your database.

Note that only users with Master rights are allowed to rebuild your database

Rebuilding your database

To rebuild your database, simply click the Rebuild button in the User Defined Fields dialog box. GoldMine asks whether you're ready to rebuild the database; click OK. The rebuild function appends all your new fields to the CON-TACT2.DBF file. This process takes only a moment or two if you do it while very few accounts are in your database. As the number of accounts grows, so does the time it takes for a rebuild.

A little planning at the beginning of your project may save you a considerable amount of time later if you have to do a few rebuilds with 25,000 existing accounts in the database. Try your best to plan for new or additional fields *before* you add a ton of data to the database. Then, rebuilding is quick; later, it may be painfully slow. In fact, if you're not completely sure how many fields you may need, it might be clever to add a couple of spare character, numeric, and date fields before you stock your database with 25,000 records.

Keep the following in mind when rebuilding:

- ✔ Always back up your entire database before rebuilding.
- ✔ No one else should be running GoldMine while a rebuild is happening.
- ✔ Make sure you have enough free disk space available before rebuilding. GoldMine will be adding each of your new fields to every record in your database. You can find a formula for figuring free disk space in the GoldMine Reference Manual, but a common guideline is to never allow your hard drive to get more than about 70 percent full. Beyond that level, your disk efficiency begins to deteriorate anyway, and you run the risk of running out of space whenever GoldMine or any other program creates temp files or backup files.

Rebuilding usually only takes a short time, and then you will be ready to display or use the fields.

Organizing and Creating Field Views

Field views are groups of fields organized into logical groupings and shown together in one window display. GoldMine comes with basically one field view: the one directly under the Fields tab. To further organize the data, GoldMine enables anyone with Master rights to design custom views. Before you can display a newly created field in a field view, you need to create that view.

One of the benefits of custom field views is that you can organize your data logically. If you have a dozen fields related to accounting, you can put them all together in one accounting view. Marketing fields can be placed together, as can the fields for sales.

Creating hot keys

If you want to gain access to a particular field view by using *hot keys* (a special key sequence that accesses a command), you can create a custom hot key. For example, you may want to go to the Accounting tab by simply pressing Ctrl+A. To designate this hot key for the Accounting tab, type **&A** in the tab name. Actually, the ampersand (&) can appear anywhere within the tab name, but the following letter will become the hot key for that tab.

In addition, you can control the access rights to individual field views. If you don't want people in the Marketing department to view or to manipulate data in the Accounting view, you can preclude them from doing so. This is often a valuable tool.

To create and maintain custom user-defined field views, follow these steps:

1. **Click the Fields tab to highlight it.**

2. **Right-click anywhere in the Fields area and select Screens Setup from the shortcut menu that appears.**

   The Custom Screens Setup dialog box appears, as shown in Figure 25-3.

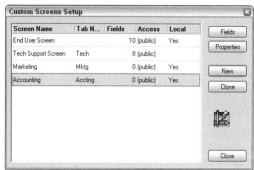

Figure 25-3: Create a custom view with the Custom Screens Setup dialog box.

3. **Click the New button to create a new field view.**

   The Custom Screen Profile dialog box appears, as shown in Figure 25-4.

4. **Fill in the following three fields on the Custom Screen Profile dialog box:**

   • **Screen Name:** This is the name for the new dialog box and will be shown in the Custom Screens Setup dialog box.

   • **Tab Name:** Designing a tab name creates a custom tab in one of the banks of tabs behind the standard tabs. Although you can enter up to 22 characters for a tab name, although you may not be able to see that many when the tab is displayed. Make sure the first 7 or 8 characters you use are sufficient to clearly describe what this view is all about.

GoldMine now allows you to place your tabs on the screen in any order you like by simply clicking and dragging each tab into the position you prefer.

- **Access:** This field allows you to direct who has access to this particular field view. To restrict access to this field view, select a user or a group of users who may access to it. To allow everyone to have access, leave the access rights set to (public).

The last check box on the dialog box controls whether this custom view is accessible from this particular contact database. Generally, you want to leave the default setting as is.

5. **When you're finished, click OK.**

Figure 25-4:
Name the custom view and tab in the Custom Screen Profile dialog box.

Sometimes you will have several custom views that are very similar and actually contain many of the same fields. Rather than painstakingly recreate the second or third such view, you can copy all the individual view and field specifications from one view to another. You can do this by clicking the Clone button on the Custom Screens Setup dialog box as seen in Figure 25-1.

Clicking the Clone button brings you to the Custom Screen Profile dialog box, allowing you to give the old view a new name and then automatically copy all the fields that are included into a brand-new field view.

Because you can assign hot keys in many places, keeping a list of the ones you have created is wise! GoldMine goes to the first hot key assigned to a function; for example, pressing Ctrl+A goes to CASES and then, if pressed again, goes to the FieldView tab assigned to that sequence.

Displaying New Fields

After you create all the field views that you need, you can begin placing individual fields on those screens.

Quite a few methods exist for displaying individual fields. In this section, I discuss a method that was introduced back in GoldMine 5.0. This method is the most streamlined and logical method of them all.

To display a new field that already exists in your database, you must first locate the proper field view. You can maneuver through the various tabbed file folders by clicking the down arrow immediately to the left of the Fields Tab. After you locate the custom screen tab on which you want to display your field(s), follow these steps:

1. **Highlight the custom tab.**

2. **Right-click in the blank area below the tab and select Screen Design from the shortcut menu.**

   A series of drop-down choices appears, as shown in Figure 25-5.

3. **Click the New Field option.**

   The Place Field dialog box appears, which allows you to select the specific field to place on this tab. Assuming that you have already created the field and rebuilt the database since then, you can find this field by clicking the arrow to the right of Field, as shown in Figure 25-6. Or, you can actually create a new field, on the fly, by clicking the New Field button in this dialog box. If you do create a new field on the fly, you have to rebuild the database before you can add information into that field.

4. **After you identify the field you want, click OK.**

   You return to the selected field view, with your new field highlighted in a red or white box. A red box indicates that the field is currently positioned on top of an existing field. You don't want two fields overlapping each other, so you have to move at least one of them. A box with a white background indicates that it doesn't conflict with any other field, but you may want to reposition it anyway.

You can reposition the field, whether it is highlighted in white or in red, by clicking and dragging it to an empty place in the window. When you have it in approximately the right place, double-click the box with the field you're displaying to show the Field Properties dialog box. Doing so allows you to do some further fine-tuning of the field, as shown in Figure 25-7.

Figure 25-5:
Screen
design
options.

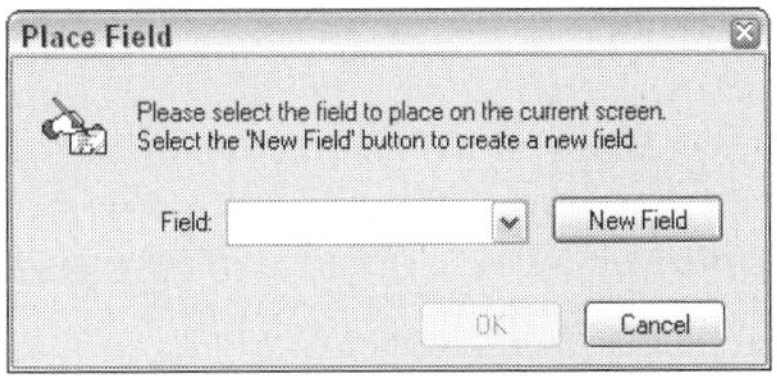

Figure 25-6:
Selecting a
field for
screen
placement.

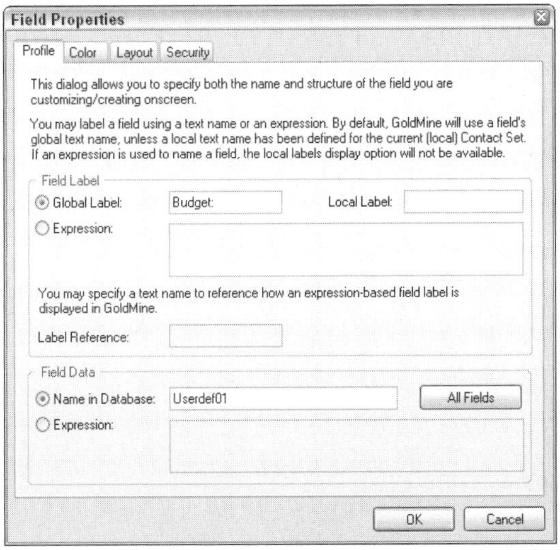

Figure 25-7:
Fine-tune
your field
definitions
in the Field
Properties
dialog box.

Click the Security tab on the Field Properties dialog box. Among other options in this tab, you can also specify who has rights to read and/or to change the data on a field-by-field basis by choosing from the following options:

- ✔ **Read Rights:** By default, this field is listed as (public), which allows all users to see the data in this field. You can enter either an individual or a group name into this field, and thus control who can see the data in this field.

- ✔ **Update Rights:** This option is similar to the Read Access field. By default, everyone can edit the data in each field. If you turn off Read Access rights, you also turn off Update Access, but situations may exist where you want someone to be able to see the data but not change it. An example might be a Credit Limit field. You may want anyone in the Accounting group to be able to read it and update it, but you may want the folks in the Sales group to be able see the data but not update it.

- ✔ **Field Audit:** If you turn on this option, GoldMine automatically keeps a historical log of all changes to the data in this field. This log includes the time, the date, and the user who changed the data. I have this set in the Account Manager field just in case a salesperson decides to reassign all the best accounts to him- or herself.

On the Layout tab, you specify the size and window positioning of each field you are displaying, as shown in Figure 25-8.

- ✔ **Field Label Size:** You may need to adjust the length of the label you are using for this field. You can increase or decrease the size of the label by simply changing the number in this field. This may allow you to adjust the window location of the data by making more room if you need it.

- ✔ **Data Size:** You can also adjust the actual size of the data display for the field. This doesn't affect the data itself but may affect how much of the data you can see at one time without scrolling right and left.

- ✔ **Colon:** You can specify the position of the colon, which separates the field label from the data itself. This essentially positions the entire object, which is the label plus the data.

- ✔ **Field Order:** The integer in the Field Order field determines the order in which you normally tab from one field to the next. GoldMine takes you sequentially from one field to the next based on the number in the Field Order field.

You can change a field that has already been placed for display by double-clicking the label while you hold down the Ctrl key. The field and label become highlighted, and you can then double-click the highlighted area. The Field Properties dialog box reappears, and you can then make whatever changes are needed.

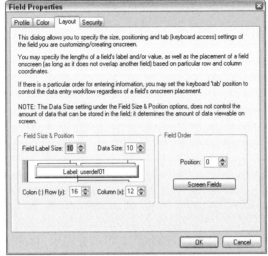

Figure 25-8:
Setting up
the field
layout.

Changing Field Labels and Data On the Fly

Any user with Master rights can change the labels of fields, including those fields above the file folders as well as all the user-defined fields in the Fields tab. For example, for a contact database that contains only educational institutions, you can change the label of the Company field to School.

In addition to changing a field label for every record, GoldMine can change field labels on the fly based on the data entered in that or in other fields. For example, if you enter Canada as the country for a particular record, you can have GoldMine automatically display Postal Code as opposed to Zip Code in the prior field. This comes under the heading of "Record Typing."

You can also change the data in particular fields on the fly based on what is entered in other fields by using the LOOKUP.INI file (see Chapter 26), as shown in Figure 25-9.

Using LOOKUP.INI, you can automatically have GoldMine assign an Account Manager based on, say, the state the account is in. This happens, however, only when you actually move the cursor into and out of the Account Manager field. You may still need to resort to this original methodology if you have more conditions than allowed in a typical dBASE expression.

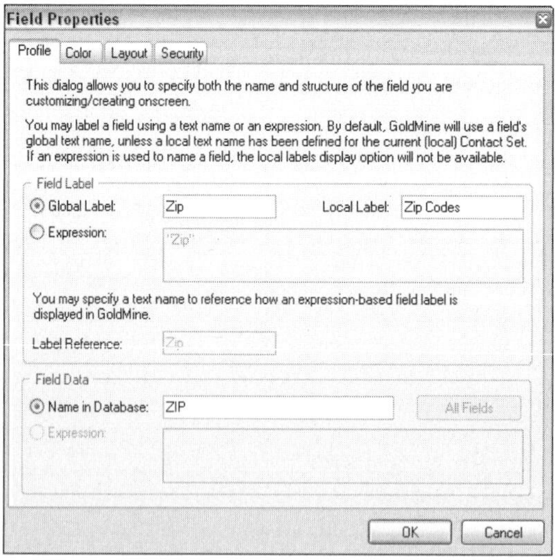

Figure 25-9:
Changing
data on the
fly.

To change the label of a field, follow these steps:

1. **Select the field label by holding down Ctrl and double-clicking the field.**

   Remember, it's the field label, not the data area!

   All the other fields in the window become highlighted in the color associated with the main screen's color scheme, whereas the selected field remains in a white box.

2. **Take your finger off the Ctrl key and double-click again in the white area where the original field is.**

   The Field Properties dialog box appears (refer to Figure 25-8). The Field Properties dialog box allows you to change not only the labels that appear in the window but also a number of other properties, including the size and position of the label. See the "Adding New Fields to Your Database" section, earlier in this chapter, for details.

   The Field Label section focuses only on the labels themselves:

   • **Global Label:** Specifies field label text. GoldMine uses the text in the Global Label field unless you have specified a value in the Local Label field (see the next bullet). Global labels appear consistently throughout all contact databases. If you want to use a different label for this field in each contact database, use the Local Label field to store the label text.

   • **Local Label:** Specifies the text of a field label for only the currently open contact database. This option allows you to use a different field label for the primary field in different databases. An entry in the Local Label field overrides whatever is in the Global Label field for the one database that is open.

The following limitations apply to local labels:

- Local labels can be used only with fields, not expressions.
- Local labels can be no more than 15 characters in length.

3. When you're finished choosing labels and properties, click OK.

GoldMine updates the contact record display to show the new field label. Changing the field label has no effect on the data in the field.

Modifying an Existing Field

Suddenly in GoldMine 6.0, we had much more control over labels and data fields. This was one of the most powerful innovations introduced in version 6.0.

Assigning an account manager

Every account, whether big or small, whether prospect or active client, should have a real live person in charge of it. This should be a basic principle of your client retention strategy. You can assign account managers in many different ways, based on product lines or on geography, for example. If you pick geography, you can base the assignment on a state, counties, a range of ZIP codes, telephone area codes, or a few other pieces of data.

As tempting as it is, resist the urge to use telephone area codes as the basis for assigning account managers. Not only do area codes change fairly frequently, but with the growing use of cell phones, area codes are less and less related to geography.

If you decide that states are the most appropriate way to assign an account manager, you can enter a field expression in the Account Manager field that automatically assigns the salesperson as soon as you enter the state. With the LOOKUP.INI technology, you could do the same thing, but the user needed to move his or her cursor into the Account Manager field for an assignment to happen. This is much better. Figure 25-10 shows how to make this happen.

Changing the face of GoldMine with Record Typing

You can use Record Typing to make really profound changes to the way in which you use GoldMine. Perhaps you want to have several different kinds of records in the same database. For example, perhaps you want records for clients, vendors, and employees as well.

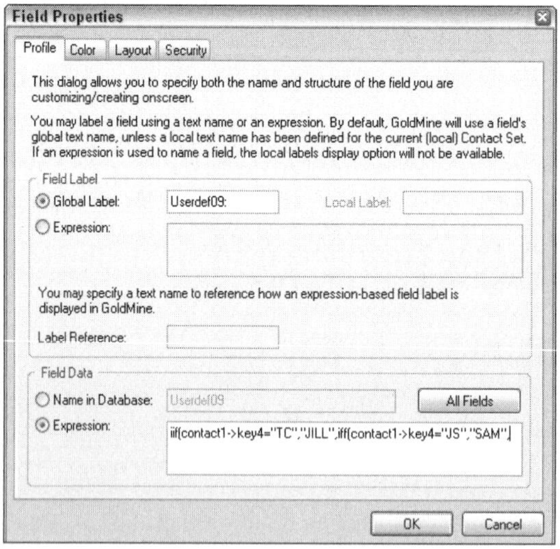

Field Properties

Profile | Color | Layout | Security

This dialog allows you to specify both the name and structure of the field you are customizing/creating onscreen.

You may label a field using a text name or an expression. By default, GoldMine will use a field's global text name, unless a local text name has been defined for the current (local) Contact Set. If an expression is used to name a field, the local labels display option will not be available.

Field Label

◉ Global Label: Userdef09:   Local Label: [   ]

○ Expression: [   ]

You may specify a text name to reference how an expression-based field label is displayed in GoldMine.

Label Reference: [   ]

Field Data

○ Name in Database: Userdef09   [All Fields]

◉ Expression: iif(contact1->key4="TC","JILL",iif(contact1->key4="JS","SAM",|

[OK] [Cancel]

Figure 25-10:
Assigning
account
managers
on the fly.

If you had a single field for Record Type, you could specify whether a particular record was a vendor, a client, or an employee. Based on the data you enter, GoldMine can completely reconfigure the entire screen. Virtually every field you see on the Vendor window can be different from what you see on the Employee window.

To be more specific, you might want the first Key field in the Employee window to house a social security number. For the Vendor window, you might want a federal ID number. For the Client window, you might want an account number.

Based on that Record Type field, the label for Key 1 would automatically change to accommodate to whatever type of information is appropriate. Taking this a step further, you can change virtually every label to coincide with the type of information this account has.

You can also control the GM+View tab (see Chapter 28) this same way. The limits are your imagination, or the experience of the GoldMine dealer with whom you are working.

If you select the Expression toggle switch, you can then enter a valid dBASE expression to have GoldMine calculate a value for the field. For example, if you have a field for Lease Signing Date and a field for Length of Lease, you could have a third calculated field for the Lease Termination Date.

Record Typing is one of the more complex and sometimes problematic areas of GoldMine. If you decide to make use of this feature, you should probably enlist the help of an experienced dealer or consultant.

Chapter 26

Creating and Modifying Lookup Lists

• •

In This Chapter

▶ Using existing lookup lists

▶ Customizing lookup lists

▶ Deleting standard entries

▶ Creating new entries

▶ Setting search options

▶ Using correct punctuation

• •

*M*any of the GoldMine standard fields and virtually any custom fields you create come equipped with lookup lists. These lists can contain prerecorded choices for entry into each such field. A number of advantages exist to having and using these lists.

These lists are a particular boon to those who never took or didn't like typing class. So if you belong to the hunt-and-peck school of typing, you'll find each lookup list to be a real timesaver. If you got an A in typing class but flunked spelling class, the lookup lists are there for you, too.

More important, the lookup lists help ensure that your entries into a field are consistent with those of everyone else on your team or with what you did last month. This consistency pays off when you want to generate reports that are sorted on one of these fields because Schenectady will be spelled the exact same way in every record. So the accounts from Schenectady will appear together in reports sorted by city. Otherwise, who knows?

Frequently throughout the various GoldMine manuals and in the help files, you see these lists referred to as F2 lookup lists. The term F2 is a holdover from the days of DOS when users pressed particular function keys (in this case, F2) to access lookup lists. F2 and lookup lists are the same thing, and so you sometimes see them together in the same phrase.

Using Existing Lookup Lists

Every GoldMine field that can have a lookup list has a right arrow displayed to the right of its data field. You can see this arrow as soon as you click in any field that has a lookup list. If you see this arrow, you know a list exists that you can use. Figure 26-1 shows a typical lookup list associated with the Phone Extension field on the main screen.

Figure 26-1:
The lookup list for the Phone Extension field.

As soon as you click the right arrow next to the field, a list similar to that shown in Figure 26-1 appears. If data was already in the field you just came from, that selection is highlighted in bold within the lookup list. Throughout the list, all the choices are arranged alphabetically. If more choices exist than can fit in one display window, you can scroll up and down using the scroll buttons on the right side of the lookup list.

If the choice you want is visible in the window, you can simply double-click it to send it into the data field. Unless some special punctuation exists (see the "Using the punctuation tools" section, later in this chapter), this choice replaces whatever is already in the data field.

Customizing Your Lookup Lists

One of the first things you need to do after installing GoldMine is to assemble all the lookup entries you want to use. Solicit from the key people using the system the choices they need in each field.

Deleting the standard lookup entries

For some reason, in version after version, the developers of GoldMine continue to supply a standard set of lookup lists whether you want them or not. Likely, you don't want most of the standard GoldMine lookups. To delete an existing entry, follow these steps after you have displayed the particular field's lookup list:

1. **Highlight the choice you want to remove.**

2. **Click the Delete button.**

3. **Confirm that you really want to delete this choice.**

4. **Repeat Steps 1 through 3 until you have removed all the entries you want to get rid of.**

If the lookup list is long and you want to delete *all* the entries, then the use of the delete key followed by the Y key is very handy. Hunt and peck typists will find this especially fun. You can clean out a list in no time!

During the installation process, you can elect to install blank lookup lists. That's probably a good idea. If GoldMine has already been installed, however, with a bunch of extraneous lookups, then you will have to go through the preceding steps to clear them out.

Creating new entries

The Lookup Window dialog box contains the New button (refer to Figure 26-1) that allows you to enter new items into a lookup list. To create a new lookup list choice, follow these steps:

1. **Click the New button on the Lookup Window dialog box to gain access to all the existing lookup choices for a particular field.**

2. **Enter your choice in the F2 Entry dialog box.**

3. **Confirm your entry by clicking OK.**

Your new entries are automatically placed alphabetically into the lookup list for that field.

If you have especially long lists and you want some particular entries at the top, you can put numbers or nonalphabetic characters in front of the entries to move them to the top; for example, 1 - Xeon, 2 - Argon, 3 - Helium, 4- Dirt.

Setting lookup list options

In addition to deleting and creating lookup list entries, you can also customize your lookup lists to make them easier for others (as well as for you) to use. Click the Setup button in the Lookup Window dialog box (refer to Figure 26-1). The dialog box shown in Figure 26-2 appears, which contains the following options:

Figure 26-2:
Customizing your lookup list in the F2 Field Setup dialog box.

✔ **Allow Blank Input:** Allows you to enter and leave the field without entering any data.

✔ **Force Valid Input:** Forces you to enter data that corresponds exactly to some entry in the lookup list.

✔ **Insert Closest Match:** Allows GoldMine to select the closest match from the lookup list and enter it into the field. This option can help shorten data entry time for experienced data entry operators.

✔ **Capitalize First Letter:** No matter how you capitalize your data, GoldMine automatically overrides it and capitalizes the first letter of each word. This might be appropriate for a person's name or for a country, but is applicable only if you're manually entering the data rather than selecting from the F2 lookup list.

✔ **Pop-Up when Selected:** Forces the lookup list to appear immediately as soon as you enter a field.

✔ **Allow Adding:** Allows users to add entries to the lookup list.

Adding to, editing, and deleting from lookup lists should be an administrative task, and I recommend that you assign such tasks to only one or two key people for coordination. Otherwise, you'll end up with a complete hodgepodge of conflicting and confusing codes and choices. Major mess.

✔ **Allow Editing:** Allows users to edit entries in the lookup list.

✔ **Allow Deleting:** Allows users to delete entries from the lookup list.

✔ **Auto Fill:** As you type, GoldMine automatically places the closest matching entry from the lookup in the field. This is often a better option than Pop-Up when Selected, providing a little more flexibility when you are manually typing an entry.

✔ **Import Lookup Entries from Another Field:** Often, one field in GoldMine uses the exact same set of lookups as another. A field for State/Province is a good example. This option allows you to essentially copy one field's lookups to another field. If you already have items in your lookup list and you import entries from another field, these new entries are merged alphabetically with those that already exist in the lookup list.

Using the punctuation tools

You can include four special punctuation tools in your lookup lists. These tools allow you to program some advanced functionality into your lookups. I explain these tools in the following sections.

Making remarks (//)

The double forward slash (//) separates your actual data from comments you want in the lookup list. Nothing that appears to the right of the slashes is actually put into the data field.

A typical example of the use of these slashes is in the Acct Mngr field. Especially when you need multiple entries, you want to use short codes for each account manager. If you were to spell out each manager's entire name and wanted three or four of them in one field, all the names just wouldn't fit. So you probably need to use their initials.

The downside of using initials is that other people on the team may not recognize the initials. The double slashes allow you to have the full name of the account manager following her initials, so you can use the short codes and still ensure that everyone else understands the meaning of each code. Figure 26-3 shows a typical example of the use of the double forward slash.

Only your data in the lookup list actually goes into the data field. Nothing to the right of the slashes is transferred.

Figure 26-3:
Sample remarks in a lookup list.

Appending data (;)

Normally, when you select a choice from a lookup list, your choice overwrites whatever was already in the data field. The semicolon, as well as the percent sign, allows you to add your selection to the already existing data without removing the original data. Figure 26-4 illustrates the use of these semicolons.

Figure 26-4:
Using semicolons in a lookup list.

If a choice in your lookup list has a semicolon immediately after the data itself, selecting that choice places it in the data field following the existing data, separated by a comma and a space. Using this technique, you can have multiple selections in your data fields.

When using multiple selections, you can quickly run out of space in your data field. Be aware that you need to count not only the actual characters in each selection but also the comma and the space that separate each choice in the data field.

One field begets another (~)

The tilde (~) is the most sophisticated of the punctuation options in the lookup lists. You can use the tilde to specify that whatever follows is a dBASE expression that will compute the entry into the field. For example, you can set a field equal to another field, or you can set a field equal to today's date, as shown in Figure 26-5.

Figure 26-5:
Coding
dBASE
expressions
in a lookup
list.

The following are some examples of adding dBASE expressions to compute an entry:

- ~**Company** places whatever data is currently in the Company field into this field.

- ~**dtoc(date( ))** places the current date in the field in character format; for example, 09/08/03.

- ~**Contact2->UserDef03** takes the information from the third user-defined field in the Contact2.dbf file and puts it into this field.

You can also use this programming technique to improve upon the standard lookup list associated with the Dear field. Out of the box, GoldMine has Dear field choices of Dr., Mr., Mrs., and Ms. You can keep these choices, but you may want to add several expressions that append last names to these salutations.

Chapter 27

Automated Processes

*A*utomated Processes are routines that sit quietly in the background, looking for events or conditions within each record that trigger some action, or even a whole series of actions. You can use the Automated Processes feature to perform a set of actions to accomplish a specific task. The Automated Processes feature is one of the key features that differentiates GoldMine from the vast majority of its competitors. I am convinced that properly implemented Automated Processes are the most powerful tools for growing your business that you will ever encounter.

You can design an unlimited number of Automated Processes to emulate a wide variety of already-existing processes within your business. You can also design some of the processes that have never been manually implemented due to lack of resources. The clear advantage of the GoldMine Automated Processes is that they never forget to do their assigned tasks, never call in sick or go on vacation, and never ask for a raise. Automated Processes just keep doing their job for you without complaint and without fail.

In most industries, selling something to a prospect for the first time takes a considerable effort, and staying in touch enough after the sale to have a reasonable expectation of a repeat sale takes further effort. Many sales consultants estimate that it takes at least six touches before you can close a new sale. A *touch* is some sort of communication, whether in person, on the phone, via mail, fax, or e-mail.

The average professional salesperson gives up after fewer than three touches due to the pressures of other commitments and other opportunities. The whole concept behind the GoldMine Automated Processes is to provide the ability to perform most of these touches without any human intervention. (Of course, the best scenario is when the prospect or customer doesn't realize that the computer, and not the salesperson, is doing the touching.) This chapter presents some simple examples of how to get the computer to do the work that salespeople or administrators are either doing now or that they are supposed to be doing but never seem to get to.

In addition, I show some examples of more complex Automated Processes that may be effective after the initial sale. Anyone with a background in marketing knows that selling something to an existing customer is easier and more cost effective than finding a brand-new customer for one of your products or services. I have seen many statistics claiming that finding a new customer is six times more expensive than selling to an existing one. I don't have a clue where that statistic came from, and my work in client retention tells me otherwise, but any salesperson would be wise to put the GoldMine Automated Processes to work to keep his or her clients.

Designing and Implementing Automated Processes

Every successful business has processes. A process may be as simple as an edict that when the sales manager gives a salesperson a lead, he or she must follow up within one day. Another example is that whenever a salesperson returns from an initial sales call, he or she should immediately send a follow-up thank-you letter.

A more sophisticated process may be one that performs a series of follow-up steps after talking with a prospect at a trade show — an initial thank-you letter via e-mail, a second mailing with brochures, and then a scheduled follow-up phone call by the salesperson. (Check out the sidebar, "My favorite Automated Process," elsewhere in this chapter, for a good example of such a process.)

A good starting point when you're designing an Automated Process (AP for short) for GoldMine is to examine all those processes you already have in place. You want to have the computer, as opposed to people, performing as many of the grunt-work steps as you can. This step is often the place where a good, experienced consultant can help you take a fresh look at procedures and policies.

Next, you should examine all the potential areas of your business where no processes exist, but where they could be implemented and could be beneficial.

Keep in mind that just because you have a process in place doesn't mean you should just blindly stick it into GoldMine. Although implementing just one good AP can have a huge positive effect on your bottom line, implementing a not-so-well-thought-out process may not have the positive effect you hoped for. In fact, automating a poor procedure, or implementing a good procedure poorly, will only cause your new system to screw you up faster and more efficiently than you could ever imagine. This is a great time to reexamine all your business processes and do some reengineering.

My favorite Automated Process

FrontRange suggests implementing several key types of Automated Processes: performing administrative tasks, managing leads, following up on contacts, sending warranty renewal reminders, automating direct-mail campaigns, and validating data. You can design and implement an Automated Process to help you accomplish any task that you want done automatically.

When I first began my computer consulting business, I occasionally exhibited at trade shows, which were expensive and a lot of work. I wanted to take advantage of any leads I got at these shows. After several days of standing in our booth, I went back to my office with a stack of business cards. These cards were like manna from heaven — hot leads that I just couldn't let go to waste.

After being out of the office for a few days, I returned to a handful of crises that demanded my immediate attention. Before I knew it, my stack of hot leads was in my desk drawer, forgotten. I did this for three straight trade shows, and I just couldn't understand why trade-show results were so poor!

So my company turned over a new leaf and implemented an Automated Process for trade shows that never fails us. At the end of the first day of a trade show, as the other vendors head for the bar, we grab our computer and head for my hotel room. All day long we collected leads and put them directly into GoldMine. We make sure our AP has started and we then head for

the bar ourselves: Step One of the Trade Show Automated Process has begun. The computer e-mails and faxes each new lead, sending a letter that basically says, "Thanks for stopping by our trade-show booth today. We were just overwhelmed by all the interest and activity today, but nonetheless, your account would be very important to us. When we get back to our office on Monday, we will send out the literature you requested. If you can't wait until then, call Jane at our office. . . ."

We repeat this process after each day of the trade show. When we get back to the office, Step Two begins. A notice is sent, directing the appropriate person to mail the requested literature. GoldMine assigns an account manager to the account based on geography and also generates a cover letter. After all these processes are done, GoldMine schedules the account manager to make a follow-up call in one week. The process checks to see whether the prospect has called us already, which prevents us from appearing out of control.

The response to this Automated Process is amazing. Literally 35 percent of the people we contact each night call us the next day, stunned that we responded so quickly. The early bird catches the worm: While our competitors celebrate down in the bar, we do our follow-up marketing to make sure that *they* have as little to celebrate later as possible. And it works!

I classify processes into three categories that represent all the major life stages of an account:

- ✔ **Hunting:** This stage is the entire sales cycle from suspect to prospect to a closed deal. Many steps exist that most companies routinely follow, or should, to move an account from suspect status to becoming a client.

- ✔ **Farming:** After prospects become clients, they should get just as much, if not more, attention as they got before. A well-known fact is that it's more cost-effective to get additional business from an existing account than it is to find a new account to replace one you've lost or failed to penetrate.

- ✔ **Resurrecting:** Sometimes accounts are lost; it happens to everyone. Sometimes it happens for reasons beyond your control, or sometimes due to neglect. Just because a client has left the fold doesn't mean you should give up. Implementing some Automated Processes to stay in touch with former clients often reaps some surprising and positive results.

Developing Tracks

One of the confusing aspects of Automated Processes is the terminology, which is probably all new to you. One of the key terms to understand is *track.* GoldMine uses this term interchangeably with *process.* Tracks consist of one or more *events,* which are step-by-step instructions that GoldMine evaluates to perform a series of activities. Each event is composed of a trigger and an action. A *trigger,* such as a warranty period about to expire, causes a specific *action,* such as sending a letter about your extended warranty plan.

Setting process options

To set up a new Automated Process or to view existing Automated Processes, choose Tools⇨Automated Processes⇨Manage Processes from the main menu. The Automated Processes Center window, shown in Figure 27-1, displays a summary of what has already been developed. The window lists all your processes, each one's options as well as the associated events. You can develop a new Automated Process by using the AP Wizard, which guides you through setting up your Automated Process as follows:

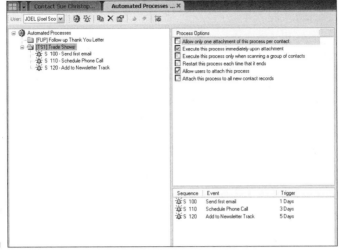

Figure 27-1:
The
Automated
Processes
Center with
a simple
Trade Show
process.

1. **To start the Automated Process Wizard, choose Tools⇨Automated Processes⇨Manage Processes and then click the New Automated Processes icon (it looks like a yellow gear).**

   The Automated Process Wizard appears, as shown in Figure 27-2. The first two fields in the AP Wizard enable you to name the process and to give it a code number. The name of each process should indicate the function or purpose of that track. Tracks are arranged alphabetically by the process code you enter and are displayed this way in various AP dialog boxes. If a process has no code (another possibility), it will be listed first.

Figure 27-2:
The
Automated
Process
Wizard.

2. **Give your process a name and a code (and possibly assign ownership of this process to someone else) and click Next.**

   On the second page of the AP Wizard, shown in Figure 27-3, the following options appear:

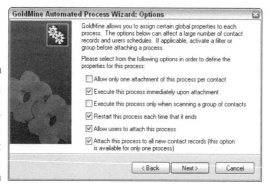

Figure 27-3:
Attaching
your
process to
contact
records.

- **Allow Only One Attachment of This Process per Contact:**
  Prevents the track from being attached more than once to a particular record. For example, you would use this option for a process
  that sends a thank-you letter to a first-time customer.

- **Execute This Process Immediately upon Attachment:** Starts processing the track as soon as a user attaches it to one or more
  records.

- **Execute This process Only when Scanning for Processes:**
  Prevents a track from being executed even if you select the preceding choice.

- **Restart This Process Each Time that It Ends:** Reattaches the track
  as soon as processing for the track is done.

- **Allow Users to Attach This Process:** Allows manual attachment of
  the track by the system users. You would use manual attachment
  for a process that is not run for every account.

- **Attach This Process to All New Contact Records:** Causes
  GoldMine to automatically attach the track to each new contact
  record, which could be useful in conjunction with use of a monitor
  track (see the sidebar, "The monitor track: An elegant approach,"
  later in this chapter).

3. **Select the options you want and then click Next.**

   The next step in the AP Wizard, the Events page, appears. If you are creating a new Automated Process, this page is empty, as shown in Figure 27-4.
   Events are the actual activities the AP is causing. For example, an Event
   might be a scheduled phone call or an appointment, or an Event might be
   a letter that is automatically sent. The Events page enables you to specify
   these activities.

It is critical that a process that performs a particular task, such as sending out an e-mail after a trade show, have a setting that does not allow that action to happen again. I know someone who created his own AP and sent out 1,000-plus e-mails to clients in his database. The next day, he cranked up his APs again and resent the e-mail to all the same clients — all because he didn't have anything in his process to see whether it had been previously sent. The first process option shown in the upper-right pane of Figure 27-1 is what regulates this.

Figure 27-4:
The AP
Wizard's
Events
page.

4. **Click the New button if you are creating a new Automated Process.**

The Event Properties dialog box appears, as shown in Figure 27-5. The "Programming event properties" section, later in this chapter, describes the options in the Event Properties dialog box.

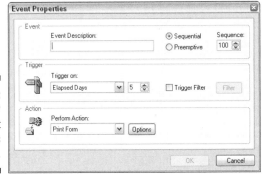

Figure 27-5:
The AP
Event
Properties
dialog box.

5. **Set the options you want for your Automated Process and click OK.**

6. **Click the Finish button.**

The AP Wizard brings you back to the Automated Processes Center window, similar to that shown in Figure 27-1, except that your new AP is listed.

Programming event properties

The Event Properties dialog box (refer to Figure 27-5) contains important options for setting up your Automated Processes. The dialog box's options are divided into three groups: Event, Trigger, and Action. The following sections describe the options in each group.

Preemptive events

Two kinds of events exist in GoldMine: preemptive and sequential. Every track can have many of each kind of event, but each track must have at least one sequential event. Every event is given a numerical sequence from 0 to 999.

Preemptive events are conditional statements, or more simply, they are *IF* statements. For example, *IF* you want to send a notice to all customers that have not purchased anything in the last three months, you can put in a preemptive statement that says, "If a sale occurred in the last three months in their History, then remove this track from the record."

You can number preemptive events only from 0 to 99 and, therefore, they are always at the beginning of the track. When you initially number your events, do not use consecutive numbers; allow some space to interject another event later. As a guideline, number your preemptive events 5, 10, 15, and so on.

Usually when you program preemptive events, you're trying to eliminate records from contention. Thus, try to create the logic within your preemptive statement to eliminate the record, rather than to confirm that this process is appropriate for this record.

Sequential events

Sequential events are always numbered from 100 to 999, and you must always have at least one sequential event in each track. Because the sequential events actually perform actions, if you didn't have at least one, the track would never do anything.

Just as with preemptive events, you should allow some room for growth, and make sure to number them in increments of 5 or 10. Sequential events are programmed into the system with the same procedure you use for preemptives. The only difference is that in the Event Properties dialog box, you select the Sequential radio button rather than the Preemptive radio button.

Choosing a trigger

A *trigger* is the condition within the contact record's data that determines what action should be taken. For example, this might be an amount of time that passed since the last time this client was visited, or perhaps a scheduled activity that requires a notice being sent to a manager.

In the Event Properties dialog box, the Trigger On drop-down list enables you to choose from the following seven options to trigger an activity:

- ✓ **Elapsed Days:** This trigger activates as soon as the number of days you enter has gone by since the last event was processed; or if this is the first event in your AP, since the track was attached to this account.

- ✓ **Immediate:** This trigger sets GoldMine to immediately execute the action associated with the event.

- ✓ **Detail Record:** This trigger looks for the addition of a specific Detail, Document Link, Referral, or Other Contact. Don't be confused by the name Detail Record. This Detail Record can trigger on almost any kind of new supplemental information.

- ✓ **History Activity:** This trigger looks for the existence of a specific type of history record in order to activate — for example, the completion of a sales call with a result code of INT, indicating that it's an initial sales call.

- ✓ **Scheduled Activity:** This trigger looks for a specific type of calendar activity. For example, it may look for a scheduled training class before reserving a projector.

- ✓ **dBASE Condition:** This one is triggered by a dBASE expression you build using the GoldMine expression builder.

- ✓ **Disabled:** This option turns off the trigger for this event. Without a trigger, the event will never happen. This can be used to document, to debug, or simply to space things for easier reading.

The monitor track: An elegant approach

If you're likely to have more than one Automated Process (and you should assume that you will), using a monitor track is a clever way to implement your system. The *monitor track* (also referred to by some consultants as an *observer track* or a *watchdog track*) is the only track that records are ever attached to. In fact, the monitor track should automatically be attached to every record. Then you won't ever have to worry about attaching records to tracks at all.

The monitor track is like the traffic cop for the whole Automated Process system: It watches out for all the possible conditions within a record and directs each record to the appropriate track or tracks. Because one track (the monitor track) can call another track (for example, the trade-show track), using the monitor track is an elegant programming approach to developing a very sophisticated series of processes.

Actions speak louder than words

The Perform Action drop-down list in the Event Properties dialog box (refer to Figure 27-5) supplies you with many options to choose from. These options are actions that will be performed when the trigger event you choose from the Trigger On drop-down list occurs, as discussed in the previous section. The actions you may choose from are as follows:

- **Print Form:** Prints or faxes a merge form when the event is triggered.

- **E-mail Message:** Generates and sends an Internet-based e-mail template when the event is triggered.

- **Print Report:** Prints a report when the event is triggered. Some reports, like the Address and Phone Report, print the entire database every time. Make sure not to have your AP print this report, or similar ones, for every record it scans.

- **Schedule Activity:** Schedules a calendar activity for a selected user when the event is triggered.

- **Create History:** Adds a history record to the contact record when the event is triggered.

- **Create Detail:** Adds a detail record to the contact record when the event is triggered.

- **Add to Group:** Adds the contact to a specified group when the event is triggered.

- **Update Field:** Updates one of the fields in the contact record with the result of a dBASE expression when the event is triggered.

- **Remove Track:** Removes the track from the contact record when the event is triggered, thus ensuring that no further actions will be taken for this account.

- **Add a New Track:** Attaches a new track to the contact record when the event is triggered. See the sidebar, "The monitor track: An elegant approach," in this chapter for some thoughts on when to use this approach.

- **Branch to Event:** Directs GoldMine to proceed to a specified event, and uses the code numbers of the events as a reference.

- **Run Application:** Starts an external application (for example, a Visual Basic program) when the event is triggered.

Executing a Process

Remember that processes, however well designed, will not work unless they are attached to records and then told to run. I discuss attaching records in the "Setting process options" section, earlier in this chapter. To run a process, follow these steps:

1. **From the main menu, choose Tools⇨Automated Processes⇨Execute Process.**

   The Automated Processes Execution dialog box, shown in Figure 27-6, appears.

Figure 27-6: Choose which processes to execute.

2. **Attach one or more records to a track by selecting the Attach Track to Selected Contacts option and choosing from the drop-down list.**

3. **Click the Process button.**

   This causes the Process Monitor window, shown in Figure 27-7, to immediately appear.

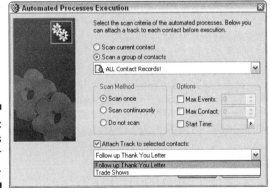

Figure 27-7: The Process Monitor window.

The upper pane of the Process Monitor window displays the elapsed time, the record currently being processed, the total number of records scanned, the number of events that have been triggered, and the title of the track currently being processed.

From the Process Monitor window, you can

- ✔ **Stop all processes** to stop all processing for all contacts.

- ✔ **Stop selected processes** to stop the current track for the current record from processing.

- ✔ **Copy logs to Windows Clipboard** to copy the log entries in the lower pane of the display to Windows Clipboard. From there, you can paste the information into your word processor or into a spreadsheet for further reporting.

Automated Processes are the most powerful features in GoldMine. Any contact management system can keep track of names, addresses, and appointments. But these Automated Processes, when properly implemented, are like a Marketing department in a box. Putting this together properly will easily pay for the whole installation of GoldMine, so don't neglect it.

The most important suggestion I can make with regard to Automated Processes is that you should seriously consider enlisting the aid of an experienced GoldMine consultant. This advice applies to the overall design of your processes as well as to the implementation of at least the first few processes. The second most important suggestion is to really focus on creating these processes because this is how GoldMine pays you back for your investment in it.

Chapter 28

GM+View and GM+Browser

*F*irst, I need to talk about terminology. Older versions of GoldMine had a display tab called GM+View. This was used to display various kinds of data that lived outside GoldMine. If you were clever, you could even have multiple GM+View displays. Now, with GoldMine 8 you can use GM+Browser to display and scroll through multiple GM+View screens.

Every record in GoldMine 8 contains an HTML-based GM+View tab, which stores customized Web pages. These pages, or views, can include rich content, such as text and graphics. The GM+View tab is particularly useful when you have a variety of graphics associated with your accounts. For example, a recruiter or a talent agency could use the GM+View tab to store a photo of each client with that client's record. A real estate agency may use it to store a photo or a series of photos of each property it has listed. Going a step further, for particularly high-valued properties, a real estate agency might want to store an entire walk-through video tour with sound on the GM+View tab.

Basically, you can think of the GM+View tab as a customized Web page for each account in GoldMine. Any type of information you have ever seen on a Web site can probably be housed in the GM+View tab.

A key to making good use of this tab is to understand how flexible it is. You can have many different views set up, and the view shown for any particular account is controlled by rules that you set up. The data in a particular field can also determine what view is displayed, or you can use a dBASE expression if a single field is not sufficient to control the view. Finally, you can leave it up to the user to determine the view when he or she activates a record and wants to see what's on the GM+View tab. If you're really technically inclined, you can add some HTML code to your GM+View and further automate the display.

In this chapter, you find out how to access information in the GM+View tab and how to set up some simple views.

Displaying the GM+View Tab

Every GoldMine record has its own GM+View tab. By simply clicking that tab, you see what information is associated with that particular record. Figure 28-1 shows a sample of a GM+View tab with two pictures associated with the active GoldMine record. A real estate agent might find a display like this to be helpful.

Each GM+View tab can have one or more links to Web sites. The links in the GM+View tab are like hyperlinks on a Web page; just click the link to go to that Web site. For example, you might have a link to a mapping system, such as MapQuest, that displays the exact location of the active account, or perhaps gives you the driving instructions. You need to click that link to display the map or instructions.

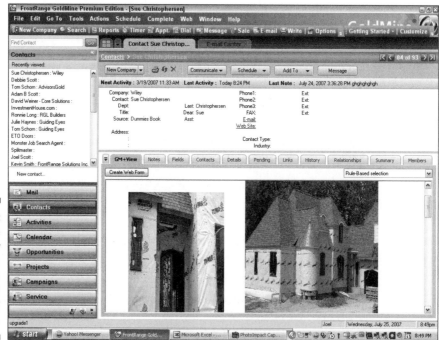

Figure 28-1: A sample GM+View with a photograph associated with the record.

Creating GM+View Templates

Only users with Master rights can design or even edit GM+View templates. The template contains all the instructions needed to actually display a series of graphics or links. To create a GM+View template, follow these steps:

1. **From the main menu, choose Web⇨SetupGM+View.**

   The GM+View Tab Settings dialog box appears, as shown in Figure 28-2. All the existing templates appear in the upper-left box. You specify the default template by selecting it from the drop-down list on the upper-right part of the dialog box. The default template shows up automatically for every record in the database, unless some rule you have set countermands that. In the lower panel, you can see a preview of each template to get a feel for what it will actually look like.

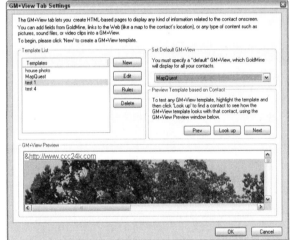

Figure 28-2:
Create a
template for
GM+View
in the
GM+View
Tab Settings
dialog box.

2. **Click the New button to display the Edit GM+View window, shown in Figure 28-3.**

   Enter a descriptive name for your new template.

3. **Position your cursor wherever you want text or a graphic to be displayed and right-click.**

   Your choices for adding text, graphics, or links are shown in Figure 28-3. Right-clicking anywhere in the initially blank area accesses this shortcut menu.

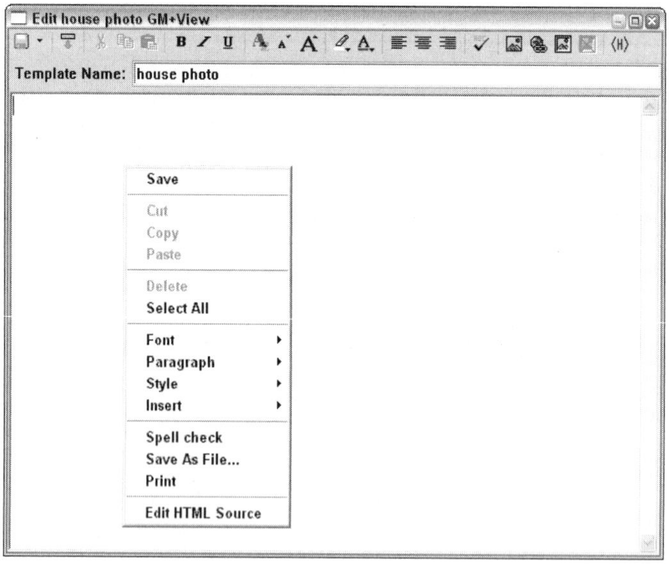

Figure 28-3:
Adding
features
to your
template.

After you have properly positioned your cursor, you can place fields or text files anywhere on the window. By right-clicking and selecting Insert, you get three additional choices, as shown in Figure 28-4.

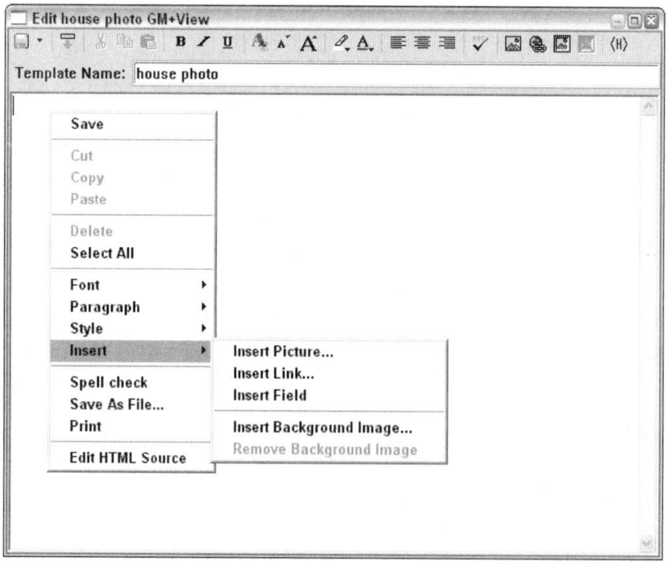

Figure 28-4:
Inserting a
picture, link,
or field.

Inserting fields and text files

When you right-click and choose Insert⇨Insert Field, you get yet another menu, as shown in Figure 28-5. The Contact Details menu choice gives you most of the critical fields from the upper portion of the main GoldMine screen. These fields are usually on display right in front of you anyway, so I'm not sure why it would be necessary to repeat them in this view. However, if you select the Include a Text File choice, you can have an associated file readily displayed in addition to the standard GoldMine fields.

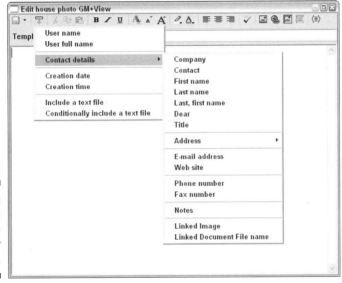

Figure 28-5: Inserting fields in the GM+View template.

Inserting links

Links, I believe, are more useful to have in the GM+View tab. By inserting a link, you can associate a GoldMine record with one or more Web pages. For example, you can include a link to a map with or without driving instructions. You could have a link to a weather site showing the weather forecast for this location. Perhaps more significantly, you could have a link to a news service or credit bureau Web site showing the latest news about each of your accounts.

Following the instructions within GoldMine itself, you end up with a link in the GM+View tab that you still have to click in order to access the Web page. If you're good with HTML code, or know someone who is, you can automate this so the requested Web appears without any further clicking on your part. Figure 28-6 shows an example of the code that automatically displays MapQuest info for each contact record in GoldMine.

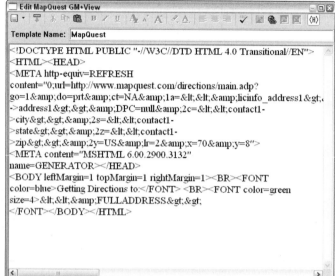

Figure 28-6:
HTML
code for
automating
a display –
in this case
MapQuest
info.

Inserting pictures

Inserting graphics is a third and powerful choice. This seems to be an obvious one for real estate agencies, talent agencies, and recruiters. But the possibilities for using photographs, or even WAV (sound) files are endless. You may want to have photos of equipment that each account has on its shop floor, for example. Insurance companies might want photos of damaged cars and buildings to assist in claim evaluation.

You can insert one or more graphic files into a template and then manipulate its positioning and alignment by following these steps:

1. **From the main menu, choose Web⇨GM+View Tab; click the Edit button on the GM+View Tab Settings dialog box.**

2. **In the Edit GM+View window (refer to Figure 28-3), click the Insert Picture icon on the local toolbar.**

   The Picture dialog box appears, as shown in Figure 28-7.

3. **Click the Browse button and locate the picture you want to insert.**

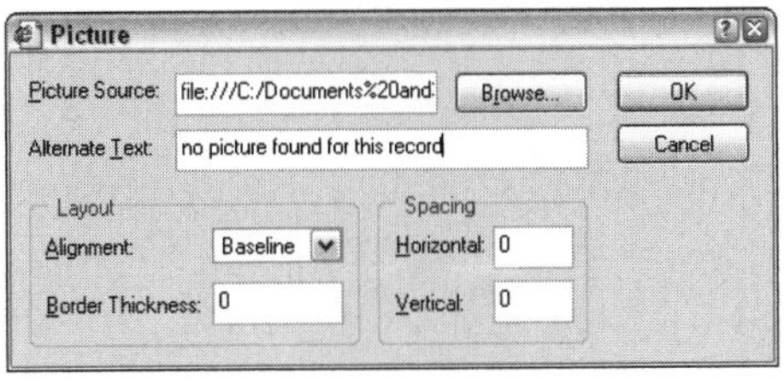

Figure 28-7:
Inserting
a picture
in the
GM+View
tab.

4. **In the Alternate Text field, type what text you want shown if the picture can't be displayed.**

   The alternate text selection allows you to specify some standard text in the event that your primary source is unavailable. This could happen, for example, if you are disconnected from either a disk drive housing the graphic or if you are disconnected from the Internet.

5. **Set the alignment of your picture, the border thickness, and spacing; click OK when you're done.**

   The layout and spacing sections of the dialog box allow you to position your pictures relative to the borders of the tab view and in relation to other pictures and text you may be displaying.

Selecting Your Template

Regulating who sees various templates requires Master rights. The starting point for template selection is the GM+View Tab Setting dialog box (refer to Figure 28-2). You can set up any template as the default template by selecting that template in the drop-down list in the upper-right part of the dialog box. Then, unless overridden by some other instruction, every user will see the default template associated with every record.

If you want to be cleverer, you can set up rules that govern the display of various templates. These rules can be based on the following:

- The value in one particular field
- A dBASE expression that might be a function of several fields
- User selection

The following steps show you how to set up these rules:

1. **From the main menu, choose Web⇨GM+View Tab.**

   The GM+View Tab Settings dialog box appears (refer to Figure 28-2).

2. **Click the Rules button.**

   GoldMine displays the dialog box shown in Figure 28-8.

Figure 28-8:
Using a field
to determine
a GM+View
template.

3. **Select an option to determine the template selection condition.**

   You can choose to have the template selected based on the field value, a dBASE expression, or to allow users to select the template themselves.

   For example, you might select the Field Value option and choose Account Mgr for the field name. Then, by clicking the New button, you are led through a series of selections.

   In this example, you are shown a listing of all the Account Managers in your company. Select one. By doing this, you can now have separate templates for each Account Manager. Moe and Larry will each see potentially different aspects of each account's business. Perhaps Curly sees nothing.

4. **Click OK when you're done setting up your rules.**

Changing the rules so that different GoldMine users see different GM+Views might be relevant in the financial services arena, where investment bankers and stock brokers are not allowed to see any aspect of each others' business.

If you don't need to be so restrictive, you can have multiple templates and allow each user to decide which template he or she needs to see at any time. In the GM+View Tab Rules for Template Selection dialog box (refer to Figure 28-8), if you select the User Selected option, all templates become available to each user. When Moe brings up a particular GoldMine record, he can right-click in the GM+View Tab area and select from the entire list of templates. This is a great way to organize a large amount of graphic data that might be too confusing to display all in one window.

Using GM+Browser

Don't feel alone if you're confused by the terminology of GM+View and GM+Browser. The GM+Browser is just a way to automatically scroll through all the different GM+View tabs you may have. In addition, by default, GM+Browser displays your default Internet Explorer page as its first tab.

1. **From the main menu, choose Web⇨GM+Browser.**

   The GM+Browser Settings dialog box appears (see Figure 28-9).

2. **Click the GM+Browser Setup button, as shown in Figure 28-9.**

   The screen shown in Figure 28-10 immediately appears. By highlighting any available GM+Views (in the left panel) and clicking the >> box, you tell the GM+Browser to display that particular GM+View.

Figure 28-9:
The GM+
Browser
screen,
showing
my default
View, which
is www.
msn.com.

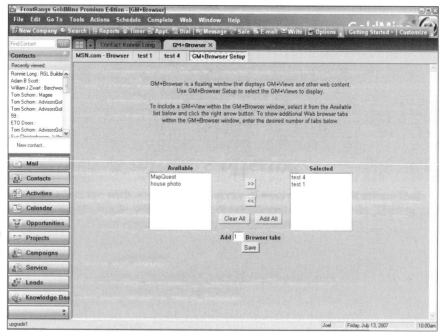

Figure 28-10:
Specifying
which views
the browser
will display.

3. Save your selected GM+Views by clicking the Save button.

GoldMine returns you to the GM+Browser display, similar to that shown in Figure 28-9, but with the additional views you've just requested. Each view is shown as a tab at the top of the display.

With the assistance of a good GoldMine professional, you can display not only Web pages within GM+Browser but also data from other applications. Good examples might be to show accounting transactions, or inventory items with, or without photos.

Chapter 29

Integrating GoldMine with Your Web Site

I make the assumption that you already have a Web site and that you have the ability to make some changes to it. That being said, you have an opportunity to truly automate the collection of leads and your responses to those prospective customers.

GoldMine's Web Import utility helps you create the pages on your Web site that collect information (those are your Web forms) as well as the behind-the-scenes scripts that grab the information from each Web form and put it all into GoldMine.

Getting the contact information into GoldMine cannot be the end of the process. After the data is in GoldMine, you need a plan to respond. And, responding quickly is a key ingredient. That's where some well-designed Automated Processes come into play.

In this chapter, I show you how to set up a simple data entry form, gather that data and put it into GoldMine, and then hand it off to an Automated Process.

Preparing to Link GoldMine and Your Web Site

One of the basic ideas behind a successful Web Import implementation is that prospects and customers have to be drawn to your Web site and motivated to provide real contact information to you.

In the past — before Web Import existed — we attracted people to our company Web site because we had brilliantly written and insightful articles that we knew everyone would want. And we gave them away for free, believing that every reader would realize that the best source for good consulting was the group that had written all those good articles. Well, I have to tell you, that idea never worked very well. I now know why: It's just in the nature of people who like to download free stuff, and I won't say any more.

We made a major improvement in our lead generation and in our sales pipeline when we stopped literally giving away free stuff for free. Instead, now the price for free stuff is providing a set of valid contact information. When designing your Web forms, focus on just those pieces of information that you really, really need in order to follow up. The more you ask for, the less likely you are to get anything meaningful. At the very least, though, get a name, a phone number, and an e-mail address.

GoldMine's Web Import is the ideal tool for making sure that you actually get that valid contact information before providing information. One of the keys to ensuring that people give you their real contact information is to let them know that your system automatically sends the documents, files, or other information to the e-mail address they provide. Therefore, if they give you something like joe.blow→bc.com, they just won't get anything in return. They other important key is to continually provide useful information from your Web site. If the information is perceived as useful, people will come (assuming that you market your Web site). Continually updating your offerings keeps a steady flow of repeat visitors.

The bottom line is to avoid allowing visitors to simply download your valuable information without giving you something in return — that being their valuable information. And with that, GoldMine can begin an automated, proactive marketing campaign! In the rest of this chapter, I discuss how to get that information from a Web form into GoldMine.

Designing Scripts

GoldMine leads you through the creation of the script that is quietly behind each of your Web forms. To begin this process, choose Web from the main menu and then choose Setup Web Import. This brings you to the first screen for building your script, as shown in Figure 29-1.

GoldMine now requires a password for your Web import, and it must match the password contained within the Web form script. In the Web Import Profiles area of the screen in Figure 29-1, you enter a unique name for your script. The whole point of developing each of your scripts is to have the input entered on the Web form either create or update records in GoldMine.

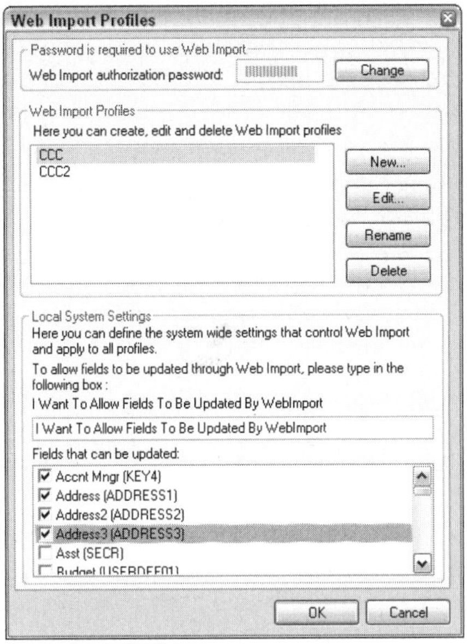

Figure 29-1:
Beginning
the design
of a script.

After you enter a name for your Web Import profile, click the Edit button. This brings you to the input form shown in Figure 29-2.

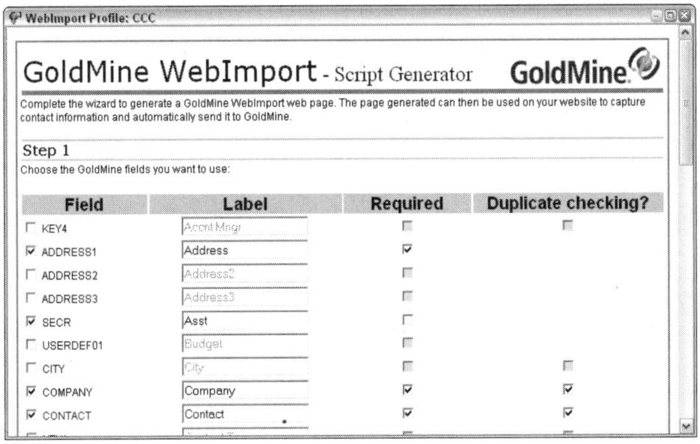

Figure 29-2:
Step 1
allows you
to specify
the fields
that will be
displayed on
the Web
form.

The fields displayed in Figure 29-2 are not only the standard fields that come with GoldMine but also any custom fields that have been added. In addition to specifying which fields are to be displayed on the Web form, you can also specify which fields are used for duplicate record checking. When the GoldMine script finds a potential duplicate record (this visitor to your Web site already has a record in GoldMine), it opts to update the existing record rather than create a duplicate. When you are done selecting fields, click the Next button at the bottom right of the screen. GoldMine moves on to Step 2, which is shown in Figure 29-3.

Figure 29-3: The upper portion of the screen in Step 2 specifies what you want your script to do.

The first three fields shown in Figure 29-3 are all required fields. With regard to the scripting language you are using, in general if you have a Windows server, you use some flavor of ASP, and if you have a Linux/Unix server, you use PHP. For the Web format language (the last field in the Step 2 form, which is not shown in Figure 29-3), you probably want to use XML, which is a more current and general language than the older GoldMine INI format. When finished with Step 2, click Next at the bottom of the screen. GoldMine brings you to Step 3, which is shown in Figure 29-4.

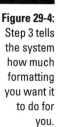

Figure 29-4: Step 3 tells the system how much formatting you want it to do for you.

Unless you have an extremely simplistic Web site, and Web forms in particular, you likely want to have GoldMine just provide the raw HTML code for the labels and fields on your form. With this raw code, you or your Web designer can then format the Web form to fit in with the design of the other pages of your Web site. Once again, clicking Next takes you to the next and final screen of this procedure. Step 4 is shown in Figure 29-5.

You can preview your new form from Step 4 and send the source code to an e-mail address of your choice.

When you Save and Exit, GoldMine returns you to the screen in Figure 29-1 where you will now confirm to GoldMine that this is what you actually want. You confirm this by entering **I Want To Allow Fields To Be Updated By WebImport**. You need to type it *exactly* as shown.

Designing Forms

In Step 3 of the preceding section, you can select something other than raw HTML. For example, you can select Centered, as shown in Figure 29-6. You can certainly experiment with the choices in Step 3. If any one of them looks good to you, you can go with that and avoid additional form design work. One suggestion is to be consistent throughout your Web site and not switch from one form design to another.

Figure 29-6:
Step 3
again. You
can actually
use one of
GoldMine's
form
designs as
long as you
consistently
pick the
same
format.

In all likelihood, though, you will want to make use of Web design software, such as Dreamweaver, to enhance the rudimentary forms created by GoldMine's Web Import utility.

Part VIII
The Part of Tens

The 5th Wave

By Rich Tennant

"This part of the test tells us whether you're personally suited to the job of network administrator."

In this part . . .

*B*ack in the day, hundreds of add-on products existed that worked, or sometimes didn't work, with GoldMine. Time and policies and survival of the fittest have whittled the numbers down. The add-ons that remain are almost all very good. In this part, you read about my ten most favorite.

It was a struggle to come up with the ten "most important" new features, but at least a few noteworthy features exist in that category. In this part, you read about all of the new tools and tricks.

Chapter 30

Ten Useful Add-Ons

*O*ver the past fifteen years, many organizations have developed add-ons to GoldMine. In the mid-1990s, a very active and enthusiastic third-party development group existed. That group and the number of products have both dwindled, but a significant core of products that bears scrutiny is still around.

This chapter cites ten of the best and most significant add-ons. I have used them all, and they work. I have used others that work also, but I had to select just ten to describe here. Of course, I have also used some that didn't work too well. I can recommend all the ones in this chapter.

Not making it into this chapter is not necessarily an indication that the software isn't good. I provide Web site information for each product. In some cases, you can purchase directly from the manufacturer, if you want. In most cases, you can also purchase (at a Dummies discount) from www.ccc24k.com.

Remote Access

One of the most frequent demands of users is to be able to access their data when away from the main office. This applies to workers who travel occasionally as well as to home-based workers. Built into GoldMine 8 is the old GoldSync methodology, so it's hard to call this an add-on, although it is an option for remote access.

Opinions vary about the pros and cons of synchronizing versus having online access. More and more, the consensus is becoming that synchronizing is too often fraught with technological challenges (it's too hard, too slow, and doesn't always work quite right) and limiting users to just Internet access is a better way to protect critical organizational data.

iGoldMine Plus

iGoldMinePlus (the successor to iGoldMine) is a product that FrontRange has licensed from GraphOn Corporation. It works with GoldMine Corporate and with GoldMine Premium, but *not* with GoldMine Standard. That restriction arises from FrontRange's desire to differentiate Corporate and Premium from the Standard Version. Please note: FrontRange has now completely discontinued sales (and soon support) of Standard. In addition, FrontRange says that you can use iGoldMinePlus to access up to 35 separate applications — including GoldMine and one of FrontRange's other products, HEAT. Unfortunately, if you try to use iGoldMine to access *both* GoldMine and HEAT, you quickly discover that you need to purchase separate iGoldMine licenses. Again, just more unfriendly and, in my opinion, inappropriate restrictions iplaced on the licensing.

If you want to use a FrontRange-certified product to access software on your server, iGoldMinePlus is certainly a choice. But if you want the insider's view, just move on to the next section.

For more information, go to `www.frontrange.com`.

GoGlobal

GraphOn Corporation created GoGlobal and has licensed this technology to FrontRange. It has basically the same capabilities that iGoldMinePlus has, without any of the licensing restrictions. After it is set up on your computer, it allows you to access the applications on your server. It has enough security for most organizations, and when you're connected, you're using the software almost exactly as you would if you were sitting in the main office.

For more information, go to `www.graphon.com`.

Remote Desktop

Remote Desktop is a Microsoft product. It is actually the successor to Terminal Services. In many cases, you already have Remote Desktop licenses and need only to deploy this utility to enjoy remote access.

For more information, go to www.microsoft.com.

Using Handheld Devices

Two basic methodologies exist for using your Blackberry or Treo or other handheld device with GoldMine. One methodology actually loads your data on your handheld; the other allows you to view and edit the data over the Internet, but does not actually store data on your device.

Each method has its pros and cons. Having critical client data on peoples' handhelds is a potential security issue. But please note that it's even easier to lose a phone than to lose a laptop.

CompanionLink

CompanionLink is a tried and tested product. It allows you to synchronize your GoldMine data with your handheld. Of course, this puts your data directly on the handheld. This is sometimes more convenient than systems that have you access the data via the Internet.

For more information, go to www.companionlink.com.

wMobile

wMobile takes a different approach to connecting your handheld to GoldMine. With its method, no data is stored on your handheld. You can view and edit data by dialing in via the Internet. Of course, no Internet, no data, but just about the only places you can't get to the Internet are on airplanes and, maybe, on subways. Soon, major airlines plan on supplying Internet connectivity while in flight.

Although wMobile costs more than CompanionLink, it is my own personal preference because it eliminates the need to synchronize and greatly reduces the security issues involved in having people running around with critical data.

For more information, go to www.w-systems.com.

General Utilities

Two major and well-recognized packages provide additional tools for manipulating the data that goes into, comes out of, and sits in GoldMine. They have both been around for years and they are both good.

GoldBox-7

GoldBox originated as a tool to import data into GoldMine. It has since grown into the Swiss Army knife of utilities. Although it provides many data manipulation tools, it also allows for recurring imports and linking to outside tables. Its prior weaknesses, documentation, and user interface have all been improved somewhat in the past few years.

It is very important that you read and observe all the caveats on the Web site cited here. Be sure before you purchase. *Caveat emptor.* There is a free demo that you can test.

For more information, go to www.redstonesoftbase.com.

Inaport

This product is a little more flexible than GoldBox, particularly in terms of integrating with outside sources of incoming data. Also, Inaport can be very valuable as a migration tool when switching from one CRM package to another.

For more information, go to www.inaplex.com.

QuoteWerks

GoldMine doesn't do quotes, which is one of the most common requests for additional functionality. QuoteWerks tightly integrates with the GoldMine Standard, Corporate, and Premium editions. That integration automatically transfers fields from GoldMine directly into quotation forms. When the quote is being prepared, using a database of products and services that QuoteWerks maintains, QuoteWerks creates a sales forecast record directly in GoldMine.

QuoteWerks is the system that I have used for many years in conjunction with GoldMine, and it has stood the test of time.

For more information, go to www.quotewerks.com.

BounceLinker

If you use GoldMine for mass e-mail marketing, you need to consider BounceLinker. BounceLinker automates the entire process of handling e-mails that can't be delivered, as well as removal requests. For example, if you do an initial e-mail blast from GoldMine to 10,000 prospects, in all likelihood at least 2,000 will not reach the recipient and possibly another 1,000 might request removal from your mailing list.

If you have BounceLinker, those 3,000 necessary transactions will be done automatically. It's money well spent if you do any significant amount of marketing with your GoldMine database.

For more information, go to www.ck-soft.com.

KnowledgeSync and TaskCentre

If you are in need of a tool to develop really powerful alarms and alerts or automation beyond what GoldMine's Automated Processes can produce, either KnowledgeSync or a newer product called TaskCentre is a good bet. With these products I get daily alerts about activities that have not been completed, contracts that are on the verge of expiring and a host of other events that might otherwise fall through the cracks. TaskCentre is a bit more graphically oriented than is KnowledgeSync, but both are excellent management tools. For more information, go to www.vineyardsoft.com (for KnowledgeSync) or www.orbis-software.com (for TaskCentre).

Honorable Mentions

- ✔ **OmniRush:** From Z-Firm (www.zfirmllc.com). For faxing, e-mailing, and printing solutions.

- ✔ **MasterMine:** From MasterMine (www.mastermine.net). For reporting and analysis.

- ✔ **Contract Time Manager:** From CCC (www.ccc24k.com). For managing billable time and contracts.

Chapter 31

The Ten Most Important New Developments Since 6.0

*T*he Premium Edition contains the first truly significant upgrades to GoldMine since version 6 came out five years ago. Not only are they significant, but these enhancements are truly positive, showing off FrontRange's renewed commitment and resources.

New User Interface

If you ever used GoldMine before Premium Edition, you can't help notice the new interface. No more four quadrants, although the same old fields are basically in the same old places. Now there's a little more flexibility when designing custom fields in this part of the screen. Oh, and, this "part of the screen," which used to just be called the "main screen" or the "four quadrants," is now called the "work area."

Navigation from one function to another is greatly streamlined by using the new Navigation Pane on the left side of the screen. In fact, the new user interface greatly facilitates navigation in almost every case. Just as an example, GoldMine now keeps track of where you've been so that you can easily backtrack.

Plus, it all looks much more modern.

Customer Support Module

The original GoldMine focused on coordinating a team of sales people. Starting with GoldMine 6, additional attention was paid to marketing. Although GoldMine was advertised as a complete CRM system, it was lacking the kind of service contract management or customer support module that many of the competing products already contained. Organizations using GoldMine but needing service management needed to buy FrontRange's HEAT product (which was, compared to GoldMine, quite expensive) or some third-party add-on such as Resource Dynamic's Tele-Support HelpDesk.

Now, finally, with the Premium Edition, GoldMine has its own answer, built right into the system with a Knowledge Base to boot. The Service Module keeps track of customer complaints or issues or questions that need to be addressed. RMAs can also be handled here. The Service Module does not really handle contract or billable time. Computer Control's Billable Time Manager fills that void nicely. Refer to Chapter 30 for more information on many good add-ons.

Tabbed View

In previous versions of GoldMine, as you moved from one topic to another, such as from a Contact Record to the E-mail Center, GoldMine would close the Contact Record and open the E-mail Center. That entire navigation system has been changed with the introduction of Tabbed Views.

The Premium Edition sports an entirely new methodology. GoldMine now keeps track of where you've been and keeps each of those windows open. Near the top of the work area, GoldMine Premium shows you a running trail of the windows you have opened.

There are pros and cons to this, but the biggest advantage is that you can pop back and forth between several different tasks without closing out what you are doing.

For example, you can work on updating an individual contact record, jump over to scheduling an appointment with someone else, and then come right back to the original contact record you were updating without stopping to save anything. This is much more efficient than the older methodology as long as you don't get lost by having too many open windows.

You can avoid the open window syndrome by remembering to close windows when you are truly done with them.

Auto-Complete

Not really new in GoldMine Premium, but new since GoldMine 6, is the ability to create a lookup list for a field and specify Auto-Complete. With this feature, as soon as you type enough in the field for GoldMine to uniquely identify which entry from the lookup list you want, it fills in the rest for you. This feature provides more streamlining and ease of use.

GM+Browser

The GM+ Browser is an extension of the popular GM+View functionality that allows you to view information from external sources such as other databases, back office systems, and Web sites. Sometimes, you may still see official documentation referring to GM+Browser as GM+View. But, no matter. You can have multiple GM+Browser windows open simultaneously, providing you the information needed to maximize your productivity. That's the main difference between GM+Browser and GM+View.

Enhanced Reporting & Microsoft SQL Reporting Services

When GoldMine was first released, it had its own report generator. It was never well supported or documented. After a few years, Crystal Reports took over as the de facto standard for creating reports from GoldMine data. In fact, Crystal was actually included with the Corporate Edition. Several additional statistical and reporting utilities, such as MasterMine and Stonefield Query, were developed by third parties.

Now, with Premium Edition, FrontRange has added another reporting option: Microsoft's SQL Reporting Service. The word "Service" is what's really significant here. Now you can schedule reports to run at predetermined times or intervals without human interaction.

SQL Query Wizard

You no longer have to speak SQL. The first versions of GoldMine had filters that allowed you to create subsets of all the records. Later, groups were developed — in a sense, these were filters on steroids.

SQL Queries have much more power than either filters or groups. With SQL Queries, you can identify any logical set of records. In addition, despite the fact that the word "queries" makes you think that all you can do is ask questions of the data, the truth is that you can also use SQL Queries to edit existing data. Very important.

With the SQL Query Wizard, even a technophobe can easily do sophisticated searches and updates. Try it. You'll like it. Back up the system first, though.

Web Integration

The Web Import feature allows you to integrate your Web site with your GoldMine database. When a prospect fills out an inquiry page on your Web site (that is, enters his contact information), Web Import automatically takes that information and creates a new record in GoldMine, or updates an existing record if the prospect is already in the database.

If that's not enough, through clever use of Automated Processes you can then have GoldMine automatically respond to the prospect and schedule the right person in your organization to follow up. This is a great and underutilized feature.

Record Typing

Although not new in GoldMine Premium but finally tuned up enough so that we can have some confidence in it, Record Typing allows you to completely change the appearance of the screens and fields based on your entry in one field.

For example, you could have a field called Record Type. Within this field, you might enter Prospect, Customer, or Vendor. Depending upon which of these you enter, GoldMine might then present completely different fields or tabs. This is a great way to further customize and streamline GoldMine. It's also a bit complicated, and you might want to work with a dealer on this one.

Several Other, Miscellaneous New Features

GoldMine Premium also boasts the following:

- ✔ Further streamlining of its Search Center
- ✔ A new API (one of the tools programmers use to integrate other systems or data with GoldMine)
- ✔ Improved Palm PDA integration

GoldMine Standard Bites the Dust

I am listing this development last, but doing so doesn't make it the least important.

GoldMine Standard was the original dBase product that first came into the market in the late 1980s. In April 2007, FrontRange announced its plan to sunset the venerable Standard version. So, effective as of May 1, 2007, FrontRange no longer sells the Standard version. This also applies to GoldSync licenses. Support will continue until April 2008, although no button exists any longer to press on your phone when you call FrontRange for technical support for the Standard version. FrontRange is trying to encourage organizations using GoldMine Standard to upgrade to Corporate, Premium, or even Enterprise.

You can download a free white paper discussing all the reasonable options from `www.ccc24k.com`.

Index

• *F* •

• *G* •

• *M* •

• T •

• X •

• Y •

• Z •